W9-CCG-649

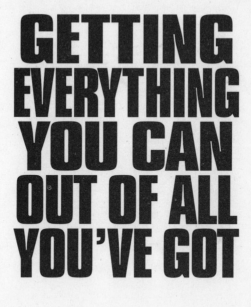

GETTING EVERYTHING YOU CAN OUT OF ALL YOU'VE GOT

GETTING EVERYTHING YOU CAN OUT OF ALL YOU'VE GOT

21 Ways You Can Out-Think,
Out-Perform, and
Out-Earn the Competition

JAY ABRAHAM

T·T

TRUMAN TALLEY BOOKS
ST. MARTIN'S GRIFFIN
NEW YORK

GETTING EVERYTHING YOU CAN OUT OF ALL YOU'VE GOT. Copyright © 2000 by Jay Abraham.
All rights reserved. Printed in the United States of America. No part of this book may be
used or reproduced in any manner whatsoever without written permission except in the case
of brief quotations embodied in critical articles or reviews. For information, address St.
Martin's Press, 175 Fifth Avenue, New York, N.Y. 10010.

www.stmartins.com

Library of Congress Cataloging-in-Publication Data

Abraham, Jay.
    Getting everything you can out of all you've got : 21 ways you can
out-think, out-perform, and out-earn the competition / Jay Abraham.
        p. cm.
    Includes index.
    ISBN 0-312-20465-5 (hc)
    ISBN 0-312-28454-3 (pbk)
    1. Success in business. 2. Entrepreneurship. 3. Creative ability in
business. I. Title

HF5386.A423 2000
658—dc21   99-055044

Truman Talley Books

First St. Martin's Griffin Edition: October 2001

10 9 8 7 6 5 4 3 2 1

To my loving wife, Christy, and my seven wonderful children, Bryan, Michelle, Troy, Jordan, Zayne, Ridge, and Sage, for giving me expansive perspective.

Contents

Part I

CONTENTS

Part II

Part I

How to Maximize What You Have

1

Your Flight Plan

AN AMAZING THING, THE HUMAN BRAIN. CAPABLE OF UNDER-standing incredibly complex and intricate concepts. Yet at times unable to recognize the obvious and simple.

Some true examples:

Ice cream was invented in 2000 B.C. Yet it was thirty-nine hundred years later before someone figured out the ice-cream cone.

Meat was on the planet before humans. Bread was baked in 2600 B.C. Nevertheless, it took another forty-three hundred years for somebody to put them together and create the sandwich.

And the modern flush toilet was invented in 1775, but it wasn't until 1857 that somebody thought up toilet paper.

Once these obvious connections have been made, they seem so obvious. So evident. We can't believe we didn't see them sooner.

An endless number of these unmade connections exist to this day, especially in the business world. You are surrounded by simple, obvious solutions that can dramatically increase your income, power, influence, and success. The problem is, you just don't see them.

I'm going to show you how to recognize the income- and success-increasing connections that are all around you. I will give you proven strategies and detailed examples of how to leverage those strategies so you can turn them into greater income, respect, power, and success. And when you do, your life will never be the same.

Much of this book is focused on how you can improve your business life and career. But the strategies also work in virtually any area of your life where you need to persuade others to accept your position or ideas.

They show you how to become a leader. A person who holds a position of respect and influence.

They show you how to get what you want. And how to get what you want in a totally ethical and honorable way.

I have included <u>over two hundred specific examples</u> of how people have successfully implemented these strategies into their business lives and careers. Several of these examples are outside the business world. But it is important that when you read these strategies and examples, you focus on how they can be successfully applied to *all* areas of your life.

You're about to begin a wonderful jourxney. You're going to learn that you have hidden assets, untapped opportunities, and overlooked possibilities that are not producing maximum results for you. That is going to change.

You'll be shocked at how truly easy this is going to be. Too good to be true? It's not. Let me take just one seemingly huge, complicated, income-increasing problem and show you how truly easy and simple it is to solve.

Did you ever wonder how many ways there are to increase your business? One hundred ways? Two hundred ways? Five hundred ways? It can be intimidating to merely figure out where to start.

I have good news—there are only three ways to increase your business:

1. Increase the number of clients.
2. Increase the average size of the sale per client.
3. Increase the number of times clients return and buy again.

Only three. It's significantly less daunting if you only have to focus on three categories. In fact, it's easy. Let's take a simple example.

- Calculate your number of clients.
- Figure the average amount they spend on each transaction or sale.
- Determine how often they make a purchase in a year.

Let's say you have one thousand clients. They average $100 per transaction or sale. And they make two purchases in a year.

# of Clients		Transaction Value per Client		Transaction per Year		Total Income
1,000	×	$100	×	2	=	$200,000

But look what happens if you increase these three numbers by just 10 percent.

# of Clients		Transaction Value per Client		Transaction per Year		Total Income
1,100	×	$110	×	2.2	=	$266,200

A mere 10 percent increase across the board expands your income by 33.1 percent.

A 25 percent increase in these categories nearly doubles your income to $390,625. Very simple. But the results can be overwhelming. Focusing on this simple formula is just one small way people easily do increase their incomes or grow their businesses by 100 percent, 200 percent, or more.

But my simple geometric growth formula works just as well on nonfinancial goals. My good friend, a famous peak performance coach, used a version of it to propel the Los Angeles Kings hockey team to a stunning 9–1 victory over their competitors. How'd he do it? He got the Kings players to break down each key element of the game into an identifiable process. They then rated on a scale of 1–10 based on how they performed each successive period. At the break the coach would target two or three different processes like power plays and challenge the player to improve his rating performance that next quarter. On the chalkboard he demonstrated to them how much-improved their performance efficiency among two or three existing points in enough different categories produced exponential compounded overall impact. Once the Kings realized how to use the power of geometry to maximum competitive advantage, they went wild with it and trounced the competition.

So you see, it works for business, sports, all areas of your life, when you apply it.

Let's get a little more specific. Here are a few examples of how various companies have increased their numbers in these three vital categories.

How to Increase Your Number of Clients

I have a client whose income curve was stagnant. It doesn't matter what they sold. Pretend it's your product or service. This company had a compensation program that paid the salespeople 10 percent of the profit. So, if the company made a $1,000 profit on a sale, the salesperson would get $100 and the company would get $900.

I had them calculate:

- What the average new client is worth to them in dollars each time they buy
- How many times that client will buy from them each year
- How many years the average client will be with them

It turned out the first sale, on average, resulted in about a $200 profit for the company. Of that, $20 went to the salesman or saleswoman, $180 to the company. On average, the client bought five times a year for three years. So basically, each time that company got a new client, they were receiving $3,000 in cumulative profits.

My solution: Instead of giving the salespeople 10 percent of the profit on a sale to a new, first-time client, give them 100 percent of the profit on the first sale.

The company management's response: "You're insane!"

I smiled pleasantly and went on to explain that as long as their salespeople maintain sales from existing clients at past levels or above, give them 100 percent of the profit on the first sale for every new client they bring in. They'll be ten times more motivated to sell new clients. And every time they bring in a new client, the salesperson makes an additional $200, but the company makes an additional $2,800.

The company implemented the plan and sales tripled in nine months.

. . . and they said they were sorry for calling me insane.

How to Increase the Size of the Sale per Client

General Motors, Honda, Ford, etc., will sell you a new car for $24,995. Have you ever paid just the advertised price? Or do you buy a few extra items, like a radio, air-conditioning, security system, sunroof, warranty package, or financing?

Despite our good intentions, when we go out to dinner many of us up the value of our transaction when the waiter shows us the wine list, and later that damned dessert tray.

How to Increase the Number of Sales per Client

Stockbrokers offer occasional IPOs to select clients.

Clothing stores, auction houses, jewelry stores, and others hold private "by invitation only" sales events for preferred clients.

Airlines offer frequent-flyer miles.

Miles Laboratories published a small cookbook filled exclusively with hot and spicy recipes, and they gave it away for free. Why? Miles Laboratories is the maker of Alka-Seltzer.

These aren't just random, unrelated business-increasing anecdotes. Each example represents a well-thought-out, documented, income-increasing principle or leveraging strategy. And you are about to learn them all.

But I'm Not in Sales and Don't Have Clients

You might be thinking, "My business responsibilities don't include clients and selling. I'm in the accounting/human resources/quality-control/MIS/production department."

Think again. The fact is, everyone is in sales. Whatever area you work in, you do have "clients" and you do need to "sell." They are frequently referred to as internal clients.

Your internal client might be the head of your department,

and you need to sell him or her on your project, your proposal, your promotion, your perspective, your value, or your raise. Your clients might be the people who work under you, and you need to sell them on giving you their best, focused, thoughtful work. Your clients might be people in other departments who could aid you in your area of responsibility. Or vendors, other complementary companies, or future employers.

When you read the phrase "selling your product or service," don't just think in terms of the product or service your company sells, but also your individual and intangible personal product or service—*you*. And understand that you need to sell you and your ideas in order to advance your career, gain more respect, and increase your success, influence, and income.

And these strategies can be applied to areas not considered traditional business activities. For instance, if you're a teacher and you need to persuade the principal or school board to accept your proposal or plan, these strategies apply.

These strategies can be used to increase the success in your personal life. If you work with charity groups, community organizations, or service clubs, you frequently need to convince others that your approach, program, or solution is the correct one and should be implemented. These strategies will help you make that "sale." They will enable you to reach your persuasion or selling goals in many areas of your life. You will gain confidence by knowing the best and most effective ways to cause people to follow your lead.

These strategies are designed to raise you above your competition no matter who your competition is. If you work for a corporation, you have your company's competition—another corporation. But you also have your personal competition—the person in the office down the hall whom you are competing against for the next big promotion. Or the guy who just sent his resume in to Personnel and wants your job.

Recognition, Respect, and a Big Office

Understanding and applying the strategies you are about to learn will lead to increased company revenues and increased personal success and income for you.

But there will also be other rewards along the way.

Realize this hard fact: The people above you (bosses, management, and organization leaders) want one thing most of all—they want solutions to problems. Solutions that make them look good and help them achieve their goals. They want the people who report to them to be problem solvers. These strategies will give you those solutions and turn you into a problem solver. Employers will kill for problem solvers.

A good idea is a good idea no matter where it comes from. And when you come up with that good idea you will be rewarded, perhaps not with an immediate increase in income, but with greater recognition, respect, more/influence, a promotion, a title, or a larger office. All of which lead to . . . increased income.

The Universal Solutions

Can these income-increasing strategies and principles really apply to all industries, all people, and virtually all situations? Absolutely.

Let me tell you about two people, each working in the same

"industry." But only one of the two has discovered how to multiply and maximize his talents. A true, but very extreme, example.

Two men were mugged. Neither one was harmed.

Mugger number one took the man's wallet and all his cash—$85.

Mugger number two had a different approach toward his "business." Mugger number two took the other man's wallet and cash, $70, plus his watch and his Princeton class ring. The watch and ring were not expensive and had no real street value.

Ordinarily, that would be the end of the story.

But, two days later, man number two walks out of his New York City apartment on his way to the office. He hears someone calling his name. He turns, and there is the man who mugged him, smiling and not at all threatening.

Mugger number two asks the man if he would like his watch and Princeton ring back. As both items held great sentimental value to him, he said yes. The mugger offered to sell them back for $500. The man only had $90 with him. The mugger accepted the $90, but instead of returning the watch and ring, he gave the man a receipt from a pawnshop. Later that day the man went to the pawnshop and paid $80 to reclaim his watch and ring.

Mugger number one made $85 cash.

Mugger number two, applying simple income-increasing strategies and uncovering hidden assets, opportunities, and possibilities, made $70 on the mugging, $60 by pawning the watch and ring, and $90 by selling the pawn ticket to my friend. Total income: $220.

Yes, the income-increasing strategies you are about to learn can be used by all people in any industry.

(Mugger number two was never a client of mine. And I do not suggest that anyone go into this line of work. But whatever field you're in, at least get all you can out of it.)

Avoid the Costly Learning Curve

The philosophy of this book allows you to avoid the costly learning curve in almost everything you do. And that saves you time and money. It enables you to run rings around all of your competitors before they ever figure out what you did to them. It virtually guarantees you greater success and multiplied profits from every business-building step you ever take.

I'm referring to the process of borrowing success practices from other industries and applying them to yours.

Most people I meet have spent virtually their entire life in one basic business or industry. Maybe you've done that, too. But when you spend all your life in one industry, all you know well are the common success practices of just your industry. You only understand how people in your field market, sell, advertise, or promote. And almost everyone in your industry probably markets, sells, advertises, and persuades pretty much the same way as everyone else.

Industrial manufacturers primarily use a field sales force.

Retailers basically just put ads in newspapers and the Yellow Pages.

Stockbrokers do virtually all their business by telephone.

Doctors, dentists, and lawyers rely almost exclusively on referrals.

And so on, and so on, and so on.

When you limit your business to doing things the same way every other competitor of yours does, you can only produce modest, incremental gains—at best. At worst, you could easily lose ground.

By helping you study and identify the fundamental principles that drive the successes in hundreds of other industries, you'll be able to pick and choose the most powerful, effective, state-of-the-art, breakthrough approaches to introduce to your industry. An approach that's as common as dirt in one industry can have the power of an atomic bomb in an unrelated industry. I'll show you how to adapt those concepts to your own specific situation. And since you'll probably be one of the few competitors, or the only competitor, in your field using these breakthrough techniques, your results should multiply immediately. With little effort on your part, we should be able to engineer stunning advances for your business, career, and life, and leave everyone else in your dust.

Where Do These Strategies Come From?

Here are some examples where people took strategies from other industries.

Federal Express applied the banking industry's method of clearing checks overnight to the overnight delivery of packages. Banks send all checks to a central processing point, then out to the appropriate branch. FedEx adapted the hub-and-spoke concept where every package went to a central location (Memphis, Tennessee) and then was flown to its final destination.

A man named George Thomas was searching for an effective way for people to apply deodorant. He was very frustrated in his research for a solution until he realized he was holding the answer right in his hand. George borrowed the concept of the ballpoint pen and created roll-on deodorant.

Dave Liniger, founder of RE/MAX real estate, grew his company to a billion dollars in sales by using the "100 percent solution," which lets salespeople keep 100 percent of their commissions while charging them a monthly fee for office facilities and equipment. His agents were making so much money, they rarely left.

The story is told that one day Dave went into his regular, three-chair barbershop. The owner was lamenting how hard it was to keep good barbers. They'd leave and go into business for themselves. Dave explained how his real estate company held on to talent using the 100 percent solution. The barber nodded politely.

The next time Dave was back and reached for his wallet to pay, the barber said, "This one's on me. I took your advice and now we're a 100 percent solution barbershop."

The unanswered question in this story is this: Where did Dave Liniger come up with the 100 percent solution in the first place? Did he create it himself, or did he get the idea from another industry . . . like his previous barbershop?

What You're Going to Learn

There are two categories of specific income-increasing strategies that you will learn. The first category: How to Maximize What You Have.

This section will show you how to get the most out of everything you already have.

You will focus on the main barriers that cause people not to do business with you and how you unknowingly limit and restrict your results, success, and income. You will learn strategies to break through those barriers.

You'll be able to apply these strategies to your existing situation and begin increasing your success and income. They will work for you almost immediately, and they will continue to work for you at whatever heights you reach.

Once you understand those strategies, you'll be ready to use them in conjunction with the second category of powerful income- and success-increasing strategies: How to Multiply Your Maximum. You will apply the strategies in this section to your career or business to create multiple sources of income or success.

Depending on any single approach for all your new clients or career advancement and continuous business is a disaster waiting to happen.

A simple analogy: If you're fishing and have one pole with one line in the water, you will be able to catch only a limited number of fish. But if you use ten poles and put ten lines with ten different baits in the water at the same time, your fish-catching potential will significantly increase.

Many of the best prospects are accessed from multiple impact points that move them from curiosity to interest, and all the way to action. If you're attacking your market from multiple positions and your competition isn't, you have all the advantage and it will show up in your increased success and income.

These income multipliers will show you how to build a system of attracting new clients and increasing business with current clients from multiple angles. They'll stimulate more allies and champions, within your company for you.

1 + 1 = 2.   But, 1 + 1 + 1 = 10

You could apply many of these strategies and concepts as individual, freestanding strategies and they would, by themselves, produce significant results. But that would be a colossal mistake. Combining several, if not all, of these strategies will produce even greater results. The whole will be greater than the sum of the parts.

Many of these strategies will be referred to in multiple chapters. Several of these strategies intertwine and, when combined, will not merely add to each strategy's effectiveness. Instead they will multiply your results several times over. I'm going to give you a quick overview of several of these strategies so you will start to think of them not as individual, separate strategies, but as parts of the even more powerful whole.

How You Think

No one is a hundred times smarter than everyone else. Few corporations today really have any technical advantages over their competitors, nor does anyone really have any major manufacturing distribution or labor edge. So why do certain superachievers gain levels of success so much higher than others'?

In chapter 4 you will learn that they have a better philosophical strategy. They approach everyone they deal with in a totally different and more effective way than everyone else does. And frequently their strategy is hard for anyone else to figure out. But you're about to learn it.

In this book, the word *client* will be used instead of *customer*. This is not only to avoid the constant and cumbersome phrase of "customers and/or clients," but because it helps define the meaning of the Strategy of Preeminence.

The Webster's Dictionary definitions of these two seemingly identical words are:

Customer: A person who purchases a commodity or service.

Client: A person who is under the protection of another.

The difference in the meaning is massive. And there's a massive difference in the way a person who does business with you could or should be treated.

If in your field these people are referred to as customers, that's fine. But whatever you call them, always think of them as a client.

What exactly does "under your protection" mean? In this case it means that you don't sell people a product or service just so you can make the largest one-time profit possible. You must understand and appreciate exactly what your clients need when they do business with you—even if they are unable to articulate that exact result themselves. Once you know what final outcome they need, you lead them to that outcome—you become a trusted adviser who protects them. And they have reason to remain your client for a lifetime.

For instance, a man who goes to a hardware store to buy a power drill doesn't really need a drill—he needs holes.

He has a financial, emotional, logical, or intellectual need for holes. He might think he wants a drill. But it's your responsibility to determine the real truth and his real need. Your responsibility and opportunity is not just to sell him a drill. You must figure out how to satisfy his financial, emotional, logical, or intellectual need for holes and make sure the drill he buys from you will solve his problem and give him the exact holes he needs.

Or maybe he thinks he wants holes, but when you find out that he needs to insert rods in these holes, you realize that fasteners would work better than holes. So you sell the client some fasteners. You have truly solved his problem.

17

You have also become a trusted adviser and a friend. And you should think of your clients as dear, valued friends. The concept of viewing clients as valued friends will appear frequently in this book and for good reason—it is the essence of the Strategy of Preeminence and the lifeblood of a long-lasting, rewarding, and profitable relationship for both you and your clients. And you will learn that the value you provide to your clients and everyone you deal with can be deeper, more meaningful, and more rewarding than you ever realized.

The Royal Bank of Scotland issues two high-security check-cashing cards to its transvestite clients—one with a photo of them dressed as a man, and the other as a woman. A bank spokesman said: "If any cross-dressing clients go shopping dressed as a woman, it's possible for them to have a second card so they can avoid embarrassment or difficulties when paying by check."

A man landed in jail following a drunken brawl during a Texas-Oklahoma football game. The next morning the Oklahoma judge set bail for $250, but the man was far from his home in Dallas and knew no one in town. The man pulled out his Neiman Marcus credit card. He reached a Neiman Marcus vice president, who arranged for the bail to be charged on his account, and the man was set free.

Once you understand how to think about the people you work with, we'll start increasing your income and success. . . .

The One and Only You

In chapter 6 you'll learn why your clients buy from you instead of your competitors.

If you don't know why this is, that means one of two things.

Either (a) you offer a client a unique set of advantages or benefits, but you've never identified them yourself, or (b) you offer that client no unique advantage and you're just lucky as heck that you have the business in the first place. There's no basis upon which you're keeping it. Any time your competition wants to offer your client an advantage you don't, they can take that client away from you.

To get your prospects and clients to see you or your business as offering them a superior benefit or advantage that no other competitor offers them is the essence of a unique selling proposition (USP).

You must determine the most powerful benefit or advantage you can possibly offer an existing or future client so it will be totally irrational for them to choose to do business with anyone but you or your company. And here's how you can do that. You identify what advantage or result your clients want the most.

You don't have to change your product or service, but you have to position your product or service as having a unique benefit they're not getting from your competitors. And you don't offer it to your clients subtly. You incorporate the fact that you are now offering them this unique advantage or benefit in everything you say and everything you do. When you do this, you clearly educate them so they see, appreciate, and want to seize that advantage.

When Avis was struggling to come up with a marketing approach that would gain them the market advantage, they needed a unique selling proposition that was very powerful. After all, Hertz was well ahead of them in size and market share.

What did Avis do? They came up with the unique selling proposition, "We're number two. We try harder." They still rented cars just like Hertz, but they positioned themselves as the company that would work harder and give better service and better rates. And they made incredible progress and growth because of that USP.

Federal Express developed a USP that stated, "When it absolutely, positively has to be there." When FedEx started using that USP, shipping companies were not delivering packages overnight. They weren't even guaranteeing when a package would be delivered. FedEx offered clients a unique advantage— that the package they needed to ship would be delivered at the doorstep of the intended recipient by 10:30 A.M. the next day. Absolutely guaranteed. Period.

Dennis Rodman was in the National Basketball Association for several years, playing hard and posting impressive rebounding numbers. But he received little publicity and few, if any, endorsement contracts. Then he created a USP for himself—bizarrely bright, multicolored hair and outrageous tattoos. With that came notoriety and a fortune in publicity and product endorsements.

Once you have a unique selling proposition and have given people a reason to talk to you, what do you offer them? . . .

No Risk, All Reward

Two friends are each going to purchase the same product or service. One is leaning toward giving his business to Company A, the other to Company B.

"I'm buying from Company A because if something goes wrong, I know Company A will take care of it quickly."

The other said, "But if you buy from Company B, nothing will go wrong."

The first person replied, "Yeah, but it might, and I don't want to have to worry about it."

Chapter 7 will show you that whenever two parties come together to transact business of any kind, one side is always asking the other (consciously or otherwise) to assume more or all of the risk. If you ask someone to take on all the risk, their first inclination is not to buy.

You probably stand behind your product or service right now. And if there's any problem, you or your company will either fix it, replace it, or refund the client's money. But you probably don't aggressively promote that philosophy. In this chapter you will learn how to do that with a strategy called risk reversal.

Your goal is to eliminate as much, if not all, of the risk in the transaction for your client. When you take away the risk, you lower the barrier to action and eliminate the primary obstacle to buying.

Aggressively let your clients know that if they are dissatisfied, you will give them their money back, redo the job at no charge, or whatever else it takes to demonstrate your total, passionate commitment to their satisfaction.

Clients will take advantage of this risk-reversal strategy and very seldom ask for reimbursement. But the offer will serve you 100 percent of the time.

Did you ever subscribe to a magazine or a newsletter and the reason you subscribed was because they gave you a thirty-, sixty-, or ninety-day, no-questions-asked, 100 percent money-back guarantee? Or even not ask you to pay up front? That's risk reversal.

After Orville and Wilbur Wright became the first to conquer powered flight, they used risk reversal when they contacted their congressman. They wrote that they had a plane fit for practical use, that could fly at a high speed, and that could land without wrecking the structure. They said, "Don't send us one red cent! Just sign the contract. Give us your specifications for the desired machine, we will create it, and demonstrate it. Only when that is done, do you pay."

You want a promotion. Go to your supervisor and offer to work in the higher position for sixty to ninety days at your current salary. You can guarantee either that the company will be completely satisfied or guarantee a specific level of performance or result. At the end of the trial period, they can make the promotion and raise official or you'll return to your previous position.

As president of Chrysler, Lee Iacocca took only a $1 annual salary and stock options that would pay off only if he improved the company's bottom line.

Once you've offered a risk-free opportunity and people are ready to do business with you, what's the best thing and the right thing to sell them? . . .

Bigger, Better, and Happier

In chapter 8 you'll learn that every time someone makes a purchase from you or your organization, you have an opportunity to increase the size of that purchase. And the motive is benevolent, not self-serving. It's not just to add to your short-term profit. It's all about you helping your client get the optimal benefit or advantage out of the transaction they're doing with you.

During the Great Depression, the Kraft company tried to market a low-priced cheddar-cheese powder, but the public wouldn't buy it. It was a failure. One St. Louis sales rep, looking for a way to unload his allotment of the stuff, added individual packages of the cheese powder into boxes of macaroni. He then offered grocers the opportunity to sell them as one item, which he called a Kraft Dinner. When the company found out how well they were selling, it made the dinners an official part of its product line.

You have a responsibility and an opportunity to introduce every client you deal with to all the alternatives they have available and to help them understand what their objective is for buying your product or service in the first place. And to help them recognize that they have options they could be taking advantage of that could produce a better result than the level they'll receive from the purchase they originally intended to make.

In this chapter you will learn the concepts called add-ons and cross-selling. By add-ons, I mean that you graduate the client to a larger or superior alternative product or package of goods or services. In other words, they may have been content coming in to buy the standard, basic product or service. And yet, by understanding what their intended use for that product or service is, you realize that the basic, standard purchase can't possibly give the client the performance outcome they seek. So you recommend a larger, higher-quality, or more sophisticated version of the product that you know will give them a better result. They don't have to buy it, but you have an obligation to demonstrate to them the differences in performance and outcome they can expect to receive and to make them an offer that gives them an incentive for considering trading up.

A cross-sell is introducing to the client an additional product or service that will add or increase the result of their transaction with you or your company.

Your clients will appreciate you for doing it. Their lives or business will be better for it. Why? They get a superior out-come. And when they get greater results, they're happier. So, your goal in these transactions, when you're using either add-ons or cross-selling, is to always offer your client alternatives—alternatives that perform better and which are in your clients' best interests, not yours.

Mattel gets you to buy Barbie. But Barbie only comes with the one outfit she's wearing—très gauche! You add on more Barbie clothes, a Barbie car, a Barbie house. But Barbie is lonely. You buy a Ken for Barbie, and guess what? Ken only comes with the clothes he's wearing.

AT&T and other phone companies sell you a simple phone line. Then call waiting, voice mail, automatic callback, a second line for a computer, a third line for a security system, information-number autodial option, caller ID, or a fourth line for a fax. And now they're getting into the cable and computer information-delivery systems. These guys are good.

No one is holding a gun to our heads to make us buy these added products and services. We purchase them because they give us the added results we want.

Increased income is a by-product of management's percep-tion of your worth. Find something that no one else in your company is doing (or doing well) and voluntarily add it onto your responsibilities.

An added note to the Kraft Macaroni and Cheese innova-tion—how well did that add-on strategy work in the long run? Research has shown that today only 55 percent of dinners served in homes in the United States include even one home-made dish.

So your unique selling proposition got their attention, and risk reversal caused them to buy, and add-ons and cross-selling gave them the best products or services to solve their problem, but how do you know that's the best you can do? . . .

Testing . . . One, Two, Three . . . Testing

Before Henry Ford would hire anyone for an important position, he would have lunch with them. If the potential employee would salt the food before tasting it, Mr. Ford would not hire the person. The reason? Salting the food before tasting it indicated the person would implement a plan before testing it— ergo, no job.

Chapter 9 teaches you to test everything. It's simple and the payoff can be enormous. It's not at all unusual when you test and compare the effectiveness of one approach against another for the superior approach to outperform the inferior one by as much as ten or twenty times.

The selling approach you're currently using to sell your product or service could be underperforming, delivering only a fraction of what an alternative approach or strategy might yield. I've seen people test different variables in their advertising, web sites, sales letters, live sales presentations, guarantees, USP, and pricing points. Increases of 500, 1,000, and 2,000 percent have resulted just by changing from one approach to another. In other words, you might be producing only one-fifth of the results, sales, income, or profits you could be getting with the same or even less effort and cost. Until you start testing different responses and performance levels, you're leaving massive potential on the table.

One company that apparently didn't test enough is the maker of Excedrin. Several years ago they ran a multimillion-dollar national advertising campaign showing different above-average headaches and assigning them numbers, like "Excedrin headache number nine" and "Excedrin headache number twenty-three," where Excedrin relieved the pain.

The campaign created great name recognition and was seemingly very successful. But, in fact, sales went down. The company later learned that people were aware of the campaign and said that Excedrin was an excellent, stronger-than-average pain reliever. And if they had a severe headache they would definitely take Excedrin. But if they had just an average headache, Excedrin was a stronger medication than they needed, so they would take a milder pain reliever like aspirin.

The company could have saved millions of dollars and not lost market share had they done one simple thing. *Test*.

Another international corporation that also apparently didn't test enough before they went national was Coca-Cola. They sparked a consumer revolt when they tried to replace Classic Coke with New Coke. A nearly disastrous idea that could have easily and inexpensively been avoided by testing.

Was Henry Ford too extreme with his hiring policy based on salting food before testing? Maybe. But, then again, Henry Ford was America's first billionaire.

Once you understand these strategies—the Strategy of Preeminence, developing a USP, risk reversal, add-ons and cross-selling, testing, and several others—you can easily apply them to your current operation and gain increased revenue and income. But then we'll move into new territory—creating multiple sources of income. Here comes the really big money. . . .

Partners in Profit

Chapter 10 reveals how you can tap into millions of dollars of investment that companies have made in their clients for decades, get those companies to direct all of their clients to start doing business with you and your company, and have it cost you nothing.

I call this concept host-beneficiary relationships. It's a simple process that's based on utilizing existing goodwill and strong bonded relationships that other companies already have established with people who are prime prospects for your product or service.

Duncan Hines was a traveling restaurant critic. His book, *Adventures in Good Eating*, a guide to restaurants along major highways, was so popular that his name became a household word. Hines's notoriety attracted the attention of Roy Park, a New York businessman who was looking for a way to promote his new line of baked goods. He asked Hines to become a partner in the company, and Hines agreed. Together they formed Hines-Park Foods, Inc. Their Duncan Hines line of cake mixes captured 48 percent of the American cake-mix market in less than three weeks.

Determine who in your marketing area is already selling to the clients you want to be reaching, and who has their trust, respect, and goodwill. They would be selling something that either goes before, goes along with, or follows the product or service that you sell to people. Your product or service does not compete with their product or service, but it complements it.

The moment you identify who these businesses are, you're almost all the way home. All you have to do is contact those companies and make it easy and advantageous for them to refer their clients to you.

If you work in a corporate structure, the principles are the same. For instance, if you sell software for a company, you could contact a salesperson who works for a corporation that sells the computer hardware to the same client base and develop a mutually beneficial relationship.

Why would companies be willing to do this?

Most companies and individuals would love to create new profit centers, but they haven't the slightest idea of what they should be or how to start one. You are perfectly suited to be a joint-venture profit center for them. If your product or service goes before, with, or after theirs, then obviously their product or service will go before, with, or after yours.

Visa and American Express have formed strategic alliances with airlines, automobile manufacturers, oil companies, and others that reward consumers for using their particular credit card.

Sears Roebuck made hundreds of millions of dollars by promoting Allstate insurance to their clients in their stores.

When major motion-picture studios like Disney and Universal produce movies aimed at the youth market they develop merchandising host-beneficiary relationships with fast-food chains like McDonald's and Burger King.

Perfume and makeup companies will hire and pay the salaries of the people who work at the cosmetic counters in large department stores. Some of the cosmetic companies actually *own* the cosmetic counter.

Recommended by a Friend

In chapter 11 you'll see that most people and businesses spend all of their time, effort, and money on conventional marketing, advertising, or selling programs when a fraction of that effort, and virtually no expense, would get them many times the results if they developed a formalized referral system.

It's probable that a large portion of your new clients actually come from direct or indirect referrals right now. But you probably have never put a formal referral system into place. In this chapter you will learn to do that.

You've invested far too much in your business and clients, and the values and benefits you provide are too important, to allow all of the friends, coworkers, family members, and colleagues of your current clients to be denied access to you.

A formal client-referral system will bring you an immediate increase in clients and profit. And it doesn't cost anything to implement it.

A referral-generated client normally spends more money, buys more often, and is more profitable and loyal than most other categories of business you could go after. And referrals are easy to get. Referrals beget referrals. They are self-perpetuating.

Every time clients deal with you in person, through your sales staff, by letter, E-mail, or on the phone, diplomatically ask them for client referrals. But you must first set the stage.

Tell your clients that you enjoy doing business with them and that they probably associate with other people like themselves who mirror their values and quality. Since they obviously know the exact people you prefer working with, you'd like them to refer their valued friends and associates to you. If you acknowledge your clients' value and importance to you, they'll be eager to reciprocate.

Then extend a totally risk-free, obligation-free offer. Willingly offer to advise, talk to, or meet with anyone important to that client. In other words, offer to consult their referral without expectation of purchase, so your clients see you as a valuable expert with whom they can put their friends or colleagues in touch.

If you do this with every client you talk to, sell to, write, or visit—and you also get your key team members to do it as well—you can't help but get dozens, even hundreds, of new clients. I have seen business literally triple in six months when people used an organized client-referral process.

Charles Lamb once said, "Don't introduce me to that man. I want to go on hating him, and I can't hate a man whom I know." On a personal level a simple introduction by a respected colleague to a prospective client, business associate, or potential boss can have the same effect as a referral or even an endorsement.

Love Is Better the Second Time Around

It can cost a small fortune to acquire a new client—but it costs almost nothing to gain back an old client.

Chapter 12 shows you that clients stop buying for three basic reasons.

Reason one, they stop buying temporarily and just never get around to dealing with you again. Out of sight, out of mind. A trite phrase, but very true. Once you stop dealing with a company, no matter how valuable the product or service, you tend to fall into a different buying pattern.

The second reason people stop dealing with a company is because they became dissatisfied. There are hundreds of reasons a client becomes unhappy and stops doing business with a company. But the important thing to realize is that rarely did you intentionally offend or dissatisfy that client.

The third reason is the client's situation has changed to the point where they no longer can benefit from your product or service. This may seem like the end of the road with a client in this position. But that's not the case. Even a client who may not be in a position to do business with you can be a great source of additional income. And you'll learn how.

When you recognize that over 80 percent of all lost clients didn't leave for an irreparable reason, you can instantly take action and get many—even most—of those clients back. And when they do come back, they tend to become one of your best, most frequent, and most loyal client groups.

They also turn into your best single source of referrals.

The Write and Wrong Way

How would you like to have one thousand to ten thousand tireless salesmen and saleswomen working around the clock, calling on the maximum number of the absolutely most qualified prospects for your product or service—and never forgetting to make any selling point or any closing argument?

Chapter 13 shows you how that ability is available to you instantly by recognizing and utilizing the powerful tool that is direct mail. Direct mail refers to all written material used to communicate with prospects and clients, including sales letters, E-mail, brochures, and proposals.

It sometimes costs $100 or more to make a cold sales call. Many cold calls take weeks or months to set up. Yet it can cost you less than fifty cents to contact your target market through the mail.

And when people call cold or visit cold, they're introducing an idea for the first time. It has to settle in. It has to be embraced. There are a lot of negative issues you have to overcome, including the resistance of secretaries or voice mail. When you make that the job of the sales letter, it lays the groundwork for you.

When you get the letter in the hands of the intended recipients, they've got the complete message, from beginning to end. Every question is answered, every issue addressed, every problem solved, every reservation overcome, every application made, and every call to action expressed.

Even the envelope carrying your sales letter can be a selling tool. It can be very businesslike, with just a name, address, city, and state; or it can be more personal, with a personalized-looking message on the outside of the envelope.

Sales letters are the most powerful prelude to telephone marketing efforts. Sending a sales letter ahead of a phone call can increase the effectiveness of the call itself by 1,000 percent.

When a letter precedes the call, you are not calling cold. Your prospect has already been presold on your product or service.

When Senator Robert A. Taft announced for the presidency in 1952, Walter Weintz created an elaborate series of test mailings for the campaign. To these he added a revolutionary element: a request for money. Not only would a dollar or two coming in indicate the winning test, it was like betting on a horse. Put money on a horse, Weintz reasoned, and you'll do everything in your power to make sure that horse wins. In this case, you'll not only vote, but persuade your friends and family to do likewise.

Weintz went on to use this technique for dozens of candidates. It changed American politics forever.

More to Come

These are just some of the key success- and income-increasing strategies you will be learning. We'll delve into these and other strategies in great detail. And you'll learn how to apply all the strategies to successfully selling on the Internet. But again, don't limit their power and effectiveness by looking at any of them as individual concepts. When combined together, these strategies will produce exponential growth in income, results, and success.

You're about to begin a wonderful journey. Embrace these strategies, apply them with diligence, and your final destination will be financial security, influence, recognition, and much-deserved success.

2

Great Expectations

WHAT SHOULD YOU EXPECT TO ACHIEVE WITH THE INFOR-mation you will learn in this book? Simply put, you should expect to achieve your dreams, raise the bar, and accomplish your goals.

This is about the big picture. About how to view your business, career, and life from the top of the mountain. And the fastest, safest, easiest path to get you there. In a later chapter, I'll give you valuable direction on establishing and attaining specific goals that are worthy of your untapped potential. But now, I want to talk about what your grand vision and overall approach should be for making the absolute most of every opportunity you have (and why your current vision is nowhere near as grand as it should and could be).

I want to help you achieve a personal vision of success that's greater than you've ever thought practical. Doing it smarter, not harder, is the secret. But most people only know the adage. I know how it's really done. Now you're about to learn it.

Your greatest success and prosperity in business and life will come from your ability to create your own breakthroughs.

This chapter will teach you inventive, new ways to generate innovative ideas, think more creatively, and implement breakthroughs that can dramatically improve the results your previous approaches produced.

Giant Steps and Quantum Leaps

Most people operate with a mind-set that assumes success comes one small step at a time. This is an unfortunate misconception, and it's clearly reflected in the way most people function and go about getting clients, growing sales, building their businesses and careers . . . and living their lives. They strive day to day to make incremental gains. Or worse, to merely hold their own against the rest of their world. That's the pathway of conventional, limited growth and, ultimately, "success erosion."

This approach keeps you working harder and harder for your business, instead of getting your business or career to start working harder and harder for you.

I don't want to see you operate that way. And you don't have to.

Advancing at a measured pace—step by step, from where you are to a little bit better—may seem the logical and safe way to proceed. But you can and should think in terms of skipping levels and making quantum leaps. You can move rapidly, easily, and surprisingly safely from your present level of accomplishment to a place that is several stages higher. You can do it instantly—and directly. And you can do it in virtually every aspect of your business or career activities. You can do it by not limiting yourself to following only those practices people in your industry follow.

I want you to stop accepting your present-day business circumstances as the way it has to be. You're going for major breakthroughs.

A business strategy that may be as common as dirt in one industry can have the effect of an atom bomb in an industry or business application where it's never been used before.

So, if you're going to give your business or career explosive jumps in results that put you far beyond most of the people you compete with, you can't do it by following the same practices you've (and they've) always followed.

Think about it logically. You can't be a follower and expect to ever really become a leader in your field. It just doesn't work that way in today's fast-changing world. Instead, you need to see the overlooked opportunities that are all around you and act on the vast sums of untapped income and unclaimed success just waiting to be harnessed.

You probably spend too little time studying the most successful, innovative, and profitable ideas people in other industries use to grow and prosper.

Yet, if you start focusing on other industries' success practices, you'll be amazed at how easily you can adapt these ideas to your own business situation. Suddenly, you'll see significantly better ways to produce significantly better results from the same time, manpower, effort, activity, and capital.

Frank Howser, Lewis Crandal, and Richard and Maurice McDonald.

How many of these names do you recognize?

Frank Howser designs and constructs displays and booths for trade shows. A few years ago, two young guys asked Frank if he could design something for their little start-up company so they would look "flashy" at a trade show. They couldn't pay him cash, but they offered to give him stock in their start-up business. Frank declined the offer. The two young men were Steve Wozniak and Steven Jobs. Their little company was Apple Computer.

Lewis Crandal sold his half of the store for $1,200 to his partner, Mr. Woolworth.

Richard and Maurice McDonald sold their hamburger stand, concept, and name to a fifty-one-year-old salesman named Ray Kroc, who went on to create a multibillion-dollar organization.

How many of *these* names do you recognize?

Ted Turner, Bill Gates, Rupert Murdoch, Donald Trump, and Warren Buffett.

The first group of unknowns never saw the opportunities for breakthroughs that were right in front of them. The second group did. And they acted on them.

What Exactly Are Breakthroughs?

Breakthroughs are unconventionally fresh, superior, more exciting ways of doing something. Breakthroughs are the dramatic improvements in each area that make you more powerful, efficient, effective, and productive, and more valuable or inspiring to your client.

Breakthroughs make your marketing produce twice or three times the results from the same effort or less. Breakthroughs transform your product from a commodity into a prized proprietary item no one else can offer (or directly compete against). Breakthroughs let you control your business with fewer people, less payroll, less confusion, more productivity, more efficiency, and more profit. And breakthroughs let you change the entire business game you play by allowing you to totally (but ethically) change all the rules and remake them at will.

Breakthroughs let you outthink, outleverage, outmarket, out-sell, outperform, outimpact, outdefend, outmaneuver, and continuously outwit your competition on every level. Do this constantly and you cannot help but ultimately become and remain the dominant and leading force and choice in your field, market, or career category.

When you practice a continual breakthrough business *performance-maximizing* philosophy, many of your previous business and money problems will dissolve.

Leadership becomes the natural (almost effortless) by-product of seeing and creating breakthroughs.

Companies who innovate and produce breakthroughs lead their field. So do individuals. Companies and people who lead command more business, keep more business, and take more business from their competitors. They also command far greater respect and trust from their clients and industry.

Right now your competitors are constantly trying to come up with new ways to take your clients, job, or entire business away from you. You've got to beat them to the punch. Breakthroughs are the pathway to do that.

Breakthroughs let you reinvent your business or career before some competitor does it to you. Breakthroughs let you maximize your successes better and longer so you can safely uncover new future successes. Breakthroughs let you ethically use other people's knowledge, capital, or resources to your own maximum advantage.

Breakthroughs let you lower or totally eliminate the risk in an activity, while vastly increasing the payoff potential. Break-throughs make you unbeatable. Breakthroughs make people wealthy.

Breakthroughs propel your career upward by allowing you to

stand out favorably and contribute more value that gets recognized by your employer.

The speed at which events are occurring around us requires that breakthrough thinking become continual, everyday thinking. Not merely a rare or occasional event in your business life.

You don't want to wait for a major catastrophic event to change your business for the negative. So you must invent and constantly be reinventing your own better future. That means becoming ethically opportunistic, looking at everything around you (in and outside your business or industry) with an opportunity-based focus and asking yourself continuously, "Where's the big overlooked opportunity here?"

It's also adopting a *possibility-based* mind-set that looks for new, different, and better ways to attain a goal or solution or address a situation.

It's starting to see opportunities where everyone else sees problems, obstacles, limitations, or boundaries. It's recognizing how much more you can achieve by leveraging the impact of whatever is going on all around you. The most exciting breakthroughs occur when you reach beyond the traditional way of looking at or doing something and become open and receptive to new possibilities.

Being Opportunity-Focused

Major breakthroughs come from the correct mind-set. It's an attitude—an opportunistic attitude. People who make breakthroughs are always opportunity-focused. People who don't, aren't. It's that simple.

In 1972 the Democratic convention nominated George McGovern to run for president against Richard Nixon. During the convention, Senator McGovern dumped his vice-presidential running mate, Senator Eagleton. A young, sixteen-year-old entre-preneur saw a one-time opportunity and bought up five thousand suddenly obsolete McGovern-Eagleton buttons and bumper stickers. He paid about five cents apiece for them. He soon resold them as historical and rare political memorabilia for as much as $25 per item.

This is an excellent example of an ethically opportunistic mind-set. True, the young man's one-time windfall profit did not result in a major industry breakthrough. But what is impor-tant is that he had the opportunity-focused attitude that is needed to see an opportunity where no one else did. That young man, by the way, was Bill Gates.

But I'm Not Bill Gates

To create major breakthroughs you don't have to be the intel-lectual equal of Bill Gates or Ted Turner or Rupert Murdoch or Donald Trump.

Most major breakthroughs are a result of looking at things with a commonsense, "superlogical" degree of open-mindedness. And the ability to take action on what you see. They have little to do with advanced education, high IQ, or vast amounts of money. And the most dramatic breakthroughs frequently cen-ter, pure and simple, on better ways to do things—faster, easier, or more effectively or logically.

Anyone who saw the first Indiana Jones movie, *Raiders of the Lost Ark*, remembers when Indy got trapped in the bazaar in a dead-end street with a seven-foot giant swinging swords at his head. Everyone thought poor Indy was a goner, until he made a breakthrough move and pulled out a gun, shot the giant, and ended his problem. As I said, breakthroughs can come in many different and unusual ways.

Major breakthroughs are merely fresh new ways to do something. And *new* means new to your industry, market, competitor, or clients; not necessarily new to the world. Applying old things in new ways is a breakthrough. Applying new things in new ways is a breakthrough. Applying old things in new combinations is a breakthrough. Applying new things to new markets, or old things to old markets can be a breakthrough, too. Look at Domino's Pizza. When Domino's started, home deliveries had become almost obsolete because the service was undependable. But they figured out a workable system and reintroduced an updated version, and a billion-dollar breakthrough was reborn.

Monocidal-Rogaine Was an Accident

Somebody with vision figured out how to capitalize on the unintentional fact that this acne product also grew hair as a side effect.

Microwave cooking happened purely unintentionally in a radio-wave test laboratory when a scientist left his lunch too close to the power source. Same goes for Post-its. They were accidentally "discovered," but became commercial blockbusters only after someone at 3M figured out what the application opportunity really was.

Born-Again Breakthroughs

Starbucks brought America European cappuccino and a breakthrough was "reborn."

Infomercials were popular back in the fifties when TV first started. Then they gave way to sixty-second advertisements. Fast-forward forty years and now they're hot again.

Banks came up with automobile leases to counteract rising car prices and lowered tax incentives.

Real estate developers came up with auto malls to leverage the combined power of multiplied advertising and maximized flow of qualified prospects.

Do You Have a Better Idea?

One study showed that out of sixty-one breakthrough inventions, only sixteen were discovered in big companies. Most of the best ideas come from people just like you. For example, the dial telephone was invented by an undertaker, and the ballpoint pen by a sculptor.

Will Parish, a former lawyer and conservation specialist, was well aware of rising energy costs and diminishing fossil-fuel resources, as well as the enormous problems associated with waste disposal. While in India, he ate a meal heated by flaming cow dung. That's right, cow dung. The result? Parish formed National Energy Associates, which now burns nine hundred tons of cow chips a day, producing enough megawatts to light twenty thousand American homes. Parish says he now combines "doing well" with "doing good," and *Fortune* magazine labeled him the world's true "entre-manure."

The El Cortez hotel in San Diego is the birthplace of an architectural first. Management determined their single elevator was not sufficient for getting their guests to and from their rooms and the lobby.

Deciding an additional elevator was needed, engineers and architects were contracted to solve the problem. They proposed cutting a hole in each floor from the basement to the top of the hotel. As the experts stood in the lobby discussing their plans, a hotel janitor overheard their conversation.

"What are you up to?" he asked.

One of the planners explained the situation and their proposed solution. The janitor responded, "That's going to make quite a mess. Plaster, dust, and debris will be everywhere."

One of the engineers assured him it would work fine because they were planning to close the hotel while the work was being completed.

"That's going to cost the hotel a healthy amount of money," the janitor noted, "and there will be a lot of people out of jobs until the project is completed."

"Do you have a better idea?" one architect asked.

Leaning on his mop, the janitor pondered the architect's challenge and then suggested, "Well, why don't you build the elevator on the outside of the hotel?"

Hence, the El Cortez became the originator of a popular architectural feature. It doesn't necessarily take a trained expert to come up with the best idea.

The founder of Nike, an avid runner, sat at his kitchen table and poured rubber into a waffle iron to create Nike's unique sole for their first running shoe.

If you are fishing at forty degrees below zero and you pull a fish up through the ice, an obvious thing happens. The fish freezes, fast and hard. But Clarence Birdseye, grinding out a living as a fur trader in Labrador, noted something else about these quick-frozen fish.

When thawed, the fish were tender, flaky, and moist—almost as good as fresh-caught. The same was true for the frozen caribou, geese, and the heads of cabbage that he stored outside his cabin during the long Canadian winter.

That observation made Clarence Birdseye a wealthy man. The quick-freezing process pioneered by Birdseye produced frozen foods that were palatable to consumers. It created a multibillion-dollar industry and gave farmers the incentive to grow crops for a year-round market. In the case of frozen orange juice, it created a product where none existed before.

What's the lesson in all this? You must constantly be on the lookout for new and better ways to dramatically improve your overall business performance by capitalizing on what everyone else sees as a limitation.

Head Up, Eyes Open, Mind in Gear

A young boy happened to look down and spot a shiny quarter. He picked it up. This was good—it was his quarter, fair and square, and it had cost him nothing.

From that moment on, he walked with his eyes surveying the ground for more treasure. During his life, he found 387 pennies, 62 nickels, 49 dimes, 16 quarters, 2 half-dollars, and 6 one-dollar bills—a total of $22.87.

The money had cost him nothing, except that he missed 28,742 beautiful sunsets, rainbows, babies growing, birds flying, sun shining, and the smiles of the people around him. He also missed an untold number of million-dollar breakthroughs.

Fiscal responsibility is very important. But don't waste all your time on nickel-and-dime thinking. Learn to be an ethical opportunist who creates breakthroughs. Keep your head up, your eyes open, and your mind in gear.

You need to reach out for ideas and answers. Examine ideas, people, procedures, and philosophies from as far outside your normal sphere of business and life as you can possibly reach. Develop a genuine interest, fascination, and curiosity for how other things outside your limited business world work and the principles they're based upon.

Keep continual access to a flow of information that connects you to successful, creative breakthrough developments and achievements. Whether you read the pages of *Forbes, Inc.,* or *Technology Today,* or attend business, trade, or technology conferences, or merely walk the aisles of a well-stocked bookstore, recognize how many people and organizations are driving their success and growth by coming up with new ideas, perspectives, and innovative techniques, and then acting on them. This "observed validation" is critical to encourage, stimulate, and sustain your own business breakthrough efforts.

Stretch yourself and start examining subjects, industries, and markets you've never been interested in before. Why? Because you'll get fresh new perspectives, ideas, and insights into segments of the buying market you've never thought about before. And you'll start seeing the connection. Ask yourself powerful questions about how other people use things, do things, sell things, deliver things, service things, make things, compete, and prosper.

There are an unlimited number of breakthroughs out there . . . just waiting for you to discover them. Marketing breakthroughs. Innovative breakthroughs. Creative breakthroughs. Operations breakthroughs. Source breakthroughs. Technology breakthroughs. Systems breakthroughs. Process breakthroughs. Selling system breakthroughs. Product breakthroughs. Distribution breakthroughs. So many breakthroughs, so little time to discover them all. So much to borrow from and funnel into your newfound maximizer's mind-set. That's why you need to start doing it right now. And keep doing it, forever!

You don't have to be an Einstein to look at your business or career world with fresh new eyes and stop accepting the traditional "herd" mentality just because you and everyone else has always done it *that way.*

It's Time to Act

Whatever you do and wherever you are in your career—whether you own a business or professional practice, have profit-and-loss or divisional responsibility for any element of a profit-oriented business, or are a staff member in another's employ—you owe it to yourself, your company or practice, your employer, your career, and your future to learn how to generate the maximum results from everything you do: Creating break-throughs is the answer you're after.

Whatever you're doing, however you're doing it, and wherever you're doing it, you can *and must* find continually better ways to maximize your results. But maximizing and creating breakthroughs means more than simply getting the most profit, highest performance, and greatest productivity and effectiveness out of an action, opportunity, or investment. It also means achieving maximum results with a minimum of time, effort, expense, and risk—something few people practice or even think about. Think: highest and best use of your time, money, and effort. Highest and best. Always highest and best!

Your Fundamental Objectives

In order to produce the maximum number of breakthroughs possible, you should focus your thinking on these fundamental objectives that your breakthrough ideas should be designed to achieve. It's a success template that keeps your mind's eye on the breakthrough ball at all times.

- Always discover what the hidden opportunity is in every situation.

46

- Try to uncover at least one cash windfall for your business or employer every three months.
- Engineer maximum success into every action you take or decision you make.
- Build a business breakthrough foundation based upon multiple streams of idea generation instead of a single idea source.
- One of your breakthrough goals is to always make you, your business, or your product special, unique, and more advantageous in your client's eyes.
- The more value or wealth you can create for your client, the greater the power of that breakthrough.
- A breakthrough's purpose is to help you or your business maximize personal or organizational leverage in every commitment of action, investment, time, effort, opportunity, or energy you make.
- Breakthroughs increase in direct proportion to the amount of networking, brainstorming, and masterminding you do with like-minded, success-driven people outside your industry.
- Your goal in creating breakthroughs is to use ideas to create more value for others.
- Breakthroughs fuel growth thinking.
- Growth thinking seeds/breakthroughs . . . the two go hand in hand.
- The best breakthroughs take away risk or resistance from the other side. So it's easier to say yes than no.
- Employ as many success practices of others outside your field or industry by adopting or adapting their philosophies and methods to your business situation.

Action Steps

Think about breaking out of the conventional approach you've been taking in as many different areas of your business or career as possible. Break your activities into as many subactivities as you can. Each one can be targeted for one or more breakthroughs. Imagine what it will be like when your mind is thinking about overlooked opportunities as fresh possibilities in each activity you do. Make a list of outside sources of information about other industries' business practices you could plug into.

Identify both your biggest and easiest existing breakthrough opportunities. Try to come up with thirty breakthrough ideas in thirty minutes for thirty different areas of your business or career. Next, try to identify twenty overlooked opportunities that your business or job is sitting on. Come up with ten possibilities you could test that, if successful, would result in a major breakthrough. Make a list (and keep adding to it) of as many breakthroughs as you can identify that other industries have produced. Finally, start applying the mind-set you're now developing to the subject matter of each chapter you are about to read.

3

How Can You Go Forward If You Don't Know Which Way You're Facing?

I F A CHILD COMES TO YOU AND SAYS, "I DON'T FEEL SO GOOD," you respond, "Where does it hurt?" The child tells you where (head, tummy, throat, leg—whatever) and you begin the process of fixing the ailing area.

So why don't people do the same thing in their business lives?

If their business or career "doesn't feel so good," they either do nothing at all or increase exactly what they've been doing, hoping to make things better, even if exactly what they've been doing is what caused the problem in the first place.

The point is, they don't know what their business success, or lack of business success, is based on. They don't ask themselves the right questions because they don't know the right questions.

The first step in navigating any journey through treacherous business waters is to know exactly what your strengths and weaknesses are. And how they relate to your competition. Yet almost no one in business does this strategic analysis. Even fewer people working for corporations operate their careers strategically. Until you know your business positives and negatives it's impossible to get the ultimate rewards and payoffs you're after. So the first thing you need to do is get a handle on where you are, so you can then determine what you need to focus on to get where you want to be.

This chapter will show you how to evaluate your business strengths and weaknesses in order to identify the basis of your current success or lack of success.

Following are fifty questions. By simply answering these questions, you will gain vast insight into the strengths and weaknesses of your business or career. Answer the questions on a company and a personal career level. If you don't totally understand or are unable to answer particular questions, don't worry. When you have read all the strategies in the book you will understand the meaning of all these questions and you will appreciate the value and importance of them.

1. What initially got me started in my business or career (what motivation, occurrence, etc.)?
2. When I first started, where did my clients or promotions progress come from (what process, method, or action did I use)?
3. Why did clients originally buy from me (or buy me)?

4. Why do clients buy from me (or buy me) now?

5. What primary method of generating clients was used to build my business/career?

6. Which of my marketing or sales efforts brought in the bulk of my sales or clients? What percentage of my business comes from this particular effort?

7. Do I test the various aspects of my marketing and selling activities to make sure they're producing the best and most profitable results?

8. How well connected or how involved am I with my clients at the sales/networking or transaction level (do I still sometimes take orders or sell or follow up)?

9. What ongoing sales/networking efforts do I personally perform today? How do these functions differ from those I performed when I started my business/career?

10. Where do my clients come from specifically (demographics)?

11. Would I rather attract more new clients or garner more money from my existing clients, and why?

12. Who else benefits from my success, excluding my clients, my employees, and my family members?

13. How many of my suppliers/business colleagues would be motivated to help me grow my business more because it will directly benefit them at a very high level? Who are they?

14. When I create a new client for my business or profession, who else have I directly created a new client for?

15. Describe completely what my business/career does (*what* I sell, *how* I sell it, and *whom* I sell to by industry, commercial category, or specific niche).

16. What is my business philosophy as it relates to my clients?

17. How have my methods for doing business, or the product

or service line(s) I market, changed since the inception of my business?

18. What are my sales per employee or personal/departmental performance levels? Is that above, below, or equal to my industry average?

19. What is the lifetime value of my typical client (or my contribution to explore) (i.e., how much revenue will he or she generate for me over the entire period he or she does business with my company)?

20. What is the biggest client complaint about my company, and how does my company successfully address this problem?

21. What is my unique selling proposition or USP? (Why do my clients buy from me—what is it about my product and/or service that distinguishes me from my competition? Do I have more than one USP for different product/service lines or segments of my business?)

22. Is my USP a consistent theme in all of my marketing and sales efforts? If yes, how, and if no, why not?

23. Briefly describe my marketing program or marketing mix (all the different types of marketing I use and how they interrelate—i.e., sales letters, direct mail, direct sales, personal networking inside, outside my company, industry, marketplace, Yellow Pages, spot advertisements, etc.).

24. Who are my biggest competitors and what do they offer that I do not?

25. What steps do I take to offset their advantage? Are they working?

26. What is my competition's biggest failing, and how do I specifically fill that void?

27. What do my clients *really* want (be specific, don't just answer "a quality product or service")? How do I know?

28. Do clients buy from me exclusively or do they also patronize my competitors? What steps can I take to get the main portion of their business (preempt and dominate)?

29. What's my market potential (universe) and my current share of that market?

30. What does it cost me to get a new client? (If I ran an advertisement that cost $1,000 and I obtained two new clients, my cost would be $500.) Translate this to whatever your acquisition cost is.

31. What is my biggest and best source of new business, and am I doing everything possible to secure this business?

32. What has been my biggest marketing success to date (defined as a specific promotion, advertising campaign, sales letter, etc.)?

33. What is my biggest marketing problem or challenge today? Describe it in its entirety as candidly and directly as possible, including personal, financial, and transactional implications it may impose.

34. How many better ways could I reduce the risk of transaction, lower the barrier of entry, or reduce the hurdle for my client to make it easier for that person to do business with me?

35. After the initial sales, are there systematic, formal methods I use to communicate and resell to my clients—strengthening the relationship and bonding them to me?

36. Do I have an adequate supply of client testimonials, and is there a system in place for their capture? Are they written, on audiotape, or on videotape, and how are they used in my marketing? Also, can I measure, compare, or quantify the tangible impact I make on my clients?

37. Do I actively solicit referral business?

38. Have I ever tried to reactivate my former clients and

unconverted prospects? Do I maintain systematic contact?

39. Have I ever tried selling a list of my unconverted prospects to my competitors, or turning enemies into allies?

40. Do I make consistent efforts to communicate with my clients about what my company is doing to help them?

41. In what ways do I try to up-sell my clients?

42. Do I need to make money on first-time buyers, or am I satisfied with only making it on the back end (reorders), short- or long-term strategy.

43. Do I ever barter my products, services, or assets with other companies in exchange for their products, services, or assets?

44. What kind of guarantee or warranty do I give my clients, to take away the risk of the transaction, and how does it compare with my competitors' or what the industry at large offers?

45. What is my client attrition rate?

46. How do I capture the names, addresses, and phone numbers of all my clients and prospects? Do I use them in my marketing programs?

47. What is my average order, transaction size, amount, and what are the steps I can take to increase it?

48. How much is the initial sale to a new client worth?

49. Do I use a list broker or data experts? If not, where do I get my prime prospect names?

50. Do I joint-venture my client names with other companies? If so, what were the results?

Just by answering these questions, you have placed yourself ahead of 95 percent of the businesspeople in America, many of whom are your competitors. Those people spend so much time working in their business, they never work *on* their business. Focusing on your business realities will enable you to apply more easily my income- and success-increasing principles to your business career and see greater success and profits in less time.

Again, if you were unable to answer any of these questions you will be able to when you have completed the book. And you probably will go back and answer some of them differently.

Action Steps

You can't make the best decisions, pursue the best strategy, or focus on a big goal until you first recognize and evaluate all the options, opportunities, and business intelligence you have available to you. So, identify what you're doing right and what you're doing wrong. What you could be doing better, differently, more effectively, and more profitably. And what you know, but don't act upon.

You can't know what area of your career or business to focus on and improve until you know the realities of these areas.

4

Your Business Soul— the Strategy of Preeminence

WHY DO SOME PEOPLE GAIN LEVELS OF SUCCESS SO MUCH higher than others'? Frequently it's due to the fact that they have a better philosophical strategy. They approach everyone they deal with in a totally different and more effective way than anyone else does. And while their competitors are usually unable to figure out this strategy, it is one *anyone* in business can successfully employ by simply changing his or her focus from "me" to "you." This is true whether you own a business of your own or work for a corporation. This simple adjustment in your focus is the key to what I believe is the most powerful business (and life) strategy you can employ. I call it the Strategy of Preeminence. Once you begin to use it you will always—not just sometimes, but always—stand out in the minds, hearts, and checkbooks of your client, your employees, your employer, or your boss as the very best there is. The preeminent choice.

The Strategy of Preeminence is quite simply the ability to put your clients' needs always ahead of your own. When you master that your success will naturally follow.

If it seems backward to put your clients' best interests ahead of your own that's understandable. In fact, that is the reason so many businesses are unremarkable, unmemorable, and, ultimately, unsuccessful.

It's amazing how many people and companies will say and do whatever it takes to make a one-time sale rather than taking the time to understand the clients' desired outcome. And then having the courage and the concern to tell that client that what they really need is much less than what they told you they wanted. You may, when you take this approach, end up with a smaller initial sale, but you will have just made a new friend, someone who will remember you the next time. And who will, no doubt, tell his friends about you and your company.

The Strategy of Preeminence is a powerful yet simple strategy that almost single-handedly can transform your business or career. It makes people enthusiastic to do business with you instead of your competitors. It will give you an uncanny insight into what people want, and why they act and react in various ways. It will turn clients into, literally, friends for life. And it will strengthen your passion and connection to everyone with whom you associate.

In this chapter you will learn how to understand the true needs of your prospects, clients, employees, bosses, vendors—everyone. And how to approach them in a way that results in their complete satisfaction and their long-term loyalty to you.

A Client, Not a Customer

I'm going to repeat a few short ideas from earlier in the book because they make an extremely important point.

Consider the definitions of these two words.

Customer: A person who purchases a commodity or service.
Client: A person who is under the protection of another.

If you use the word *customers*, that's fine. But always think of them as *clients*. And when you start to *serve* clients rather than *sell* clients, the limits on your business success will disappear.

What exactly does "under your protection" mean? In this case it means that you don't sell them a product or service just so you can make the largest one-time profit possible. You must understand and appreciate exactly what they need when they do business with you—even if they are unable to articulate that exact result themselves. Once you know the final outcome they need, you lead them to that outcome—you become a trusted adviser who protects them. And they have reason to remain your client for a lifetime.

When a father comes into your store to buy his six-year-old son his first bicycle, what is he looking for? What does he need? Does he just want a bicycle? No. He's looking for one of the most joyful sharing experiences of a lifetime—teaching his son how to ride a bicycle. Just like his father taught him to ride a bicycle when he was six. He's looking for a memory that will last for the rest of his life and his little boy's. He's looking for that once-in-a-lifetime moment when his son, smiling ear-to-ear and speeding down the street, yells, "Look, Dad, I'm riding a two-wheeler!"

So, do you sell the father and his son the top-of-the-line, highest-profit-margin bike in the store? Maybe, if that's the best solution to your client's problem. But you definitely should tell the father that you've seen hundreds of dads come in to buy their child's first bike and you know what a wonderful experience he and his son are about to have. And possibly a less expensive model would be better for his son. It's the little guy's first bicycle and he may crash it into a tree or two. You make the sale and you just became a trusted adviser to the father.

The father realizes you didn't just sell him a product. You "protected" him. He became a client. In a couple of years his son will need a new bike. Where do you think he'll go to buy it?

And at that point the upscale, high-profit-margin model might be the best choice. Maybe the entire family will want bikes to ride together.

And when the time comes for the little boy to buy his son his first bicycle, where do you think he'll go?

The Strategy of Preeminence doesn't apply only to selling clients your product or service. This strategy is of equal importance to anyone, in any business situation. If you're in administration, legal, shipping—any department—you should use the Strategy of Preeminence as a basis for dealing with everyone. Be a problem solver, not a problem bringer. Add value to every task you undertake on your employer's behalf. Anyone, in any situation, who can look at you as a trusted friend who is providing a service that will benefit them in some way, will be more than willing to sing your praises to those who have the ability to advance your career. Not just because you helped them. But also because they will want to continue to take advantage of the valuable service you provide them.

Whatever you do, if you focus on giving value and advice

instead of manipulating and maneuvering, you win over many more prospects, clients, bosses, colleagues, and friends. And you will be rewarded in ways you never dreamed.

Falling in Love

One of the biggest mistakes, probably *the* biggest mistake, people make in any business is that they fall in love with the wrong thing. They fall in love with their product, service, or company. You should believe passionately in your product, service, or company. But you should fall in love with your clients. By *client* I mean several groups. Not only the people and businesses who pay you for your goods or services. But also your employees, bosses, team members, and vendors.

Awesome service is admirable but trite. Falling in love with your clients means taking responsibility for their well-being. Putting their best interests ahead of your own.

Most people think, "What do I have to say to get people to buy?" Instead you should say, "What do I have to give? What benefit do I have to render?" It has nothing to do with sales shenanigans or trickery or schemes. It has everything to do with what benefits you give your clients.

The more value you give others, the more value you generate. Not only for your clients but for yourself. The more contributions you make to the richness of the lives of your clients, the more bonded you will be to them and they to you. And the more successful you will become.

The focus of your concern should state to the client, in essence, "You matter. Your well-being is important to me."

See yourself as becoming an agent of change. A creator of value. A value contributor.

You Give More Than You Realize

I was advising a group of Realtors. I asked them if they really thought that they provided superior value to their clients. Some said, "Absolutely." Some didn't know.

I asked them the question differently. I said, "Well, let me ask you these questions: If I chose another real estate agent over you, would he or she represent me at the same level? Would he or she research the market? Would he or she market me to other Realtors? Because that's what you really are when you list the property—you're a marketing agent whose job it is to sell that property to other agents."

Next, I said, "Would other agents negotiate, research, and identify opportunities for me to buy in the same way? Would they negotiate the transaction? Would they hand-hold it? Would they fight to get me the lowest rates? Would they negotiate to give me a lower cost than most people have to pay?"

And they said, "No—we do things that other people don't." (I had a core group of really successful, aggressively dedicated Realtors.)

I said, "Let's take some scenarios. A family came to you eager to sell their house for any number of reasons, either positive or negative. And you helped them realize a greater outcome than they thought they could get. (They thought they were going to have to sell for $200,000 but you were able to get them $240,000. Or they thought it was going to take six months and you were able to do it in two months.)

"Didn't you enrich their life?

"But how well did you enrich it? First of all, you took four months' worth of uncertainty out of their life by selling the house quickly. Or you put several thousand extra dollars in their pocket, money they otherwise wouldn't have had. Money for retirement. Money for paying bills or to invest in their new house, or to fund education or holidays.

"If you help somebody who thought he or she could only afford a $300,000 house get a $350,000 house because you got them a better rate, then you are looking out for your clients' well-being. You increased their lifestyle. You moved them into a different environment. You gave them more than they expected.

"Conversely, if somebody thought they were going to have to spend $350,000 but you were able to get them a house for $300,000 that was even bigger and better, you changed the quality of their life. You gave them enough money so they could do so many more things.

"Just look at the impact of your efforts. You gave them so much more than you've ever given yourself credit for. Didn't you really enrich their life at a deep level? Didn't you have a major impact?"

And they said yes. And I said, "And you invested three or four months of your life in the relationship, didn't you?" And they said yes.

And I said, "Did you get emphatically involved in their hopes, their dreams, their needs, their situation? All the key issues? Their complexities? Their family problems or situations? Yes?"

I said, "Didn't you really befriend them?" And they said yes.

"So didn't they reciprocate and befriend you?" They said yes. "Then doesn't that mean you have a very deep, rich friendship which you invested in?" And they said yes.

"Would you just drop any other friend of yours and let them fall out of your life after you had one social transaction with them?" And they said no. So I said, "Then why would you let that happen with this friendship? If they are a dear and valued friend, would you let any other friend make a dangerous mistake? Would you let any other friend really jeopardize their life? Would you let any other friend let somebody important to them do something stupid or dangerous or inadvisable?" And they said no.

"Then why would you allow any important friend of yours who is a past client, or any important friend of theirs or a relative or family member or coworker, do anything that was dangerous? In the scope of any given period of time, or in the life of any important friend of yours (i.e., a former client), there are so many people whose lives are changing.

"They're getting older and they're outgrowing their house because their children are gone and they need a smaller place. They're getting married and they need a bigger place. They have been married and living in an apartment but now they have children and they're ready to make a commitment. They have a death in their family and they have a necessity to downsize. They have a divorce in their family and they have a necessity to downsize. They have a move or a reversal in their business, and they have a necessity to downsize. They have a great achievement and great richness and they have a necessity to expand. They're blessed with richness and maybe they're pregnant and they need to expand."

The point is constant, constant flux. Constant dynamic change. People who are important, valued friends to people who are your valued friends deserve to have the best-reasoned, the best-informed, and the most objective and knowledgeable advice they possibly can get about important emotional decisions. Because they could get into someone's unscrupulous clutches and make a critical decision that could negatively impact a big portion of their lives and finances.

Don't you then owe it to your past clients, who are your valued friends, to contact them and tell them that you care deeply about them and if anybody in their lives is at these crossroads, you want to encourage them to refer them to you if for nothing more than just to get your best judgment on something. It doesn't matter whether they ultimately take advantage of your services. It just matters to you that they at least get the best take they can on the situation before they make an ill-advised decision.

That awareness of the value people have created, of the friendships and the investment and the importance of their past clients and others who are important to them, helped a bunch of real estate agents double and triple their sales. And in the process they had even more fun by making more great contributions to their clients' lives than ever imaginable. You can do the same.

You need to recognize the impact you have on people's lives in the business you are conducting. What you render, and the way you render it, has changed their lives. It has helped enrich them. It has helped their security.

What service or product are you involved with? Computers? Insurance? Accounting?

Think about the real estate agent example but substitute your product or service. Then realize the value you can or do give your clients.

If you think you don't have a client whom you sell to, think again. You have a department head you report to, employees who report to you, a company VP, a COO, a CFO, a CEO— these are your clients. And when you realize the value you can bring them you'll be rewarded not with sales, but with greater recognition, stature, and power within your company. You'll be rewarded with a larger office, a higher title, a raise.

Change the way you think about, deal with, and speak to your clients. Greet them on the phone and in person with the same joy, sincerity, and enthusiasm that you'd show any other valued friend.

Respect the importance of their time, their sense of security, and their comfort. Don't make them wait too long on hold or in your waiting room or at their home. Provide for their comfort. That may mean coffee and beverages and a comfortable, clean setting complete with fresh, interesting reading material. It may mean a pleasing shopping environment and enough help on hand for a client to get the most out of their buying experience with you.

It means pitching in when a client's in trouble—like the FedEx dispatcher who got a frantic call from a tearful bride-to-be whose gown had been misrouted the day before her wedding.

The alert dispatcher located the gown in a distant city and had it flown to the distraught client's city by private plane. The gown arrived in time for the young woman to wear it at her wedding.

The rescue effort was expensive, but it became the talk of the wedding reception—and no doubt caused many executives attending the ceremony to start using FedEx.

It means following up after the sale—not just to patronize but to contribute, acknowledge, and assure that client that you care about them.

It means thinking about the client as more than just a checkbook. It means seeing him or her as a valued business partner, someone whose well-being and success is directly tied to your own.

Human Nature

Mastering the Strategy of Preeminence is really the understanding and having the utmost respect for human nature. Start by considering yourself and how you go about making decisions. Naturally, you want to feel good about yourself and the decisions you make—in business or just in everyday life. You want to look smart and feel like you've done the best you can. But sometimes you're just not sure what the right decision is. So your first instinct is to take less action because you're afraid to take the wrong action, and you don't want to look dumb.

What you look for in those situations is a trusted friend. A confidant. Someone you can feel comfortable asking advice from because you know he or she has your best interests at heart and will give you advice that will benefit you, not him or her.

Now, consider that everyone you sell to, individuals or corporations, reacts in exactly the same way. Because they are all, first and foremost, human beings. And, as such, they will always exhibit human behavior. Just like you.

Your job, therefore, is to understand and acknowledge the reality of human nature in your clients. Accept that people will work harder not to look foolish than they will work to gain an advantage. Become their trusted adviser, their friend. Treat them the same way you would want to be treated.

A successful business starts not with just a great idea or product. Rather, it starts with the desire to provide a solution to another's problem. In doing so you enrich your own life and the lives of those around you, your family and employees or employers, by enriching the lives of your clients.

You need to understand that you have a higher purpose for being in business than simply making money. Your purpose must be understanding what you can do to help solve the problems of others, help maximize the options, and finding ways to do it. And unless you understand that higher purpose, you can't begin to take advantage of your potential.

With that understanding, however, comes the realization that you can have an impact on people. That you can produce a positive response. A positive action. A positive result.

Think back to my session with the Realtors. They came to the realization that they don't simply sell houses. They enhance their clients' lives. And in doing so, they enhance their own lives, as well as those of their families and colleagues. Now that's a positive result. For everybody.

The beauty of the Strategy of Preeminence is that it applies to any business, whether you're selling life insurance or you own a hardware store. The steps you must take always remain the same. You must first identify what your client really needs, even if your client doesn't recognize what it is he or she needs. The client may think that a particular item is what he or she is searching for, but if you probe a bit you might see that an entirely different solution will solve your client's problem, maybe even a less expensive solution. Now you have become more than a salesperson. You've become an adviser. You've begun the process of winning trust and, ultimately, additional business from your client.

This approach to business may seem pretty obvious to you. But you'd be amazed at how few people in business understand this very basic concept. It's hard for them to understand that what they really are selling is solutions to problems, not merchandise. And it's hard for them to see that selling a person what he or she needs versus what they have to sell will set them apart from the pack and result in repeat business and referral business.

I guarantee that when you practice the Strategy of Preeminence the rewards you will accumulate will astonish you. And I don't mean just financial rewards. There is no question that you will generate more money than you ever imagined when you start putting your client's needs first. But it won't stop there.

Consider how you will feel about yourself and your business when you become a trusted adviser to your clients. I submit that your business, your life's investment, the body of your work, will stand for something wonderful. You will have created value for yourself and your family. You will have provided livelihood and sustenance to your employees. And not only will you have enriched your own life materially beyond anything you ever thought possible, but you will have enriched your life because you will recognize the worth of your endeavor.

Action Steps

Think about the different people you deal with, sell your products or services to, buy from, and work with. Think about them one at a time. Then focus on what that person's real need in dealing with you is. What results are they truly after? What's the impact your action, product, service, or function has on their career, job, future, well-being, etc.? How have you impacted their quality of life in the past? What has it meant in terms of their business or personal success? How much more could you do to improve your impact on that result? Think about their hopes, dreams, fears, interests, families, goals, and dependency or trust in you.

Realize these people are all your friends. Trusted and trusting friends. You've built a deep connection with them. Find something about them you can get even more enthusiastic and excited about. Then try a little test. Let your renewed passion and purpose work for you and them. Connect (in person, by letter, E-mail, or fax) more compassionately, respectfully, and loyally to that person. Then see what a dramatic difference it makes in the way they respond to you.

5

Break Even Today, Break the Bank Tomorrow

MOST BUSINESSES GENERATE A SUBSTANTIAL AMOUNT OF profit from clients who keep repurchasing, again and again—over the months, over the years, over the decades. Obviously, all those repurchases can put a substantial amount of profit into your bank account. Very little of that profit would be there if you didn't bring those clients into your business or practice in the first place.

How much would it be worth to your business if you could bring in an extra 10 or 110 or 1,010 clients this month and every month? Even if you don't make a single dime on the initial transaction, but instead you make enormous combined profits on all the repeat transactions you do with them in the future?

Acquiring clients at a breakeven or a slight loss and making substantial profits on back-end repurchasing is one of the most overlooked and underutilized methods of client growth and generation available to you. But it can't work for you until you first recognize a very important fact. If your business or practice is one that has a high probability of clients coming back, again and again, to repurchase from you the same or different products or services, you owe it to that business or practice to do everything within your power to get clients into the buying stream as quickly and easily as you possibly can.

Until you identify and understand exactly how much combined profit a client represents to your business for the life of that relationship, you can't begin to know how much time, effort, and, most importantly, expense you can afford to invest to acquire that client in the first place. You need to know the lifetime value of your clients (or your clients' marginal net worth).

M ost businesses and people make it far too hard for clients and employers to start a relationship with them. They make it too difficult to get prospects to start using their products or services to the maximum advantage. If you lower or totally eliminate the hurdle in starting a relationship, far more people will begin one with you.

If you deliver great value, service, and tangible results, these people will keep coming back and dealing with you. And the fact that you were the only one with enough faith in yourself, your product, or your service to take the risk instead of putting the risk on their shoulders will long be remembered favorably by these clients. The faster you get a buying or advisory relationship started, the faster someone will convert from prospect to lifelong client.

In this chapter you will learn how to determine the best possible offer to a first-time client—even if it doesn't result in an immediate profit. But you'll see that it will result in a long-term relationship and long-term profits.

Many companies increase their clients and profits merely by shifting their focus from trying to make a huge profit on the acquisition of a new client to making their real profit on all the repeat purchases that result from those new clients. The classic examples are the book and music clubs. Why would big, astute companies like Columbia House or Book-of-the-Month Club possibly be willing to send you six to twelve tapes, CDs, or books for a dollar or two initially? Do you think they lose money long-term on those transactions? Or do you think they recognize that for every 10 or every 110 people coming in, a large number will keep buying over and over again at full rate? They want to do everything possible to make it easy and attractive to get you started buying and using their service in the first place. By doing this they do tens of millions of dollars a year from the people who come in on that break-even proposition.

Many credit cards offer a 6 percent or lower interest rate for the first six months you have the card.

On-line server companies will offer thirty days' free service when you sign up.

A Hollywood motion-picture camera manufacturer lends (at no cost) their high-priced, state-of-the-art professional movie cameras to budding film-school directors. Many of those same students will someday rent their high-priced cameras when they become the next Steven Spielberg.

Ambitious employees volunteer to take on additional responsibility or fill in as interim supervisor or manager on their own time and at no additional pay. As a result they are in a position to get a promotion or raise in the near future.

Knowing how much a client will spend with you over a period of years tells you how much you can spend on the process of acquiring a client.

The most profitable thing you'll ever do for your business or career is to understand and ethically exploit the marginal net worth of a client.

What is the current lifetime value of one of your clients? It's the total profit of an average client over the lifetime of his or her patronage—including all residual sales—less all advertising, marketing, and incremental product or service-fulfillment expenses.

Let's say that your average new client brings you an average profit of $75 on the first sale. He or she repurchases three more times a year, with an average reorder amount of $300, and on each $300 reorder you make $150 gross profit.

Now, with the average patronage life lasting two years, every new client is worth $975.

You could, theoretically, afford to spend up to $975 to bring in a client and still break even.

If you haven't calculated your clients' marginal net worth yet, here's how to do it:

1. Compute your average sale and your profit per sale.
2. Compute how much additional profit a client is worth to you by determining how many times he or she comes back.
3. Compute precisely what a client costs by dividing the marketing budget by the number of clients it produces.
4. Compute the cost of a prospect the same way.
5. Compute how many sales you get for so many prospects (the percentage of prospects who become clients).
6. Compute the marginal net worth of a client by subtracting the cost to produce (or convert) the client from the profit you expect to earn from the client over the lifetime of his or her patronage.

Real-Life Successes

A client of mine is in the construction business. The firm is a very large one. It is their standard practice that the first job with any new client is done at a breakeven to their company. And they make certain that the client knows they're not making any money on the job. They do this to demonstrate and prove their ability and their performance. Eighty percent of the people who do that first job with them come back again, and my client does $50 million a year, almost all of which is the result of initially bringing clients in at a breakeven.

Another of my clients does $6 million a year in air-conditioning and heating maintenance repair work. The entire business is based on a very simple premise. Two times a year he does a mailing to all his clients, and he does advertising to the outside market offering a $19.95 tune-up and cleaning service for your air-conditioning or heating system. In the winter he offers to do your heating system; in the summer or spring he offers to do your air-conditioning system. He only charges $19.95 for the service. Quite frankly, it costs him about $30.00 to actually perform the service.

Why in the world would he lose nearly $10.00 on every client who responds? Because he has discovered, after analyzing the results of what happens when he runs this promotion, that 50 percent of the people having a service done have an immediate additional problem that needs to be repaired—one they didn't even realized existed. That results in a minimum $125.00 additional highly profitable service charge that occurs right at the same time the tune-up is being performed. Even though he loses $10.00 on the initial service, he usually makes a very handsome profit before he ever leaves the home.

He's also discovered that half of all the new people having the service performed for the first time come back again as regular, full-paying repair clients over the years. Half of his business, over $2.5 million from new clients, results from these $19.95 small-loss-based acquisition programs.

A coin company I worked with in the Midwest built a $500-million-a-year investor base by offering people the chance to make their first coin purchase at a breakeven. The coin company made no profit. They actually lost $10 because they gave every client buying those coins a set of books and reports valued at $100 that educated the buyer about investing in coins. Each set cost my client $10. That gave the clients a basis upon which to consider and evaluate whether coin investing was right for them. My client got approximately fifty thousand people the first year they made this offer to buy the coins at a breakeven. Of the fifty thousand initial clients, nearly ten thousand came back and bought $5,000 worth of additional coins within six months at full margin. Of those ten thousand people, about two thousand people came back and bought $10,000 or more additional coins at full margin. Of those two thousand people, five hundred came back and bought at least $50,000 of coins, all before the first year was over. And approximately two thousand of those people kept buying over and over again. The result was tens of millions of dollars in profit that resulted from fifty thousand new clients acquired at a slight loss.

Same Strategy, Different Approaches

Once you've calculated the lifetime value of a client, you have many ways to accomplish your break-even objective.

Remember, the goal isn't just to cut the price of the first purchase. The goal is to make that first purchase so much more appealing that people find it harder to say no than yes . . . please!

While reducing the price of your product or service is the most common and obvious way to get the first sale, there are other powerful ways to obtain first-time buyers.

For example, you can calculate your allowable marketing or selling cost, which is how much money you're willing to either spend or forgo receiving (by reducing the selling price), in order to make that very first purchase more appealing to a prospective client.

Let's say your product or service sells for $200 and your cost is $100. Also assume your average client repurchases several times a year for several years and you will realize a good long-term profit. Obviously you can reduce your price by $100 on the first sale to reach a break-even point and gain a new client. But you could put that $100 to a number of other uses.

You could keep the price at $200 and use the $100 as "spiff" or extra selling incentives to your salespeople. Giving salespeople greater financial incentive to bring in new, first-time clients can produce tremendous results in the right situation.

You could also use that same $100 to buy more of your product or service. So you still charge the full $200, but you give prospects twice the quantity on the first purchase.

Or you could take the $100 and use it to buy other complementary products or services (at wholesale) to package and add to your product or service without raising the $200 price—so the value of your offer becomes far greater and thus more attractive.

Or you could use that $100 to invest in advertising, sales letters, additional salespeople, free seminars, or any other marketing and selling programs. Or you could rent promotional space in someone's store or trade-show booth and pay them the $100 for every new client you gain through their facility.

The only limitation you have on how to use your allowable marketing or selling cost to help you strategically break even on the initial sale is that it must be ethical and legal. And after testing it out it must be economically viable in the long term.

This strategy, when applied, will make your conventional-thinking, nonstrategic competitors look far more expensive and appear to offer significantly less value. And you will gain visible distinction, attract more clients, and seed significant profits for the future.

Action Steps

Make a list of every product or service you or your company sells. Then figure out how you can lower the resistance barrier to a prospective client, employer, or prospect by lowering the entrance fee you ask. Remember, focus attention on the fact that where you begin has nothing to do with where you end up. A new client first coming in for a lower-priced starter offer will turn into a client who buys over and over at full margin. Likewise, an employer who promotes you to a higher position (or a new employer who hires you) but will pay you only your previous salary for the first thirty or sixty or ninety days is the same employer who will probably agree to pay you 30 or 50 or 100 percent more in the long term. But before you get that 30 or 50 or 100 percent salary increase, you have to get in the door.

Try it out in a small, safe test approach first. You might offer to do a project for your current employer or work in a new position for three months with no raise. You'll be pleasantly surprised by how many people take you up on your proposition. If you use the logical strategy of lowering the barrier of entry to get started in a relationship, it will produce significant business and career results.

6

Vive la Différence

How can you elevate yourself or your company to a position of notable superiority over your competition?

In order to stand above the crowded marketplace, you or your company must offer your prospect or client a unique and distinctive benefit or advantage above and beyond that of your competitor. If you don't, people have no motivation to do business with you instead of your competition.

You must identify and understand what it is you or your company do or can start doing for your clients that provides them with a result or an advantage superior to the competition's. This is called the unique selling proposition (USP). Your unique selling proposition is that distinct, appealing idea that sets your business apart from every other "me too" competitor.

When you identify what that distinct advantage is, you then must integrate it into all your promotional, marketing, advertising, and selling operations. This includes what you or your salespeople do and say, plus all the collateral material you use, the brochures, the sales letters, advertising—everything. You don't just want to say it, you want to constantly demonstrate it. You want to live it. That means that whatever your USP stands for, you do at all times.

USPs differ for different companies and different market applications. I suggest the first thing you do is look at ads in newspapers, brochures, professional journals, trade papers, on television and radio, even in the Yellow Pages, to see what unique selling propositions various organizations use. Talk to business owners and salespeople and ask them, "What do you think the primary advantage of doing business with you or your firm is over your competitor?" Listen to how their answers might directly or indirectly apply to creating your own unique selling proposition.

In business and in a career, standing out more favorably, advantageously, and appealingly in the prospect's or client's eyes is a big reason why clients and employers will choose you over your competitor. The more clearly you telegraph what makes you the better choice (offering more benefits, advantages, and bottom-line payoff), the more often they'll choose you over your competition. You need to create maximum real and perceived advantage in your clients' and employers' eyes and minds at all times.

In this chapter you will learn to develop a personal unique selling proposition that sets you apart from your competition and attracts clients by offering them a powerful and unique benefit.

Developing, identifying, and incorporating your personal USP into everything you do is challenging. But the reward will be well worth the time. It will give you differentiation from, distinction from, and the advantage over everyone in your marketplace. So don't be hurried. Think about what you do. And think about what your competitors do, or don't do, and how you could do it better.

Your entire marketing and operational success should be built upon your unique selling proposition. Your USP may touch any part of the marketing gamut—price, service, quality, exclusivity, or any other aspect of your business.

There are many kinds of USP successes. Some companies position themselves as having the best selection or broadest array of buying options. Their USP is "broad choice." Other companies may offer more limited selection, but their USP is "low price" or "low markup." Another company may decide they don't want to be known for just price or selection. Instead they offer the finest quality at a higher but still reasonable price. Quality or exclusivity—even snob appeal—is a USP for some. Still another firm may offer a product at reasonable prices, but their distinct selling appeal is that they offer better service, assistance, or installation help.

The possibilities for building a USP are unlimited. It's best, however, to adopt a USP that dynamically addresses an obvious void in the marketplace that you can fill. Beware though. It's counterproductive to adopt a USP if you cannot fulfill the promise.

Before recommending some specific USPs, let me describe a curious and pathetic phenomenon. When you ask a business person to articulate clearly and concisely, in one paragraph or less, his or her company's USP, most have no answer. Why? Because they've never thought about or offered a specific unique selling proposition. Most of them have no USP, only a "me too," rudderless, nondescript business that feeds solely upon the momentum of the marketplace. There's nothing unique, there's nothing distinct. They promise no great value, benefit, or service—just "buy from us" for no justifiable reason.

It's no surprise that most businesses lacking a USP merely get by. Their failure rate is high. Their owners and employees are apathetic. And they get only a small share of potential business.

But other than a convenient location, why should they get much patronage if they fail to offer any appealing promise, unique feature, or special service? Clients expect special consideration and regard in exchange for their business.

Would you want to patronize a firm that's just "there," with no unique benefit, no incredible prices or selection, no especially comforting counsel, service, or guarantee?

It's ludicrous to operate any business without carefully crafting a clear, strong, appealing USP into the very fabric of that business's daily existence.

That tiny fraction of all business professionals who adopt a dynamic USP fare immeasurably better than those without one. They have a profound advantage over all their competitors.

The Big Promise

How do you pick a USP? You must first identify which needs are going unfulfilled within your industry, such as:
1. A broad selection
2. Big discounts
3. Advice and assistance
4. Convenience (i.e., location, fully stocked shelves, immediate delivery)
5. Top-of-the-line products or services
6. Speedy service
7. Services above and beyond the basics
8. A longer and more comprehensive warranty or guarantee than the norm
9. Any other distinct advantage, tangible or intangible bene-

fits, or valuable advantages you can give that the competition doesn't.

The point is to focus on the one niche, need, or gap that is most sorely lacking—provided you can keep the promise you make.

You can even create hybrid USPs—combinations that integrate one marketing gap with another. Before you decide on a USP, be sure you can always deliver that USP through your whole organization. You and/or your staff must consistently maintain high levels of quality or service.

If your USP is that your company offers the broadest selection of products or services "instantly available" or "always in stock," but in reality you only stock six out of twenty-five items and only a few of each item, then you're falling down on the essence of your USP—and your marketing will fail. It is critical to always fulfill the "big promise" of your USP. If you don't honestly believe you can deliver on your USP, pick another one. Be sure it's unique and that you can fulfill it.

Preemptive Marketing

Another way to develop a unique selling proposition is through preemptive marketing.

A classic example of the power of developing a USP through preemptive marketing occurred years ago with Schlitz Beer.

In the early 1920s, there were about ten different brewing companies aggressively competing for the same market. Schlitz wasn't doing very well and was number eight in the market.

All the breweries advertised the same basic message: "Our Beer Is Pure." They didn't explain to the beer drinker what *pure* really meant. They just kept saying, "pure," "pure," "pure."

Schlitz hired a marketing consultant in hopes of improving sales. The marketing consultant was taken on a tour of the brewery and was told how Schlitz brewed their beer. He was very impressed with what he learned.

The Schlitz facilities were right on Lake Michigan and the water back in the twenties was very clean. However, even though they were right on the lake, they drilled two five-thousand-foot artesian wells because they had to go deep enough to find the right combination of water with the mineral content to make the best possible beer.

They explained how they went through 1,623 separate experiments over five years to identify and develop the finest mother yeast cell that could produce the richest taste and flavor.

They showed him how they went through a process of distillation of the water before they used it to brew the beer. It was heated to five thousand degrees Fahrenheit and then cooled down and condensed—and they did that not once but three times to make sure it was absolutely purified.

They described the bottling process where they steamed each bottle at temperatures of sixteen hundred degrees Fahrenheit to kill all bacteria and all germs so they could not possibly contaminate the taste of their beer.

Then they explained that they had every batch tasted to make certain it was pure and rich before they would ever bottle it and send it out the door.

The consultant was overwhelmed by this brewing process. He told Schlitz management that they should tell consumers about the extraordinary measures they took to brew their beer. Schlitz management said, "Why would we do that? All breweries do the same thing we do."

But the marketing consultant understood the concept of preemptive marketing. "But no one in your industry explains it," he answered. "The first person who tells the story and explains how, and the reasons why, you do something, will gain distinction and preeminence in the marketplace from then on."

Schlitz was the first and the only company that ever told the story of how their beer was made. That became their unique selling proposition.

Through their USP, Schlitz made the word *pure* take on a very different and much more tangible meaning to all beer drinkers around the country.

Consumers saw in the description of the brewing and bottling process that Schlitz went through something totally different and far more valuable and appealing than any other beer on the market.

Schlitz began using this preemptive marketing USP, and in six months Schlitz beer moved from number eight in market sales to number one.

Be Clear and to the Point

Before you can incorporate and communicate your chosen USP through various marketing avenues, focus and articulate it crisply and clearly—with impact. Don't be cute or abstract. Think it through until you can articulate it in one crystal clear, compelling, alluring paragraph—or less.

The USP is the nucleus around which you build your success, fame, and wealth. So you'd better be able to state it. If you can't state it, your prospects won't see it. Whenever a client needs the type of product or service you sell, your USP should bring you or your company immediately to mind. Clearly conveying the USP through your marketing and business performance will make business success inevitable. But you must boil down your USP to its bare essence.

Try it. Write a one-paragraph statement of your new USP. At first, you will have trouble expressing it tightly and specifically. It may take two or three paragraphs or more. That's okay. Ruthlessly edit away the generalities, and focus on a crisp, clear statement that promises the most you could possibly offer. Hack away excess verbiage until you have a clearly defined unique selling proposition that a client or prospect can immediately seize upon.

You must integrate your USP into every marketing aspect of your business, including display advertising, sales letters, and field salespeople.

Let's say you run display ads, and your USP offers a greater selection than any other competitor. There are several ways to integrate this into your ads.

State the USP in the ad headline:

We Always Have 168 Different Widgets
In No Less Than Twelve Different Sizes
And Ten Desirable Colors
In Price Ranges from $6 to $600

Or:

Five Times the Selection,
Four Times the Color Choice,
Three Times the Number of Convenient Locations,
Two Times the Warranty,
And Half the Markup of Any Other Dealer

Or amplify your USP in a subhead:

**Most Plumbing Contractors Handle One
Or Two Lines of Air-Conditioning**

Acme Plumbing, Heating, and Air-Conditioning handles the ten best-selling brands—plus we are an authorized installer and service center for five additional lines. Why accept little or no choice on a matter as important as your office or home comfort, when a call to Acme can put all the options at your command?

Or maybe this one:

Most Service Companies Work from 9:00 to 5:00

ABC Service Company will send a repairperson whenever you need one. We have twenty service people on twenty-four-hour call, seven days a week, fifty-two weeks a year—including holidays, even Christmas and New Year's. With twenty full-time service people always on call, we'll respond within three hours—even on weekends.

One more important point: Our repair prices are the same whether you use us weekdays at 2 P.M. or weekends at 5 A.M. And our rates average 10 percent below our top ten competitors.

Those are just a few suggestions for display headlines and subheadlines for a selection-based USP. Now let's look at some ways to develop that headline thought in the body of any ad.

**When You're in the Market for Widgets,
You Want to Know All Your Choices—
Unless You Are Happy with Just Any Old
Widget, or the First Widget You Find**

If you're not aware of all the available choices, how can you possibly know which widget is right for you?

That's why ABC Company doesn't just offer one or two kinds of widgets. We've researched the widget industry extensively for years. There are 106 different kinds of widgets, and depending on your budget and expected usage, different ones may serve you better or more economically.

If your widget must last fifteen years, spend 20 percent more for our twenty-year-guaranteed, triple-layered, quadrupled-welded (not riveted), lead-reinforced "soup."

If you only need the widget for a year or so, our private label copper/tin version is fine. It's one-half the thickness of the top-of-the-line unit and has 60 percent of the capacity, its seams are precision-riveted and solder-sealed, and its durability rating is eighty-eight plus. Best of all, it only costs 40 percent as much as the top-of-the-line unit.

Your needs are unique, and a widget that might be perfect for someone else might be too much or too little for your special needs. That is why we feature 15 brands, 47 different models, and 106 different types. Plus . . . (You get the point.)

The Price-Discount USP

If your USP is price-discount positioning, you might use these kinds of headlines and subheadlines:

**We Sell the Same Brands of Widgets as
Company X or Company Y—
At 25 to 75 Percent Less**

Or:

It Usually Costs You $110 per
Square Foot to Build a New Home

We'll remodel up to four thousand square feet with triple-grade materials—two-by-six (minimum of two-by-four) high-alloy, twenty-thousand-pound high-tech nails (instead of tin), real walnut paneling (not veneer), filament wool carpet (not polyester), and pure brass fixtures—for just $39 a square foot. (Minimum five hundred square feet.)

Or:

When a Dealer Buys Widgets from the Factory,
He Gets a 10 Percent Discount for Buying a Dozen,
A 20 Percent Discount for Buying a Gross,
And a 50 Percent Discount for Buying Five Hundred

We buy widgets in minimum lots of ten thousand units, so our cost is about 20 percent less than any other dealer's. Then, we mark them up only 25 percent over our cost.

Where would you rather buy your widget? From the guy who buys them in dozen-unit lots, then doubles the price, or from us?

Now, extend the price-discount USP headline and subhead into the body copy of the ad:

A lot of companies sell widgets; some with a big markup, others for less. The average industry markup is 225 percent. That means widgets that cost the dealer $100 cost you $325.

The typical "discount" dealer marks up his widget 170

percent, so the widget that costs you $325 at the full-markup dealer costs you $275 at the discount dealer.

We buy more widgets at better prices than any other dealer in town.

We mark up our widgets a mere 50 percent. The same widget that costs you $325 at the full-markup dealer, or $275 at the discount dealer, costs you only $150 at our company.

The Service-Oriented USP

Here are ideas for a service USP approach:

**When You Buy Widgets from Every Other
Dealer in Town, You Get a "Limited"
Twelve-Month Warranty. When You Buy That
Widget from Us, You Get a Lifetime,
"Unlimited" Warranty with Service
Guaranteed within Twenty-four Hours, and a
Loaner Furnished Free. Plus,
We Make House Calls.**

Or:

**Most Tree Trimmers Charge You $100 or
More for Every Call. And Your Trees and
Shrubs Should Be Trimmed at Least
Three Times a Year.**

ABC Tree Trimmers will trim and maintain your trees and shrubs six times a year—once every two months—and all it costs you is $16 a month, billed quarterly.

Or another possibility is:

Whenever It Snows, We'll Be Out
Within Twenty-four Hours to Clean Your
Driveway and Walk—Free
. . . Just another added benefit of placing your home owner's policy with XYZ Agency.

The Quality or Snob-Appeal USP

How about the quality/executive USP? Here are a few interesting headline and body copy possibilities.

Only 1,200 XYZ Deluxe Widgets
Are Produced Annually
Nine hundred stay in Europe, where they originate. Of the remaining 300, 50 go to Japan. Of the remaining 250, 100 go to South America and Australia.

Each year, only 150 come into the United States. Of that 150, only 25 are sent to California—and we've got 18 of them.

We'll offer them at very fair prices to our best clients as long as they last.

Or:

The Framework of the ABC
Custom-Designed Sofa Is Fused
Together with ⅞-Inch-Thick Dowels
It's then epoxy-melded with a graphite compound tested to a strength tolerance of over twelve thousand pounds of force. It's designed to firmly support the sofa for at least fifty years.

The fabric is handmade by craftsmen in a family-owned

mill, where they still weave fabrics the same way they did one hundred years ago. Each yard of fabric contains 5,680 feet (over a mile) of silk and nylon threads, and patterns are intricately worked into the fabric with artistic precision—one strand at a time. Embossing is meticulously supervised by the same ruthless perfectionist who oversaw the creation of the magnificent fabric that adorns the sofa in the reception area just outside the White House's Oval Office.

This factory produces only forty-five hundred yards of handwoven, hand-embroidered, hand-inspected, quadruple-lined and finished fabric each year—only enough material to cover eighty-five sofas in an entire year. We have secured the entire production of the factory for the month of May and we are accepting inquiries regarding our custom-designed, custom-covered sofa. But, please, don't call us unless you can wait patiently for three months, can afford the best, and can appreciate a genuine, one-of-a-kind work of historic art.

Reinforcement

Are you starting to see a trend here? The more measurable, comparable, demonstrable, or quantifiable your advantage, the more powerful it is, too!

By now you should have the general idea that you should carefully integrate your newly adopted USP into the headline and body copy of every ad you run, in every direct-mail piece you send out.

But integrating your USP into just your ads and mailing pieces is not enough. You must integrate it into every form of your marketing.

When you or your salespeople call on prospects, everything

you say should clearly reinforce your USP. You should explain the USP to the client in a clear, concise statement.

Throughout the sales presentation, your salespeople should refer to the USP benefits or advantages. Always show the prospect why it's very much in his or her best interests to take advantage of your USP rather than your competitor's USP (if he even has one).

Whether it's you or your salespeople, don't merely try to wing it. Do your homework. Express the essence of your USP. Be sure you and your team can clearly and powerfully express your USP in sixty seconds (the oral equivalent of a written paragraph). Then compellingly state how it benefits the prospect and why it's important. Furnish your prospects with plenty of examples of how you honestly deliver your USP.

When an old, tired company or profession adopts a powerful, new, and appealing USP, it gives new life, new excitement, new interest, and new appeal to the marketing plan. You're suddenly different. Now you're on the client's side. You're his advocate, championing whatever advantage you or your firm's USP can offer him. It's exciting and appealing to clients, as well as to your company.

Finding Your Niche . . . or Niches

Think about your own past buying experience in light of the USP examples I gave you earlier. When you are in the market for a product or service, don't you tend to favor any business that strongly presents one of the basic forms of USPs?

However, remember this axiom: You will not appeal to everybody. In fact, certain USPs are designed to appeal to only one segment of a market. There is a vast gulf between the upscale clients and the bargain seekers, and you probably can't reach them both. Which do you want to stake out as your market niche?

Don't forget my earlier advice—don't adopt a USP that you can't deliver. Also, analyze the market potential of various USP positions in terms of volume, profits, and repeat business. Your USP must not only fill a market void but also result in adequate volume, clients, action, and profit to suit your psychological and financial needs.

If you're like me—never satisfied, and constantly searching for new challenges—you can actually compete against yourself.

There's no rule that says you can't, by adopting different USPs, develop different businesses or separate divisions of your business which compete against one another.

For example, you could develop an exclusive and expensive boutique operation to go after the low-volume, high-profit end of your market, while simultaneously developing a high-volume discount department to go after your mass market. At the same time, you could create a supereffective service operation to go after people requiring special attention or accommodations.

Get with the Program

A department store developed a one-time USP holiday sale. Full-page newspaper ads featured increased inventory and price reductions and offered clients the ease of phoning in their orders. When clients called, the telephone operators knew nothing about the unique offer because no one had informed them. The result: Clients were irritated and sales were lost because one store executive failed to tell the telephone operators about the plan.

All your in-store clerks, telephone staff, receptionists, client-service people—everyone with any public contact or client interaction, or anyone who impacts your business—must fully understand, embrace, and believe in your USP.

If your USP is giving advice, assistance, and superior service, it can't stop with mere sales rhetoric. It must become total company conduct. If someone calls in with a question, the people answering the call must extend themselves. You and your employees must live, breathe, and act your USP at all times.

Talk to your staff, write scripts, hold contests, and reward people who distinguish themselves in promoting your USP. Set an example so your staff can see the USP in action. Most people are silently begging to be led—especially your employees. Teach them how to be perpetual extensions of your USP.

Repeat Sales and the USP

Most businesses depend on repeat or back-end sales of some sort, so it's vitally important to indelibly etch a strong, clear, compelling USP in the minds of your clients *after* they've bought from you. This way, your distinct advantage and benefits will pop into their heads when it comes time to buy again.

How can you ensure that you are in the hearts and minds of your clients after the sale? Here are a few good approaches: Immediately following the sale, write, e-mail, phone, or visit your clients. During this follow-up effort, make sure the clients feel important and special, and that their initial purchases are "resold." Repeat your USP and remind the clients how it helped them make their purchasing decision.

Good marketing requires that you give clients rational reasons for their emotional buying decision. A strong USP helps you do that.

Extending Your USP

A USP can come in the form of an occasional special offer. Depending on the business, I advise my clients to frequently offer special promotions to their clients by mail, telephone, or in person. Every human wants to feel appreciated and personally acknowledged. By offering your clients genuine, specially priced deals or first choice, you endear yourself to them. At the same time, you enhance your clients' perception of your ongoing USP.

Remember the following principles when extending a special offer:

First, the client should always see the offer as a logical extension of your basic USP.

If your USP is service, your preferred promotions will be service-based rather than price-based. Give them extended service—for instance, a special offer of your basic service, or one year of free consulting or assistance not normally given.

Second, make it very clear that this special offer is only available to current clients.

Third, don't cut corners by not providing a better price or higher-quality product, longer guarantee, or added services.

Remember the basic point—integrate a powerful unique selling proposition into every aspect of your communication with prospects and clients. Special promotions can amplify your clients' appreciation of your USP.

Actions Speak Louder Than Words

Your client-services operation is an important vehicle for your USP. Your client-service people should know just as much about available choices, options, or whatever your USP is as your salespeople. Give them reasonable authority to replace, repair, or reinstall if there is any dissatisfaction. Make them aware that their jobs depend on ensuring that the promise behind your USP is fulfilled. They should provide evidence to any client with a problem, complaint, or question that the USP is real and that the entire company is enthusiastically committed to doing whatever it takes to promptly fulfill that USP promise.

Some Examples

When Stouffer's rolled out its Lean Cuisine frozen entrées, they weren't simply selling frozen food. There were already dozens of companies selling frozen food. Stouffer's USP was selling the idea of high-class dieting to an increasingly health-conscious populace. Lean Cuisine wasn't targeted at people looking for frozen entrées and dinners—it was focused on consumers who would be attracted to the idea that the food was convenient, tasty, and compatible with a healthful weight-conscious lifestyle.

A printing company I have advised was having trouble developing a USP that set them apart from the competition. Their original USP was "Quality is no accident." Not a bad place to start, but it was too vague. Just saying the word *quality* doesn't mean much. People really want no mistakes and they want it on time. The USP they now advertise is "On-Time Printing, No Excuses." And their advertising uses the USP to explain exactly what they will do for a client—perform faster, define the job requirements and length, and guarantee that there will be no mistakes in the work.

When Domino's first came out, do you remember what they said? Hot, juicy, delicious pizza—delivered to your door in thirty minutes or less—or it's yours absolutely free.

Back when they started, no company was delivering pizza in a half hour—guaranteed. Few companies delivered pizza, and if the pizza was delivered late and cold you lived with it—you owned it.

Domino's was the first and only company to do that when they started. Their USP was so distinctive they virtually owned the market for years.

Nordstrom built their department store success through one basic unique selling proposition. If you have any problem with a purchase, for any reason, bring it back for a no-questions-asked, 100 percent money-back refund—anytime in the future. Anytime in the future—not in three days, not in seven days, not in thirty days. If a year later you're dissatisfied—if five years later you're dissatisfied—*it's no problem*.

Financial adviser Howard Ruff built a twenty-million-dollar newsletter empire back in the eighties, by putting himself in a unique and distinctive position in his marketplace.

Most of the other financial advisers took the position that they were big-time Wall Street pros. And they were trying to appeal only to the affluent investors.

Howard took the opposite approach—he said, "I am the financial adviser to the middle class. And I want to protect your interests at a different level. I know how hard you work to make a dollar. I know how important it is that you don't lose it. I know how critical your retirement monies are to you. I respect your situation and I will approach it differently than anybody else."

That USP rang so true that hundreds of thousands of middle-class investors flocked to him.

I have two different clients in the expensive business-software industry who both have used the same process.

They will not try to sell any prospect until they first invite them to attend a day-long, extensive seminar program.

During this program my clients start at the beginning and explain thoroughly to all the prospects in attendance how and why and where their software can produce the greatest advantage to a client.

They explain how the software was created, why the software was created, and all the benefits and functions that were engineered into the software.

They tell the prospects how other companies in their fields are using that software today. They cite for them specific performance improvements they can expect to occur when they start using that software in their businesses. And they answer every question a prospect attendee could pose. Plus, they introduce questions the prospects have never even thought to ask.

At the end of these seminars they then offer these prospects the chance to experience the software in their operation, side by side with their existing software, for thirty days.

They put a pilot program in operation.

They also introduce the prospect and arrange private interviews with at least a dozen other people in the same business who are successfully utilizing the software. In this way the prospect can get a candid, objective assessment, firsthand from actual real live users, of the benefits and advantages they can expect to receive when they start using that software in their own enterprise.

I advise a chain of beauty salons that educate women before they ever take a client. They teach them about the role makeup and hairstyle have in complementing and improving the design of their facial structure.

They talk about how other clients have used different styles. They show them pictures. They ask them a lot of questions not only about what they think will look the best, but questions about their lifestyle. They then can appreciate what the best recommendations might be to give the client the best looks, and the best feels, for their active or inactive lives.

You should even integrate your USP into every contact with dissatisfied clients.

Whenever someone asks for a refund, replacement, or adjustment, instead of resenting the fact that you have to give back money, use that opportunity to reconvey the essence of your USP—either in person or via letter. If you have an exchange department, instruct that staff to courteously and sincerely reiterate your firm's USP and assure the dissatisfied client of the firm's commitment to offer more service, greater selection, or better guarantees. Then, if you issue credit or a check, include a prepared letter expressing your deep commitment to your USP and apologizing for any inconvenience, disappointment, or dissatisfaction.

In the mail-order catalog business, the Sharper Image has a dynamic USP built around exclusive, expensive, nonessential adult toys. All of these toys are unique and high-tech, and they can't be found in ordinary stores or gift shops.

The list of ego-indulging items sold by the Sharper Image is unbelievable. Everything from computerized bathroom scales to full sets of mounted armor. Their USP of selling exclusive, exotic toys fills a void. Believe it or not, a lot of people are willing and able to buy these items. Especially if they believe they are buying something unique that will impress their peers.

The Sharper Image then adds four elements to make its USP even more irresistible:

First, the president of the Sharper Image personally tests, evaluates, buys, and uses every product he sells. His personal guarantee stands behind every product he offers.

Second, you can try out any product for one full month, solely at the Sharper Image's risk, never your own.

Third, if at any time within a twelve-month period you find the item at a lower price than you paid for it at the Sharper Image, they will refund the difference on the spot.

Fourth, they have a frequent-buyer's point program where clients get special bonus gifts for buying from them.

The Sharper Image increased their volume to several hundred million dollars in annual sales. Their USP produced that success.

A Los Angeles–based pest control company also had a nifty concept. If you called them for any specific, one-shot exterminating problem, they would up-sell you to a quarterly maintenance program plus free service calls any time a specific pest problem arose.

Signing their agreement gave you the peace of mind that no ants, roaches, fleas, spiders, or other pests would infest your home. Instead of getting just $60 for solving a one-shot pest control problem, the quarterly maintenance plan earned them $200 a year.

Converting one-shot service calls into price-induced annual maintenance or annual service programs has terrific USP appeal, and it can be applied in all sorts of businesses.

Your unique selling proposition is vital to your marketing foundation. You must clearly identify and articulate your firm's USP.

In some cases you have to create your USP from scratch. Take the miniwarehouse owner, for example, who, like most miniwarehouse owners, was simply offering spaces for rent.

The USP: Offer free transportation from the client's home to the miniwarehouse, provided the items are in shippable containers. And provided the client signs up for a six-month rental in advance.

And why not also offer free insurance for long-term renters—and even a free delivery service for anyone who wants an item temporarily brought back from storage?

If you needed miniwarehouse space, who would you go to: someone who offered just a cubicle and a key, or someone who offered all these additional conveniences at no extra charge? That's the power of a strong USP.

In other cases, a company may already have a strong USP but doesn't know it. A custom jeweler thought his USP was "Unusual Gold Jewelry." But on interviewing the jeweler, I discovered within seconds that what the jeweler was offering was much more specific.

His real USP was "Custom jewelry of twice the quality as the run-of-the-mill stuff but at half the price." See how much more powerful that is to a prospective client?

The bottom line is this: Develop a USP and extol it in everything you do. It can put you head and shoulders above your competition forever.

Action Steps

Make a list of the real benefits or advantages that you already offer a client or employer. Then list the benefits and advantages your competition offers them that you don't. Now list the ways you could improve upon your competitors' unique advantages. List any niche advantages you already possess. For instance, the ease of application of your product or service. Or your location.

Now make a list of your most important or favorite suppliers, vendors, retailers, and businesses in your professional life. Focus on the one biggest reason why you like or prefer dealing with each of these entities over their competition. Reduce that main reason or benefit down to one sentence or less. Then see if you can adopt that same benefit or advantage to your business or career.

Think about the biggest successes you know or see in any field. What's their biggest single benefit (their USP) to their client market? Is there a direct application here for you? When you understand and start focusing on and promoting the unique advantages or benefits you can offer your clients or employer, you'll see results.

7

Make 'Em an Offer They Can't Refuse

A FARMER WANTED TO BUY A PONY FOR HIS LITTLE DAUGH-ter. There were two for sale in his town. Both ponies were equal in all aspects. The first man told the farmer he wanted $500 for his pony—take it or leave it. The second man was selling his pony for $750.

But the second man told the farmer he wanted the farmer's daughter to try out the pony for a month before the farmer had to make any purchasing decision. He offered to bring the pony out to the farmer's home along with a month's worth of hay to feed the pony. He said he'd send out his own stableman once a week to show the little girl how to groom and care for the pony. He told the farmer the pony was kind and gentle, but to have his daughter ride the pony each day to make certain they got along together.

Finally, he said that at the end of thirty days he'd drive over to the farmer's and either take back the pony and clean up the stall—or ask, then, to be paid the $750.

Which pony do you suppose the farmer decided to purchase for his daughter?

Obviously, it was no contest. And it will be no contest for you against your competition if you incorporate strong risk reversal into your business operation.

The biggest secret to success in business or a career is to always maintain the edge in everything you do. Logical-sounding, yes, but infrequently understood. Even less frequently practiced. One of the biggest "competitive-edge" advantages you'll ever gain is to always make it easier for the client to say yes than it is for them to say no. You do it by taking away the financial, psychological, or emotional risk factors that are always attached (stated or unstated) to virtually any decision-making proposition you ever ask a client to make. When you remove the risk for anyone deciding to do business with you, it results in a powerful advantage in your business and financial success.

In this chapter you will learn how to use risk reversal to eliminate the client's risk in any transaction, thus eliminating the primary obstacle to their buying.

As I mentioned earlier, whenever any two parties come together to transact business of any kind, one side is always asking the other (either consciously or otherwise) to assume more or all of the risk.

When you take away the risk to your prospect or client, you lower the barrier to action, thus eliminating the primary obstacle to buying. And that's what you must do. Assume the risk in every transaction you have with your clients. Let them know that, if they are ever dissatisfied, you will give them their money back, redo the job at no charge, or whatever else it takes to demonstrate your total, passionate commitment to their satisfaction.

From a practical standpoint, you probably offer some form of risk reversal to your clients. But odds are you don't forcefully use that in your selling efforts. Most people almost sweep it under the rug, or hide it in their closet.

I want you to push it into the heart of your selling message.

You're going to be the one company or practice in your industry or the one executive or staff member in your company who offers a strong and powerful risk reversal to the client.

Here's how you do it:

You totally and completely guarantee the purchase for your client.

What does *guarantee* mean? It means you totally eliminate the risk for the client. You do it by making a completely risk-free performance guarantee to compel them to purchase from you instead of your competitor and to purchase now.

Think about what your clients want most (results-wise) from purchasing your product or service. Then guarantee them that outcome—or they can have their money back. If it's not practical to fully guarantee the entire purchase, then guarantee whatever portion of the purchase is practical.

What's Better Than Risk-Free?

In many selling situations, competition is so keen that you need a greater benefit for the client than basic risk reversal. The answer is to use a better-than-risk-free guarantee (BTRF).

The BTRF guarantee enables you to do something that a basic guarantee or risk-reversal approach does not. When you utilize a better-than-risk-free guarantee, you are acknowledging and rewarding the client for the value of both his or her time and his or her faith expended in favoring you with his or her purchasing decision.

When you tell me that if I am dissatisfied for any reason whatsoever, you will not only give me full and immediate return of my purchase price, but you promise me an additional reward on top—a compensation incentive for having taken the time, effort, and faith to purchase in the first place—I'm impressed. I'm hard-pressed to say no to a proposition like that.

On a practical transactional basis, here's how a better-than-risk-free guarantee works:

I sell my own live training programs on a better-than-risk-free basis.

First I let people preview my methods both in written and recorded form, before I even ask them to sign up. I promise they'll get a tangible and profit-rendering idea they can apply and make money from before they ever sign up. The materials are theirs to keep even if they don't go forward and attend my seminar. When they sign up I send them nearly $5,000 worth of materials a full six weeks prior to attending. They are encouraged to read, listen, and watch everything I send them and apply what they learn prior to attending. If they don't make a significant preattendance profit, they are welcome to cancel and keep nearly a third of the advance materials for their efforts.

I don't stop there. If they do what I suggest, applying all the advance materials and making a profit up front, I still don't consider their attendance binding on their part, not until they've sat through a full one-half of the entire program. If by 2:00 P.M. on day two of my three-day program they haven't absolutely received well over $5,000 in value, they are welcome to leave and receive a full and immediate refund. No questions asked.

No hard feelings, either. And I want them to keep the materials for having gone that far.

Compensating your clients for their dissatisfaction and valuing their time and trust is the concept behind a better-than-risk-free guarantee. BTRF guarantees are a seldom-used but extremely powerful advantage you can give yourself and your business or practice.

Because this approach is probably a bit foreign to you, let's walk through a few ways you might use a better-than-risk-free guarantee.

If you sell products or services, consider offering the client something else in addition (a bonus) when they agree to purchase. Offer them an exceptional money-back guarantee, but allow the client to keep the bonus if he or she asks for a refund.

Another twist on this approach is to offer financial compensation if they ask for a refund. I've seen people use "double your money back" guarantees quite successfully.

I've seen publications not only offer to give you a refund but buy you a subscription to their competitor's publication if you are dissatisfied.

You have enormous flexibility when considering the use of a guarantee, because you can offer a straight thirty-, sixty-, or ninety-day version. You can offer one year. Or a lifetime.

An even more innovative guarantee approach I've seen used is to denominate a very specific result or minimum result or personal performance level the client should expect within a defined time period.

For example:

A health club I worked with tested four different guarantees. Thirty-, sixty-, and ninety-days risk-free. The fourth test added a written agreement guaranteeing the specific result the client wanted (e.g., lose twenty-two pounds of fat and turn it into rock-hard, rippling muscles within 120 days).

The try-it-free-for-sixty-days outpulled the other three tests by a large margin. And nearly 50 percent converted to paying members at the end of the period. But the specific-result guarantee worked well, too, far better than the others without the specific result guarantee.

What's the point I want you to see?

It's this: Test the most specific types of guarantees and better-than-risk-free guarantees you can before arbitrarily deciding on one.

It might help you to appreciate the power of specific risk reversal if I tell you that the automobile industry has spent millions of dollars trying to understand what makes people buy and not buy.

Their biggest discovery is that the primary reason people don't buy is that they don't want to look bad in the eyes of their peers, and they don't want to make a mistake.

By using risk reversal and purchase guarantees, you get clients to see that they now can't possibly make a mistake. Nor could they ever look bad again, since they can get out of their purchase if it doesn't perform. You have a powerful new tool—a huge selling advantage over your competitors who don't offer this level of specific risk reversal.

Increase the Guarantee, Increase the Profit

I've observed that when you put very specific and dramatic performance-based guarantees or risk reversals on your selling proposition, your sales almost certainly soar. But another quite wonderful thing occurs. Because you guarantee your client such a specific outcome or result, you will normally perform even better than you used to in order to assure that your company delivers what you promise.

So the client ends up receiving a far higher than expected level of service, quality, and performance—and you both win big in the process.

One client of mine, an architect, offers a simple pledge: If his client isn't happy at any stage of the project, the architect refunds any previously paid fees and reperforms the unsatisfactory work for free. He very successfully incorporates this fact into his selling activities and, since starting to do it, his practice has thrived.

It will absolutely make a huge improvement in your business or practice, too. I can't tell you whether your sales, closures, and referrals will shoot up 40 or 440 percent.

I *can* promise you they will go up.

And because you understand that you are the one company or person that is consciously working to assume all the risk in the transaction, your awareness of the risk factor will be very apparent to your clients. They will be drawn to you and your enterprise because they'll sense your commitment to make the transaction work for them, not just for you.

An opal dealer I work with has a very daring guarantee: Anyone buying a stone from her takes it anywhere—to a friend, another jeweler, anywhere—and if they're dissatisfied, unhappy, or just plain change their mind, it's no problem. They can get a full 100 percent money-back guarantee anytime within one year.

No other opal dealer in the country makes a claim like that. She outsells all her legitimate competition.

Risk reversal helps people decide to act and act now, today, immediately, without fear or concern.

Another client of mine is a broker of investment properties. His risk reversal to his clients is powerful. He guarantees that if any property he sells you isn't rented within 120 days of your closing escrow, he'll pay the fair market rent for up to two years, as long as you allow his management company to manage the leasing and rental activities.

Are you starting to see all the innovative ways you can use risk reversal and money-back or performance-based guarantees to eliminate uncertainty, improve decisiveness, and give your business a competitive edge?

If there's no risk in doing something, a lot more people tend to give it a try. Once they try it out, if your product or service performs as you say, most people will continue buying again and again.

Say What You Mean—Mean What You Say

But your guarantee must be sincere, one that you stand behind 100 percent and one with no loopholes. A bogus or insincere risk-reversal policy will do more harm than good. A few horrendous risk-reversal examples:

A well-known candy producer's candy bar carries a "guarantee of satisfaction" on its wrapper. If you're not completely satisfied, just mail the uneaten portion of the fifty-cent candy bar (which will cost you thirty-nine cents postage) along with an explanation of your dissatisfaction to the company. You won't get your money back. Instead, the company will send you another of the same candy bar. And what if you don't like that one? They'll send you another. . . .

An electronics corporation requires a steady hand or a magnifying glass to fill out the warranty for its calculator. The warranty is a postcard only two inches wide and three and five-eighths inches long. You're supposed to send in the warranty right away. But it's unlikely that the warranty will ever reach its destination—unless it's put in an envelope—because postal regulations prohibit the mailing of a postcard less than three and a half inches by five inches.

Another electronics company says that if its cheapest quartz watch needs repairing under its one-year warranty, you must pay a $4.95 handling charge (plus postage for shipping to the factory). The watch itself only costs $2.97.

A company that manufactures water heaters for boats pledges a money-back guarantee. If, within thirty days, you're not completely satisfied, you can get a refund by returning the product "unused and uninstalled."

Another company has a simple warranty to fill out on its electric products systems. Just complete and mail the registration form and retain the warranty. So what's the hitch? The warranty is on the back of the registration form.

The Specifics

If you use risk reversal, but only in short, abstract, satisfaction-guaranteed terms, change what you say and your terms. If your product or service is good and performs for your client, the longer the guarantee and the more specific the performance expectations you make, the more people will buy. It's that simple.

Usually a sixty-day guarantee will outproduce a thirty-day guarantee by 20 to 100 percent. Test it yourself and see what a boost it gives. A full year or even longer usually beats sixty or ninety days. The more specifically you tell people what "satisfaction" looks like, the more compelled they become to act in order to receive that benefit for themselves.

I like to see strong well-detailed guarantees used by my clients. The clearer, stronger, and more specific the guarantee, the more credibility and impact it will have on a prospect or client. How much better and more powerful is it if, instead of saying "satisfaction guaranteed," you say "unconditionally performance-guaranteed for thirty days"?

But what happens if instead of saying "unconditionally money-back guaranteed for thirty days," I say, "no-questions-asked, 100 percent money-back guarantee anytime within sixty days if my product fails to perform exactly as promised"?

That's even better.

You could go even one better by saying:

"No-questions-asked, 100 percent money-back, ninety-day guarantee if you can't honestly state that your face looks more youthful and radiant, and that your skin has better color and elasticity. If you don't enjoy results that good or better within the first ninety days of using our product, we don't deserve to keep your money. You have every right to ask for a full, no-questions-asked, on-the-spot 100 percent refund anytime you decide. And if you decide you want a refund, there'll be no questions asked and no hard feelings whatsoever on our part."

Do you see what a difference a strong and specific money-back, risk-reversed performance guarantee can make? When you start using risk reversal this way, your business almost always shoots up immediately and stays up. You close more sales, sell larger units of purchase, and sell more often when people stop worrying about making a wrong or bad purchasing decision.

When you use risk reversal, you are basically telling your client that they will never again make a bad or incorrect or dangerous purchasing decision. That's a powerfully persuading point to make. It moves anyone who's on the fence off. It gets people who were only mildly interested and turns them into hot prospects. It makes people who were trying to decide between you and one or more of your competitors choose you. It eliminates all of your competitors from the running. You virtually have the playing field to yourself.

Just adding risk reversal and a selling guarantee to your sales proposition makes a powerful difference.

There are all kinds of variations on the risk-reversal theme:

An electronics company I've worked with guarantees that its products will reduce production costs by at least 15 percent.

A consultant I've advised offers to continue retraining your staff until you can see a measurable, significant increase in productivity.

A TV-set distributor offers to buy back any sets not sold by his retailers in the first 180 days.

A consultant agrees, in writing, not to cash any checks he's received until his clients tell him they're satisfied with the work he's done.

If you're worried that switching to aggressive risk reversal will cost you a lot of business, stop worrying. Unless your product or service is flawed—or just plain does not perform for the client—the number of people taking you up on a refund guarantee is negligible. But the increase in people taking you up on the initial sales offer is anything but negligible.

I've seen strong risk reversal double and triple sales while only adding .5 to 3 percent in additional refunds to a company's numbers. (By using the testing strategy you can quickly, safely, and definitively determine the difference risk reversal can and will make. And that's what you should do first.)

Risk reversal and guarantees should be used in all your marketing efforts. Every salesman or saleswoman who works for you should be using risk reversal to alleviate fears or apprehension and to compel clients to action now. All your ads and mailings should use it. Risk reversal can become an important part of your unique selling proposition (USP).

Reverse the Risk in Your Business

Make a list of all the different ways you can 100 percent guarantee, better than guarantee, or at least partially guarantee your client's transaction. Come up with not merely the basic thirty-, sixty-, or ninety-day money-back guarantee. Also, take the time to define and explain exactly what the picture of satisfaction should look like for your client. Make a point of detailing the performance or specific results they should expect to occur if they purchase your product or service.

Always remind yourself of the fact that they are not buying a product or service—they are responding to the advantages your product or service will produce for them. So help them clearly focus and appreciate exactly what they should expect to receive.

Then test various guarantees and risk reversals with your clients and prospects. Have your salespeople try them out, too.

If appropriate, try it in one of your ads or sales letters. I guarantee you that if you'll try a specific and powerful form of risk reversal, you'll not only sell to more people, your average transaction size will go up dramatically as well.

Risk reversal should instantaneously make a huge improvement in your bottom line.

A hospital emergency room saw its noncritical caseload start dropping dramatically because it was taking nearly two hours to get seen. They instituted a thirty-minute guaranteed treatment, unless a severe emergency was in progress, and aggressively promoted this fact in their community. Noncritical caseloads rose by nearly double, thanks to this guarantee.

A prominent builder-developer guarantees the development costs to his clients. If he goes overbudget he pays the costs, not his clients. He's the only person in his area doing this, and he gets most of the business because of that.

I advise a large power-equipment company in the South that has built a multimillion-dollar business by telling their clients they have five working days after they take delivery of any large piece of power equipment to bring it back for a 100 percent refund—no questions asked.

They've had three people in the last five years ask for a refund—which is the negative side. But they've had a 300 percent increase in business—which is the positive side. And every piece of equipment that was returned was sold almost instantaneously to somebody else, again on a no-questions-asked, five-day, money-back basis.

A car dealer I worked with doubled his business by offering—no questions asked—a two-week, 100 percent money-back guarantee on any new or used car purchase.

No dealer had ever offered that. He stood out very favorably against every other dealer in his area. If you were going to buy a car, why in the world would you buy it from another dealer when you might make a mistake and regret it a week later? When, if you bought a car from my client and regretted it, you could return it and get 100 percent of your money back cheerfully—no questions asked.

His volume shot up. He did have a small number of people who did bring the cars back. But surprisingly, the vast majority didn't want their money back—they wanted to trade up to a larger model or a more luxurious one, and he actually made more profit on the people who came back and traded up than he did on the initial sales he made to them.

A company that sells a home teaching program to improve the reading skills of children offers this compelling guarantee: "Your child will raise his reading or spelling grade by at least one grade level on his next report card or your money back." If you're a parent, you realize the power of that risk-reversal offer.

Weight-loss programs guarantee specific weight loss in a specific period of time.

FedEx won't charge you if your package doesn't arrive when promised.

Blockbuster Video guarantees their new releases will be available or you get a copy of that new release free the next time.

Auto manufacturers give you bumper-to-bumper, three-year, thirty-six-thousand-mile warranties. Some companies offer even longer warranties.

Major corporations to small operations offer these guarantees for a reason. They do it because risk reversal gives them a tremendous competitive advantage. And a strong risk-reversal policy will do the same for you.

One added benefit to when you incorporate a strong, powerful risk reversal, you automatically start performing and delivering at an even higher level of satisfaction than ever before to live up to your promises.

Action Steps

Look at your business, products, services, or employment skills and talents. Make a complete list of every obstacle to your clients or employers that might prevent them from purchasing, dealing with, or choosing you over your competition.

Break them into the following categories:

Financial reasons: the initial cost or expense of choosing you. And the potential financial loss if the transaction doesn't work out.

continues to next page

Emotional reasons: how bad the client or employer would look or feel if his purchase or commitment to you fails to perform.

Measurability reasons: Can it be measured and evaluated to show the tangible impact you or your offering could or should have on the client's life, business, or career?

Ask yourself what the real downside is in offering the client that product or service or your own employment services on a risk-free basis. Or even a better-than-risk-free basis.

Look at your product, service, or personal performance history to see how many people have been dissatisfied, asked for a refund, cancelled, or complained. If the number is low or nonexistent, that means a high risk reversal would do wonders for you. If you have a high incidence of problems or dissatisfaction, it means either you promised too much or your product or services are inferior and need quality attention.

If you provide and deliver true quality and value that can be appreciated, perceived, and understood, don't be afraid to offer risk reversal. Try it out with a few prospects or clients. Or ask one salesperson to try it for a day or week or in one market to see how much better clients respond before you incorporate it continually or systemwide.

8

Would You Like the Left Shoe, Too?

W HEN CLIENTS TURN TO YOU AND DECIDE TO MAKE A PUR-
chase, it's because those clients trust and respect you and
your ability to serve their individual needs. In their eyes, you are
a leader, a knowledgeable authority, a trusted person. Otherwise
they wouldn't be on the phone with you, replying positively to an
offer you made by mail, or at your office or counter. But are you
doing all you can to give your clients all the benefits and choices
they could be getting from you and would pay for?

I raise that point to draw your attention to the fact that most
businesspeople actually limit the amount of business their clients
do with them.

I know that's hard to believe. You're probably asking, "What
business owner in his right mind would deliberately *limit* client
buying?" The answer, of course, is that it doesn't happen deliberately. It happens unwittingly. I'm willing to bet that it's happening in your own business, right now.

Still shaking your head? Then let me pose a question: Tell me
honestly—could your clients be getting more value, benefit,
protection, or advantage out of each purchase they make with

you? If the answer to that question is yes in even a handful of cases, then you owe it to your clients to show them how to derive a greater benefit each time they buy.

When you close a sale, it's the perfect time to make an additional sale—particularly if there's a very good reason and benefit for the client to buy your package deal. Sixty percent of all clients will increase if you do it right and offer true value.

In this chapter you will learn how to offer all the alternatives and supplements that are available to people doing business with you, thereby improving the client's satisfaction and increasing the value of the transaction.

Give Your Clients a Better End Result

I'm going to show you three simple techniques that will help you deliver greater benefits to your current clients, often at a discount for them, and at the same time put more immediate cash into your business:

1. Adding products and services: Offer your clients the opportunity to add related items to their basic purchases from you—items that when combined together will increase the level of satisfaction or significance of the ultimate result more completely, conveniently, and efficiently.
2. Adding volume or time options: Help your clients decide the best quantity and quality grades in which they want to purchase your goods or services. Or how long they want a service to automatically continue. Don't limit their options or choices to less quality or quantity or a shorter duration than they need or desire.

3. Adding combinations: Give your clients the opportunity to purchase combinations or packages of goods and services that help them better achieve the satisfying end result they want. With one convenient purchase decision.

You'll notice that I've emphasized the end result that clients desire. I've done that because some people in business overlook the fact that clients don't buy products or services; they buy end results.

They buy a product or a service because they believe it will help them achieve a greater sense of convenience, safety, pleasure, economy, accomplishment, or simply self-esteem.

Someone who buys a camera, for example, doesn't really want a camera. Rather they seek the ultimate pleasure of taking beautiful pictures that will preserve forever their most pleasant memories.

The product might be toothpaste, but in the client's mind, the end result is a brighter, more flattering smile and fewer trips to the dentist.

If you keep your client's desired end results clearly in mind, you can almost always add products and services that help clients achieve their end results more completely, conveniently, and efficiently. You'll also be far less likely to impose artificial limits on how much your clients buy from you—something that, in the end, doesn't help either the client or you.

And that's why product and service add-ons are important. They offer greater value and satisfaction to clients. In short, a better end result, which translates into greater client satisfaction. Which in turn produces more repurchasing and more referrals.

Of course, add-ons do best when they're offered in a price-advantageous way. Clients who buy more of a product or service receive better prices while you increase your margin.

The wonderful part about this simple concept is that the hard work has already been done for you. Your clients have already declared their trust in you by agreeing to buy something.

Adding On Products or Services

Auto dealers are putting this theory into practice with a vengeance. Instead of simply selling cars, most dealers offer their clients the opportunity to add on a stereo system, convenient financing, security devices, a sunroof, car phones, an extended warranty, and all kinds of other options to the basic purchase. As you know, they typically make such offers immediately after the client has decided to buy a car, truck, or van.

It's not a question of manipulating clients while they're still feeling the happy glow of new-car ownership. The dealers are merely acknowledging the fact that what car buyers want isn't just a new set of wheels, but a total personalized transportation package. They're not just buying convenience and mobility. They're also buying a sense of well-being, a traveling lifestyle they desire. And they are making a statement about themselves with their purchase. It's all a part of the end result the client desires.

If the clients couldn't get those added things at the dealership in one transaction, they would in all likelihood buy them piecemeal, inconveniently, and at a higher cost later on. There's a wonderful, mutually enriching quality to this one-stop-shopping experience. The clients get a better end result or benefit. And the dealerships—in many cases—net more from selling add-ons than they do from selling cars.

Add-on Opportunities Are Everywhere

Say there's a store selling computers, and someone comes in and gets interested in Computer X. The store owner knows that extra software or a special printer will make Computer X a better-performing purchase for his client. Okay, our stage is set; now let's look at how that retailer directs this particular drama.

First he concentrates on helping the client decide that he or she does indeed want to buy Computer X. But once that decision has been made, he then offers him or her the chance to add on the software or printer. At a far more attractive price than if the client came back and bought those same things at some uncertain point in the future.

The computer dealer is alert. He makes certain that he takes the client forward into the future and shows him or her what it would be like operating a computer 50 percent faster, and being able to perform three times the functions in half the time.

By being proactive, instead of reactive (what I hope you will never be), the computer dealer positions himself to solidify his hold on the client's respect and buying loyalty.

And, of course, that same dealer offers to deliver the computer, set it up, and demonstrate it for a fee. He even throws in software for different family interests—altogether adding $100 in profit to the sale. He recognizes that many people don't want to leave a store hauling a computer and then be left alone to try to get it to work. Consumers buy computers for what they can do to enrich their lives, and they often need help in knowing the best way in which to do that.

A professional speaker I worked with charged $2,000 for giving ninety-minute speeches. But when I suggested that he offer all of his program attendees an opportunity to buy his books and tapes—as an add-on service at the end of his lectures—he never dreamed that 60 percent of them would do just that. By using this single add-on, he's increased his annual income six times over.

Making Add-ons Work for You

Write the names of your three best-selling products or services. Now add the end result that clients desire when they buy these items. Then, alongside the names of those items, list some of the ways in which you might increase the value and benefit of those goods and services to your clients by adding a product or service to a typical sale.

As you do this, think from your clients' perspective. What is the end result the clients want from each of these items? If they're buying a disassembled kid's swing from you, the end result is putting their child (or grandchild) on the swing and watching them smile while they look on as a doting parent or grandparent. They don't necessarily want to be truckers or construction workers, so you might make this kind of offer: "I'll sell you the swing and put it together for you." Or "If you really prefer to put it together yourself, I'll deliver it to your house and sell you a handy tool kit at cost."

And, of course, if they enjoy watching their children's pleasure in swinging, think of the joy there would be in sliding, climbing, or playing in a playhouse. Better offer a slide, ladder, and tent along the way, too. Maybe even at a discount. Help your clients achieve their desired end result completely, conveniently, and efficiently.

Here's a short list of proven ways to come up with your own valuable add-on.

1. Observe what your clients do before they buy your goods or services. Can you provide that to them, too (as part of the

transaction) for a fee? For example, if you are selling instructions of some kind, be sure to sell the equipment necessary to perform the task you are teaching (sports equipment, computers, uniforms, preparation forms). If most people need to gather information on their purchase before making their purchase with you, provide them the information.

2. Watch what people themselves do with your service or product after they buy it, and offer to do it for them for a fee. This isn't just delivery, assembly, installation, shipping, or training as in some of our previous examples. This principle leads caterers to printing and sending out invitations. Realtors to arranging mortgages, settlement attorneys, moving services, and decorating services. And doctors to offering vitamins and providing relevant books.

3. See what people buy to go with your product or service in the pursuit of their end result. Make it available to them through you. A fishing-equipment provider will most certainly sell fishing licenses, rent boats at a nearby lake, and provide guide services, since that's all included in a pleasant day of fishing. Never make your clients have to go to three more places, make three more transactions, and have to trust three more people to achieve their end result if you can possibly provide it yourself. They'll appreciate you for your effort. Remember, your clients like and trust you already.

4. Ask yourself how you would make a client's end result even more complete. A flu shot that protects future good health very conveniently and economically. Keepsake pictures of a ski trip or anniversary dinner. When you join the clients in pursuit of all desired end results, you'll be amazed at the multitude of services and products you can provide to your clients that they will value and pay for, beyond what they currently purchase from you.

Take the idea that you like best and that serves your client's needs best for an add-on product or service and offer it to ten of your best clients. Take your second favorite add-on and offer it to another ten. Try four or five ideas this way and you'll get a quick indication of what offers the best value to your clients and the best business opportunity for you. In some businesses you can do this in a day or two, and have additional high-margin sales in the first week.

Now let's go to an even simpler way of allowing your clients to buy more from you: letting them choose the volume and frequency of their purchases.

Adding Volume and Frequency Options

Let your clients buy as much as they want, when they want it. If you let them tell you how much they want to buy, and how often, the answer may surprise you. In my experience, I have found that many businesspeople presume to know what clients want, but are startled to find that their presumptions are way off base.

When given the option or incentive, people are willing to buy more than they ordinarily do.

Clients can have all kinds of reasons or be given appealing benefits for buying larger quantities. Some might simply be taking advantage of a price break or lower unit cost. Others might be buying to assure a season-long supply. Or to hedge against future price increases. Or just to enjoy having an inventory of goods to draw from.

Can you offer a client a larger unit of purchase—perhaps a family-size month's supply, or a three-month, six-month, or a year's supply? (I've seen "lifetime" supply actually done successfully in certain situations.)

The thing to remember is your clients deserve the chance to purchase the right amount for them.

Just giving people a structured offer with volume choices nearly always boosts the business you'll do with a client on the initial transaction and over time. Photographers offer at least three basic purchase options. Only about twenty percent of their clients choose the basic offer.

When you subscribe to a newsletter like mine, you're given an optional volume choice that is only offered after you've already decided that you want the product. With my *Business Breakthroughs,* that option was a discount on the second year.

You might say that my publisher is enriched by a two-year deal. Technically, I would have to agree. But the real beneficiaries are the subscribers. They get two years of valuable business advice for much less than the per-issue subscription price they were initially willing to pay. Plus, they receive an extra business-building report. And because they sign on for two years instead of one, they will get longer and greater value out of the newsletter. They'll become more committed and connected to my business-building strategies.

Also, they typically get additional free bonus incentives for choosing this preferential option.

Just try offering four for the price of three, or buy three and get one free, of almost anything, and you'll see clients that typically bought just one item going for the higher quantity.

I first discovered the power of offering volume choices when I worked for the publisher of an expensive business magazine. I wanted to offer just a basic one-year subscription option—with no other choices.

"Wrong!!!" the publisher informed me. Then, rather than merely state his point, he did the greatest favor possible for me—he proved it. He let me do two mailings. Mailing number

one only offered people a one-year subscription and nothing else. Mailing number two offered one year for $55. But you could also choose a two-year option for $95 and a three-year "best buy" alternative option for $120.

With the first mailing, no one had a choice. So my average purchase was $55.

With the second mailing, because I offered people three different choices (two of which were more value-superior than the basic one), 40 percent chose three years . . . 25 percent chose two years . . . and only 35 percent chose the one-year option everybody had to choose in mailing number one.

By merely offering people three different choices, two-thirds of the buyers bought a higher unit of sale. We made, on average, twice the profit per client we would have made if we only offered one choice—which is really no choice.

A bookseller uses a variation of the volume add-on to sell more books to public libraries. If a library calls and asks her to send over twenty modern Greek novels, she has trained her staff to say, "Since we don't know exactly what you have on the shelf now, we'll send over one hundred books on consignment. Just send back those you don't want."

Almost without fail, the libraries keep many more books than they originally ordered. So, her business is increased, the reading public gets the advantage of a wider selection of novels, and the library gives the public better service. Three winners.

Smart Add-on No-Brainers

We have our cars hand-washed every week at our home. When the car-wash man came out, instead of just offering me one choice of $10 a week per car, he offered me a better plan for two cars and an even better deal for three. I chose three, and he more than doubled his revenue and profit per week from me. I appreciate the good value he gave me—and, frankly, it's much more convenient than taking the cars into the car wash.

Would we normally wash each of our three cars every week on our own? Doubtful. But he offered me a choice, which was so much more appealing. Now it's a no-brainer.

How many of your clients could be advantaged by receiving a larger quantity of the product—or a continuous supply of the service? If most would, you can have confidence that making this offer actually adds greater value to the client, who would ordinarily need more product eventually. Instead of paying three times as much, when you offer it for just two or two and a half times more, they save 17 to 33 percent.

You actually profit more in the process of extending a greater value to your client. How? Put your pencil to it. Say the client originally intended to purchase x size or amount of product or service, and you make a 50 percent profit. Now, through the use of a volume option, that client buys three times as much for just two and a half times the price. You just added whatever the difference is between the hard cost of the extra products or services and the additional price you receive—as windfall profit.

Let's use an example of a dry cleaner who normally does one suit for $5.00, but who offers his client three suits cleaned for $12.50. Say his cost to clean a suit is half the charge (it's potentially much less, as volume increases with dry cleaning—as with many if not most other services).

Remember, at first the dry cleaner only had $5.00 worth of business, which made him a $2.50 profit. But when the client upgrades to the three-for-two-and-a-half deal, now the dry cleaner gets $12.50 revenue—and $5.00 worth of profit instead of the mere $2.50 profit he would have ordinarily made on the single-unit purchase.

The important point here is to always focus on the increased profit—not lost profit—that an add-on transaction brings you.

In the dry cleaner example, even though the dry cleaner, in effect, gave away $2.50 in profit, he ended up with double the profits he'd ordinarily make.

As I said before, in most service examples, when you offer quantity or frequency volume incentives, your incremental or per-service real cost drops dramatically. That's why the add-on typically can double or triple your ultimate profit per sale or per client—even though your gross margins might be reduced.

When you increase the size or frequency of the purchase, you rarely lose future sales. Interestingly and quite ironically, quite the opposite effect normally occurs. People start utilizing more of your product or service than they did in the past. Actually, they are usually benefited at a much higher level when they utilize more—so they end up winning on the transaction even more than you do.

Let People Buy by Time Periods

Why hold your clients to one-at-a-time purchases if they would be better served by being able to buy a time-structured package? Like the lawn-care business that sells you a season of full lawn maintenance, instead of just a one-shot summer mowing job. Season-long service is what many home owners really want. After all, the end result of enjoying a sensational lawn without having to worry about seeding and weeding and mowing and clipping is not achieved with a single visit.

Almost any service and most products can be offered for a time period. You can sell tickets by the day or by the performance or by the season.

Optometrists can provide exams alone or exams with an annual supply of contact lenses and solutions or eyeglasses.

If you sell any product or services that can be offered on what I refer to as a TFN ('Til Further Notice) basis, you can use your add-on or up-selling technique to turn one-time purchases into ongoing, perpetual, weekly, daily, monthly, or quarterly locked-in sales. This is the concept that drives the music club business.

I got a pest control company to turn most of their one-shot clients into regular quarterly-service clients by using that add-on method. I used the same concept with a health club.

A cosmetics company built a $100-million business by persuading 60 percent of all the women buying its products to up-sell or add on and convert that one shot over to a regular, ongoing automatic monthly shipment.

How many ways can you turn your one-shot sales into ongoing purchases using volume options including this ongoing service technique? If you normally get one purchase from a client and he or she rarely comes back—and through this volume option you get a 30 to 80 percent response (that's the target range of people you could expect to convert over to TFN), you can literally triple to quintuple your business overnight.

By the way, the TFN add-on technique can work for many if not all businesses or professions if applied inventively. The bottled-water industry does a billion dollars using this strategy. And so does the vitamin industry.

Getting Down to Your Business

Take out that pencil and paper again with the names of your three best-selling products or services. Write down next to each product or service the amount that your good client buys from you, on average, in each transaction.

Just ask yourself, "What quantity or frequency choice would

give these wonderful people the greatest end result and the greatest incentive to buy more?"

Let me again help you with a few specific activities.

1. Consider offering three times the average volume being purchased now for two and a half times the price. If you are selling a pound of something, put three pounds together. If you are selling flashlights, package three together. Remember, your clients' desired end result is not being left in the dark without a light. Three flashlights might achieve that desire better than one. If you are selling an annual exam or service, package it with three quarterly checkups. If you sell a service in monthly or yearly increments, offer three-month and three-year options. And by the way, three times the volume for two and a half times the prices isn't the only combination to try. For example, I recently bought a book of twelve oil changes for the price of seven. This simple action took me from a single-purchase situation to an annual-supply situation. Wherever possible, let clients buy time periods worth of product versus a specific quantity.

2. Package your product or service for a period of time. Try a year's worth first. Any service can be turned into a yearly contract, from HVAC maintenance to initial legal consultations. Almost any consumable can be provided in a year's supply delivered every week, month, or two months. You can buy your vitamins, coffee, or wine that way. Many gifts can be turned into a gift-of-the-month club experience.

3. And finally, offer your product or service 'Til Further Notice with periodic, automatic billings. It's not just insurance, fuel oil, and newspapers that can be sold that way. Remember, people don't want valuable services or products to stop.

Write down the names of your ten best clients and, next time they call or come in, offer them your favorite volume option. In fact, try out your offer on a second group of clients who aren't on your "best" list—and compare the results, list against list.

Combinations Help Boost Profits

Now let's move onto my third technique to bring more value to your clients and more business and cash to you.

Remember, we are trying to help clients achieve their desired end result more completely, conveniently, and efficiently. But most clients don't really know the best way to make use of all the value you can provide to that end. At least they don't know as much as you do.

That's where you come in. You can do your clients a huge service by helping them choose the best combination of what you offer to meet their desires. Just group these items together and let clients purchase them in one buying decision. Bundle your products together to achieve the end result. Clients will thank you for it and you'll profit tremendously by doing it.

Just look at McDonald's for a great example. For years, clients would get in their lines and order a hamburger, and then a Coke, and then a this and then a that. Finally, the McDonald's people got the message: Clients didn't go there just for hamburgers and Cokes. A lot of them wanted a more complete meal.

So now you can get in the same lines at McDonald's and get their package-deal meal of large sandwich, fries, and beverage. For only several cents more, the client can "supersize" their meal, adding eight more ounces of Coke and a larger unit of fries.

I recently bought a large ad in a national magazine. Originally,

I was going to buy just black and white. But the magazine made me two better offers. First, a far better price if I'd run a big section (twenty-four pages); second, a very small additional charge (less than half the normal rate) if I'd do the ad in color. I bought a twenty-four-page, full-color ad when I had originally set out to purchase only a two-page black-and-white ad. What I expected to be a $10,000 purchase turned into $130,000—but I'm exhilarated. I received such a good value that I can do more effective advertising with twenty-four pages instead of two. And with full color instead of black and white. They combined a color ad with more pages to better meet my promotional needs.

Give clients three better options and a number of them will choose one of the two additions over their initial intent. Give them superior value in each option you add, and they become benefited many times more than you do from the process.

Let me share a couple of ways up-sells or cross-sells are used in the business world. For a long time the consumer electronics industry has operated from the premise that different clients require and desire different things in the consumer electronics they buy. They start out advertising a basic, very high-quality model. It can be a VCR. It can be a stereo. It can be a big-screen television—whatever. And it's a great value for the money. But it's probably got the basic set of features. Why? Because it's impossible to know what clients want in the performance of a specific piece of electronic equipment until you interview them and observe and examine how they're going to use it, what their tastes are, what they think about high technology.

So when the client comes into the store, a service-minded, value-oriented, result- and benefit-focused salesman or saleswoman has the responsibility to engage that client in a discussion designed to identify two things. First, what the client's primary needs, wants, and desires are. And second, to educate that client as to what's available and possible, because most clients have no comprehension of how sophisticated and how many functions and capabilities a given television or sound system or VCR can really offer them.

If I'm somebody who's always away from home, it would be a wonderful benefit to me to be able to record seventeen different shows a night, and have it all long-term play on a VCR. But since I don't know that's possible, I settle for the basic VCR with just limited timer capability. I've lost the opportunity to have a benefit that's meaningful to me. And you've lost the opportunity of making my life richer and in the process perhaps doubling or tripling the size of that sale and having me appreciate you for doing it. That's the concept behind an up-sell or a cross-sell. The electronics industry is probably one of the greatest practitioners of it because it helps serve the needs of their clients so well. In many businesses and professions, and I suspect yours is one of them, there are enormous opportunities to apply and utilize up-selling and cross-selling.

The key is to help that client fit the purchase to what they want the product or service to be. And until they know what's possible, they can't make the most intelligent and effective purchasing decision about any product or about any service. So your opportunity is also your obligation. You can't allow a client to just select what they want to buy until and unless they've been educated to know how much more or better is possible. That comes from offering them up-sells and cross-sells.

A company I work with sells blinds and curtains. Their standard offer is an incredibly attractive price on a really fine basic blind or curtain installation. And if all you want is a plain white set of curtains or a plain white set of blinds in the basic style, it's a great value. However, the vast majority of people want more. They want their house to look better. They want their offices to look more dramatic. They want their furnishings and their accessories to coordinate. And that opens the door to recommending alternatives to those clients. My client does that by offering up-sells and cross-sells.

Up-sells are different grades, different fabrics, different colors, different styles of blinds or curtains. Cross-sells are other decorations that go along with them; for example, a beautiful valance or coordinating the curtain fabric with reupholstering a given chair in the room to draw the entire room together. These two functions, up-selling and cross-selling, are the vehicles you have available to your company or your profession to render substantially greater benefit and service to your client. And in the process greatly enrich yourself.

Another approach to increasing the average transaction value is to use point-of-sale promotions. Point-of-sale promotions are nothing more than displays or signage that grab the client's attention right at the point of sale. Keep in mind the psychology of a client. Once he or she has decided to buy any product or service, they are committed. They have become impassioned. They have already started envisioning themselves owning, possessing, using, or benefiting from that product or service. It is very easy at that point to assist them in getting even greater value or enrichment from the transaction by offering them other items that complement the purchase the client has just decided to make. Or by offering another product or service they can benefit from at an advantageous price.

Let me tell you where this is most prevalent. You drive down the street and you see a retail store of any kind—it can be a grocery store, a furniture store, an ice-cream store—and you see a sign in the window that reads, "Sale." Or it says, "Two for One." Or it says, "Special Purchase." Anything like that grabs your attention. That's the standard form of point of purchase that small retailers use.

Electrified by Add-on Opportunity

The owner of an electronics firm in Arizona heard me talk about add-ons at one of my marketing seminars. When he got back to his office and thought about the potential benefits of add-ons, he decided to test my concept.

Most of his sales are to industrial clients. He gives them a formal, written price quotation. The new thing he started doing was to add systematically to each quotation a related product or service that was 10 to 15 percent of the overall quoted price. The additional items weren't discussed with the buyers, yet 30 percent of the time they would buy them.

"It's an almost effortless process," the owner wrote in a recent letter to me, "but it will mean as much as $60,000 in new revenue to us this year. Thank you, Jay."

Tripled Income Is Music to Her Ears

I taught a children's singing teacher how to triple her income without exerting any additional effort or expense. Instead of charging parents $20 an hour to teach their child, she offers a $65 monthly rate. Some months the child gets four lessons. Some months five. On average, parents used to take two lessons a month from her and she'd get $40. Now she works more continuously (which she loves) and her revenue per child has risen 50 percent. Most importantly, before making this offer, the average student stayed with her three months. Since she began offering this option, they've stayed indefinitely.

Face-Lift for the Bottom Line

A plastic surgeon I've helped offers facial cosmetic packages. Basic choice is a face-lift. Choice two is a lift with eyes. Choice three is face, eyes, and nose. Over half of the patients choose choice two or three. This cosmetic surgeon averages $1,000-per-patient higher sales than his colleagues—yet he actually gives a greater value to the patient. And because the patients get a better value, they can justify doing more of the facial cosmetic work they really want or need. So the biggest winners in the process are the patients who come out looking even more beautiful or handsome (nearly 40 percent of his patients are men) than they probably would have had the surgeon not offered them better choices.

I have a very interesting client who's a hazardous-waste consultant. He goes into industrial firms around the world and he analyzes their exposure to hazardous-waste problems—liabilities, fires, explosions, contaminations, penalties from government agencies, etc. After working with me for a year, he realized that consulting was not the real opportunity he had in his business. His real opportunity was his ability to introduce his clients to key experts who could solve the problems he uncovered.

In other words, he would identify that they had a real exposure to hazardous-waste contamination. In order to eliminate that exposure, they have to bring in a contractor who is a specialist. But his clients had no idea what contractors to bring in. He did. He made an arrangement to represent the best hazardous-waste contractors in the country. And now when he does a project and uncovers an opportunity for hazardous-waste contractors, he's in an excellent position to secure the job for one of the companies he represents. Bottom line: His consulting business makes him a couple of hundred thousand dollars a year. His representation business where he represents contractors makes him millions.

Many of the music clubs, once you're comfortable and buying on an ongoing basis, will introduce you to their video club or their book clubs. Why? Because they know that a very large number of their satisfied CD clients will gladly cross over and start also buying videos or books on a regular basis.

I have a fashion clothing store that started a little shoe-and-purse club for their top clients. Every season when the new purses and the new shoes came in, they automatically sent them out first to these clients on approval to try out. If they liked them and wanted to keep them, they automatically charged the purchase to their credit card. If they didn't, they merely sent them back collect. No problem. They found that 80 percent of the members of this club keep at least one item when they send them to them. It's added hundreds of thousands of dollars to their bottom line every year.

There's a wine company that I have a relationship with that started a wine club. Every month they send a different selection of wine to people who visited their winery. Some of it's theirs. Some of it's from other vintners. Some of it's white wine, some red. Some of it's dessert wine, some of it's champagne. They've expanded their business ten times over and in the process built a loyal following of people who keep buying over and over again.

With a simple idea, I quadrupled the business for a tree trimmer. His basic business was totally reactive, as was everyone else's in his field. Somebody had a tree that was overgrown or needed to be removed, they'd call him, he'd come, he'd take care of it, he'd leave, he'd wait to be called again. I pointed out to him that the vast majority of people who needed trees trimmed would need those same trees trimmed again in six or nine months. So why not set them up on a regular ongoing service where he didn't wait for them to call him, but he just went out systematically, quarterly or semiannually, and trimmed those trees for them and charged it to their credit card.

He thought it was a great idea. And in a matter of three months, he converted 70 percent of his active clients to this ongoing service.

He took people who purchased haphazardly and erratically and got them to start purchasing four times a year forever from him. The impact to his business was a doubling of sales. And he quadrupled his profit because he was able to completely stop running ads in the local newspapers and he was able to cut down on his sales force. Between the clients he locked in ongoing forever and the referrals these satisfied clients gave him, he had all the business he could handle.

A good example in the consumer products field is a company called Saint Ives Labs. They make shampoos, hair-care products, etc. But they have solely based their business on a concept that exclusively packages their products together.

They offer large-sized units of shampoo with complementary conditioner for a single price that is more advantageous than buying separately.

The key to packaging products together, wherever possible, is to offer them to the client in a more price-advantageous manner.

I worked with a chain of convenience groceries and gas stations. They had gasoline islands out front and convenience grocery stores inside where you went to pay.

I asked them to try an experiment for just thirty days.

They raised the prices of half the items in their convenience store—the chewing gum, the soft drinks—by an average of 20 percent an item.

They were appalled when I asked them to do that. They said,

"No one will buy that," and I said, "I disagree. As a convenience it has a premium value to that client. It's not going to be judged as a commodity."

They grudgingly agreed, and that grudging agreement made them $900,000 extra profit in the next twelve months because, as I suspected, sales did not drop. Clients did not balk; they cheerfully paid 20 percent more for the gum and they cheerfully paid 20 more more for the beverages and they cheerfully paid 20 percent more for the doughnuts and the coffee. Because it was a convenience. It wasn't whether it was fifty cents or fifty-nine cents. It was the fact that they were in a rush, they were going to work or from work or to a meeting, and they wanted a cold drink or a hot drink or a sandwich.

I strongly urge you to look at your business or practice and ask yourself—could I take any or all of the products or services I sell and reposition them to be more upmarket?

I had an investment client one time with a boutique type of division that sold to very high-end clients to whom they gave an enormous amount of service, attention, and research free. They also had a discount division that sold to people who just wanted great pricing. And they had the middle-of-the-road division that sold to the masses.

All three were very profitable. All three sold very differently. All three sold to different segments of the market, but all three sold brokerage services.

Ask yourself—is there a level of my market more upscale than the one I'm currently reaching that I should be catering to? And if the answer is yes—which it could be in many cases— all you have to do is try a safe little test and see what happens. Downside is nothing. Upside is tremendous.

In the majority of the cases when you raise your market positioning and become more upscale, your existing clients look at you with more respect. Thus, they have more loyalty and that turns into more referrals. Suddenly large segments of the marketplace who never noticed you before start noticing you and buying from you.

In the last several years the entire retailing marketplace has been turned topsy-turvy by the advent of warehouse pricing. Price Club, Costco, and SAM'S Club have come into being. They offer you massive jars of peanut butter and they offer you huge drums of laundry detergent for prices dramatically lower per ounce or per pound than you can buy at the conventional grocery store.

And guess what? People are flocking to buy this way.

The industrial chemical business flourishes because they sell to industry in fifty-five-gallon drums or pallet sizes. So if you have cleaning to do or if you need certain kinds of chemicals, you don't buy a one-day supply or a one-week supply. You buy it in monthly or quarterly or annual consumption units and you save tremendous amounts of money.

In the investment business, mutual funds have flourished by offering investors tremendous price breaks when they invested larger amounts of money in a given fund. Transaction fees may drop from 2 percent all the way down to .75 percent if you go from investing $5,000 to $100,000.

So what happens? People have a tendency to put more money into a fund at a single transaction.

That's the goal.

Disneyland used to sell individual ride tickets to park visitors. They found through testing that when they gave you the chance to ride more rides with a single purchase, they would charge more money and more people would buy.

They now have family plans and they have season-ticket

plans—these give families much more advantage for buying larger units.

The cruise line offers a much greater price advantage for taking a family of six than most hotels do. There are great incentives. For every family member you add to the cruise, the price per person drops.

Retail companies like Circuit City offer extended warranties on their stereos and televisions. Rental car companies offer insurance riders.

Airlines offer not only the air transportation, but complete vacation packages that include airfare, hotel, and food.

This strategy works for big corporations to small businesses and it will work for you.

Action Steps

List all the products and services you sell that produce a greater result for the client when used together or in logical progression. Try offering various combinations, packages, and up-sell with these.

Then list what I call the cycles of product or service life—all the products or services other people sell that precede, parallel, complement, or follow the use of your product or service. Find the companies who sell all these products or services and see what kind of distribution, outright purchase, or host-beneficiary deals you can make with each in order to add their items onto your client's sale.

Think of any logical services your client could benefit from after puchasing your product or service—like tech support, extended warranty, annual or semiannual maintenance, pickup and delivery, etc. Could you provide any of these services to increase the value of your transaction?

Finally: If you have nothing else you can add, consider offering a larger or more deluxe version of your product or service at a greater price.

One or more of these experiments will result in a windfall profit and achievement opportunity for your business or career. How does it boost your career? When you get one job or project, suggest that your employer or boss give you responsibility for all or part of another job or project that's complementary. And ask for a lesser amount of compensation for the added responsibility than your employers currently pay for someone who does it full-time or to an outside service.

9

How to Never Fall off a Cliff

MY DEFINITION OF A MARKETING GENIUS MAY BE DIFFERENT from yours. I think a marketing genius is someone who has the ability to always get the maximum result from the minimum effort—not the person with the most creative ingenuity. You're a marketing genius if you understand that one approach to getting clients may produce five times the results of another—so, of course, you stick with the approach that yields the best results.

So a marketing genius, to me, is someone who is both logical and prudent. Someone who only follows the path that produces the highest and best results or returns for their time, money, and effort.

Anyone can become a virtual marketing genius equivalent by doing one simple thing: *testing*.

Test Everything

It is amazing how few companies ever test any aspect of their marketing and compare it to something else. They bet their destiny on arbitrary, subjective decisions and conjecture.

You don't have the right or the power to predetermine what the marketplace wants and what the best price, package, or approach will be.

Rather, you have the obligation, opportunity, and power to put every important marketing question to a vote by the only people whose ballots count: clients and prospects, who vote with their checkbooks, credit cards, purchase orders, contracts, or raises and promotions.

You can't maximize your performance or make the most money unless you know how to make the best use of your time, opportunities, efforts, and investments. You can't get the best results until you comprehensively evaluate all the different approaches you have available in all your business activities. One approach will often outproduce another approach many times over. The odds are great that you are currently underperforming and not reaching your real potential because you're depending on the wrong actions or approaches for your success. You can right that wrong and never make those mistakes again.

In this chapter you will learn how to use small, inexpensive tests to generate invaluable information that will lead to significantly better results in every area of your business or career.

Testing applies not merely to outside sales efforts but to every aspect of marketing.

If you run ads in newspapers or magazines, test different approaches, different headlines, different hot-button emphases, different packages, different rationales, different pricing, and different bonuses on top of the basic offer.

Test different directives to the reader or listener on how to respond and what action to take.

Test positioning in the front, back, right, or left-hand side of the page. Test where your commercials run—what stations and what time of day.

For those of you who don't run ads, modify the testing concept and apply it to your sales presentations. Then test different recommended opening statements against whatever it is you or your sales staff currently use. You will find a big improvement in results here, too, when you test.

After testing your headline or opening statement, and replacing what you were doing with whatever test approach outperforms the original, I want you to keep on testing additional factors.

Make specific offers and analyze the number of responses, traffic, prospects, and resulting sales for each specific ad. Then compute the cost per prospect, the cost per sale, the average sale per prospect, the average conversion per prospect, and the average profit per sale against your control. This reveals the obvious winner, the control that you will keep running until a better control beats it.

Remember, salaried salespeople cost you the same fixed amount, whether they make one sale a day, three sales a day, or more.

An ad costs you the same amount of space, production time, or airtime whether it produces one hundred prospects, one thousand prospects, or ten thousand prospects.

Therefore, it stands to reason that you should test different ad approaches and find those that outpull all the others. Then use those approaches to maximize your investment.

Test Everything, Starting Right Now

How do we put a marketing question to a vote? By testing one sales thrust against another, one price against another, one ad concept against another, one headline against another, one TV or radio commercial against another, one follow-up or up-sell overture against another. I could go on and on.

The point is—and this is not guesswork—when you test one approach against another and carefully analyze and tabulate the results, you will be amazed that one approach always substantially outpulls all the others by a tremendous margin. You'll also be amazed at how many more sales or how much larger the average order you can realize from the same effort.

The purpose of testing is to demand maximum performance from every marketing effort.

If you or each of your field salespeople averages fifteen calls a day, doesn't it make sense to find the one sales presentation or package that closes twice as many sales and increases the average order by 40 to 100 percent with the same amount of effort?

You can easily achieve immediate increases in sales and profits merely by testing.

You, or your sales staff, should try different approaches, different hot-button focuses, different packages, different specially priced offers, different "bumps" or upgrades, different follow-up offers, different prices, and different risk-reversal or guarantee statements.

Each day, review the specific performance of each test approach, then analyze the data.

If a specific new twist or experiment on your basic sales approach outcloses the old approach by 25 to 50 percent, doesn't it make sense for every salesperson to start using this new approach?

Test every sales variable. Any positive or negative data can help you to manipulate dramatically the effectiveness of your sales efforts.

But don't stop at merely finding the approaches, offers, prices, or packages that outperform the others. Once you identify the most successful combination, your work has just begun. Now you should find out "how high is high."

Keep experimenting to come up with even better approaches that outpull your current control.

Your control is the concept, approach, offer, or sales presentation that has consistently proven, through comparative testing, to be the best performer you've been using.

Until you establish your control concepts, techniques, and approaches, you can't possibly maximize your marketing and thus your profitability.

Once you find control concepts or approaches, keep testing to see if you can improve on their performance, thereby replacing one control with a better one.

One thing you'll discover when you start testing variables is that the difference in response or results can be extreme from just a small shift.

Several years ago I was working with a precious-metals dealer who was selling gold and silver to investors on a bank-financed purchase basis.

He ran ads in the *Wall Street Journal*, and the headlines of those ads read: "Two-thirds bank financing on silver and gold."

When my client ran those ads, they were reasonably successful.

They generated enough sales so my client was able to (a) pay for the ad, (b) pay the salespeople a fair commission, (c) have money left to operate and to pay his overhead and salary, and (d) have money to invest in more advertising.

However, I didn't believe he was optimizing. I sat down with him and asked what other headlines he had tested. He looked at me bewildered and said, "None."

So I gave him three additional headlines to test.

He tested them in different ads in the *Wall Street Journal*.

Two of those headlines outperformed his existing one by small margins.

The third headline did much better.

Gold was selling for $300 an ounce and silver was selling for $6 an ounce.

Remember his old headline was "Two-thirds bank financing on silver and gold."

All I did was change the expression of the headline to better denominate what was in it for the client.

My headline read: "If gold is selling for $300 an ounce, send us just $100 an ounce and we'll buy you all the gold you like."

The headline for silver: "If silver is selling for $6 an ounce, send us just $2 an ounce and we'll buy you all the silver you want."

Those headlines pulled five times as many sales from the same size ad, the same basic advertising approach—but five times, 500 percent, more responses and clients.

Now you might ask yourself, "Why did that simple change make such a big difference?"

Most headlines people use don't communicate a "What's in it for me?" result that the prospect, the client, the reader, the listener, the viewer, can expect to receive. My headline did.

You can have far more inquiries, clients, and sales for the same money just by testing alternatives against each other:

- By testing different ways to say the same thing
- By testing different copy

- By testing the pull of one magazine against another
- By testing one mailing list against another
- By testing one radio time slot against another
- By testing one offer against another
- By testing one price against another
- By testing one guarantee against another
- By testing one sales presentation against another
- By testing one direct-mail package against another

It's relatively easy to test and track ad results and to ruthlessly leverage every marketing dollar.

Failure to test, retest, and test again is tantamount to admitting that you aren't the business person you should be. Or at the very least it's a willingness to remain stuck at the same lower-yield platform.

Keyed Response—the Key to Testing

If you have two different approaches that you are testing, you must design your test to give you specific results keyed to each approach. You must know which ad each and every prospect is responding to.

You can do this in different ways:

- Use a coupon—a differently coded coupon for each version of your ad.
- Tell the prospects to specify a department number when they call or write—there doesn't have to be an actual department.
- Ask the prospect to tell you he heard it on radio station WWXY in order to qualify for a discount or special offer.
- Include a code on the mailing label returned with the order—the code identifies the source of the label or the version of the ad you mailed.

- Use different telephone numbers for respondents—each offer is accompanied by a similar but distinct phone number.
- Make different package tests and note which bonuses or prices people ask for.
- Have the caller ask for a specific person—the name can be fictitious.

You must be able to attribute each response to one of the approaches you are testing.

Keep meticulous track of each response and its results: simple inquiry, sale, amount of sale, previous client. Keep track of every piece of information that you need in your marketing. And be sure to differentiate in your record keeping between responses (prospect generation) and actual sales. Prospects are fine, but sales are what you're after.

Then when you have all the results tabulated by method A or method B, compare the two approaches and select the better one. Then test again, using your winner in competition with a new contestant.

Testing Small

Never test big if you can test small.

A/B splits allow you to test two approaches with one newspaper press run.

When an advertiser wants to use a split-run test, he furnishes two different ads of the same size, the "A" ad and the "B" ad.

Your two ads are then distributed to demographically similar audiences. And because the ads occupy the same position within the publication, each ad is fairly tested under similar conditions.

A/B testing keeps you from wasting thousands of dollars on losing ads. In this manner, you can also spend far less money pretesting ads in inexpensive, smaller-circulation, regional editions.

If you can't use A/B splits for some reason, here's another way to test small.

Rent a list of the subscribers to your target publication.

Find a list that replicates your target audience and rent part of it, say five thousand to twenty-five thousand names. Split the names fifty-fifty (ask the list manager to do that for you; it's done all the time); send half of the list your A version of the ad and the other half your B version. Record the results and compare them.

Or, assume that a full-page ad in a newspaper costs $18,000. Rather than run two for $36,000, pretest five thousand names for $1,500 to $2,000. This way, you can afford to pretest more ads, headlines, and additional variables.

Telephone Testing

An even faster, cheaper, and sometimes more informative alternative is to pretest by telephone. Rent lists of people's names with their phone numbers. Split the list in two and present a different version of your ad, in the form of a sales presentation, to each group of names. Examine the results.

One valuable benefit of telephone pretesting is feedback. By talking directly to the prospects, you can instantly identify the problems in your presentation—and correct them and retest—before buying the ad.

E-Mail, Sales Letters, and Direct-Mail Testing

So far we've talked mostly about display advertising, but if E-mail, sales letters, or direct mail is your method, read on.

You probably use E-mail, letters, or direct mail to inspire people to:

Take action on some issue, request, or offer or propopsition.

Come immediately into your store.

Or call your order desk.

Or send a coupon so that you can call back or send a salesman.

Or send a check or charge-card order.

Using the same principle that you would in testing display advertising, do an "Nth name" A/B test. An Nth-name sample is a theoretically perfect cross section of the quality of the list you are testing.

Before you mail to one hundred thousand untested people and spend $25,000 or $40,000 in postage and costs, do a five thousand Nth-name test sample of one version of your mailing piece against another.

Test the same mailing pieces with two different headlines.

Repeat the headline on the outside of the carrier envelope.

Try different body copy with the same headlines.

Try different orders.

Try different physical components, along with the basic sales letter. A folded "read me" note, or an accompanying brochure, or a reply device with a postage-paid reply number, or a coupon, etc.

Test as many things as possible in the smallest possible arena before you risk a big part of your advertising budget on one expensive marketing approach to a large audience.

Why guess what the market will welcome, what price it's willing to pay, or what proposition it will respond to when the marketplace is willing and even eager to tell you the answer?

The same fundamental approach applies to TV and radio commercials, field sales, in-store ads, and telephone sales as well.

Why, for example, run five 60-second TV commercials each day saying something only one way, when another presentation of the same message might pull in many times the clients?

If you use TV, wouldn't you want to know whether showing your product or service in use makes a difference?

Since the cost is the same whether that sixty-second commercial produces 10 clients or 110, isn't it worth your while to find out answers to questions like these?

If you have salesmen in the field, wouldn't you like to know which service-package combinations produce the most sales?

If, instead of closing one sales call out of fifteen, you could identify a script that closes one out of eight, you'd immediately double the productivity of your salespeople.

Test presentations. Test guarantees. Test offers. Test product information. Test prices and packages. And always test against an alternative.

Test! Test! Test!

A major advertiser offered a four-week free examination of their product. They found that their ads, commercials, and sales presentations increased results by 98.6 percent over ads that didn't offer the trial period.

Another advertiser used two approaches. In one, he demonstrated his product in use; in the other, the product was a stationary piece of merchandise. The ad that depicted the product in use more than doubled results.

In an ad for an English course, the advertiser used the same copy with two different headlines:

1. "The Man Who Simplified English."
2. "Do You Make These Mistakes in English?"

The second headline produced nearly three times the sales results.

An insurance company tested these two headlines against each other:
1. "What Would Become of Your Wife If Something Happened to You?"
2. "Retirement Income Plan"
The second ad pulled 500 percent more than the first.

A famous correspondence school tested these two headlines:
1. "Announcing a New Course for Men Seeking Independence in the Next Three Years"
2. "An Up-to-the-Minute Course to Meet Today's Problems"
The first headline trounced the second headline by about 370 percent.

An insurance company tested these two headlines:
1. "Auto Insurance at Lower Rates If You Are a Careful Driver."
2. "How to Turn Your Careful Driving into Money"
The first headline was 1,200 percent better.

General Electric ran two ads, both with the same copy and headline, but changed the picture in the ad.

In the first, they used a smiling baby.

In the second, a woman was putting a GE lightbulb in a lamp.

The ad demonstrating the actual use of the product outpulled the smiling baby ad by 300 percent.

In all these cases, you would not have known the best results without testing. The results are often surprising.

Test! Test! Test! You can have far more sales, inquiries, and store traffic for the same money just by testing alternatives against each other.

Go Out in the Field and Test

Let's talk about field testing.

One salesman can use presentation A for one to two weeks, while another salesman uses presentation B.

A salesman can alternate presentations every other sales call, keeping careful track of the results.

The same principle applies to inside salespeople and telephone order clerks, too. An add-on after a basic sale can add 35 percent more profit to the transaction by adding a companion item to the transaction before the client walks out of the store or before the telephone is hung up.

For the Advanced Tester

Once you get going and become more sophisticated in your testing, the next step is to start considering quality of response instead of mere quantity.

If you come up with an ad that produces twice as many starter clients as another, think twice. A lot of lead-producing or prospect-generating marketers fail to analyze convertibility in their overall marketing analysis. Down the pike you might discover that an ad you choose not to go with produced people who repeated buying ten times longer than the better-pulling ad.

I've seen cases where an ad producing only ten leads made the advertiser more money than an ad pulling one thousand leads because five out of the ten leads resulting from ad A bought, while only three out of the one thousand from ad B bought.

The key point: You'll never know until you consider and test every facet of your scheme. That's why you have to test and perpetually track results. Keep tabs on all of your data, such as:

- Which ad brought in the sale
- How many orders a given ad produces
- How much money a given ad generates or loses
- How much the average order is worth
- How much a client or order costs
- How much or how many times the client reorders

Start by carefully recording the cost and results of every ad you run. Make sure you note what made the difference—headline changes, positioning in publications, pricing offers, etc.

Start checking the overall effectiveness of your sales presentations. Carefully trace closes per attempt and average orders per sale.

Discover, record, and analyze the number of prospects who convert into clients, the average dollar sale a client is worth the first time, how many times a year a client repurchases, and how much each repurchase is worth in gross and net dollars.

Only after you know this kind of data—through comparative testing—can you expect to find ways to improve your sales dramatically.

As far as I'm concerned, you don't have the right to determine what the market wants. But you have the duty to find out.

Price Testing

A fascinating fact about price testing. Whatever you think is your best-selling price probably isn't.

In test after test I've conducted, I've rarely been able to predict which price would prove the biggest seller. But it has to do with the psychological image a client ties into your product and price and market positioning. All I can really tell you for sure is that when you test one price point against another, frequently you'll get a difference in the double- or triple-digit range.

I've honestly seen $19 outpull $17 by 300 percent. I've seen $69 outproduce $79 by more than double.

Years ago I sold a business course. We tested $295, $395, and $495. $495 outproduced $295 by three times. It outproduced $395 by one and a half times. What does that mean? If I had arbitrarily stuck with $295, I would have had only half the orders at a fraction of the profit for my efforts. That's what you're doing to yourself if you don't test. And when I reviewed the information and insights in that business course, I realized that it was worth $495, if not more. So don't restrict or limit your sales and profits—test. Small, inexpensive tests will result in valuable information that will lead to increased income.

Sometimes the best price is higher. Sometimes it's lower. If I don't know—and I'm supposed to be the expert—you can't possibly know either until and unless you test. So start testing prices in your ads or sales letters, and in your live sales contacts with clients and prospects. And when you begin testing every aspect of your marketing and selling you'll be astonished at the ease with which you will achieve stunningly higher results.

Action Steps

Make a list of all the major elements or variables in your business or career activities that produce measurable results. Include all regular situations where persuasion or influence are important to your success. For example, sales presentations, board presentations, setting phone agreements, advertising, catalogs, sales letters, E-mail, faxes, the conduct and attitude of your order department, client services, technical support, accounts receivable, etc.

Next, identify the key transitional elements in each of those activities (i.e., headlines, presentation openings, sales, closes, USPs, etc.).

Then come up with at least two alternative ways or approaches to those activities. Create at least two different ways to say or communicate your "message": different pricing strategies, different positionings, different presentations, etc.

Then conservatively and modestly test these different approaches against your current control approach.

You'll be surprised at how many of your new tests outperform your old standards.

Find every process in your business or career that could be improved and focus on making small incremental or large exponential improvements in each process. If you do that, the combined effect will be dramatic and geometric.

Part II

How to Multiply
Your Maximum

10

With a Little Help from My Friends

SHARKS ARE RENOWNED FOR THEIR VICIOUS ATTITUDES AND indiscriminate palates. They eagerly make a meal of virtually any creature in the ocean—except the pilot fish. Instead, sharks and pilot fish have developed a mutually beneficial relationship. Immediately after the shark has killed and eaten its prey, the small pilot fish act as automatic toothbrushes, eating the leftover food lodged between the shark's teeth. It is a profitable relationship for both parties: The shark gets clean teeth and the pilot fish gets lunch without the effort of the hunt. This collaborative relationship is a basic example of what I call a host-beneficiary relationship.

Over the years the average business spends hundreds of thousands of dollars in marketing, sales efforts, and advertising to build goodwill and develop and keep a cadre of loyal clients and prospects.

The cost of acquiring a client or a prospect is enormous. (Most businesspeople don't realize it, but they are in the client-and-prospect-generating business. That's the basic goal of all marketing. Don't ever forget it.) Most businesses (and yours is probably one of them) spend their marketing dollars to reach 100 percent of an audience, and yet they're only going to get business from a fraction of this audience. In conventional marketing, this is taken for granted.

Why spend all your time, effort, expense, and credibility-building activity to attract new clients from the outside market when there is a much easier and less expensive way to do it? You can get other people, companies, publications, and organizations to get new clients for you. And they can do it faster, more efficiently, and for a fraction of the cost you'd spend doing it yourself.

In this chapter you will learn to use host-beneficiary relationships to tap into the millions of dollars of investment, existing goodwill, and strong relationships that other companies have developed with their clients. And how to have those companies direct their clients to start doing business with you.

But what if you could eliminate a lot of the expense, time, and inefficiency of "prospecting" and only spend your time and money on people who are ready to buy? Conversely, what if you could recoup the investment you've made on past prospects whom you didn't convert into clients?—money you thought was long gone and written off as advertising costs. Furthermore, what if you could do all of this with very little effort? Well, good news, you can.

You can arrange to gain additional benefits from the clients you've acquired, the prospects you couldn't sell to, or the clients you sold to long ago.

And you can find out who has already done your work for you. What I mean is that some other business, or professional practice, has already spent time, effort, and advertising dollars to attract clients who can now be yours for little more than the asking.

And I'm not talking about rudely snatching someone else's clients away from them. Not at all. I'm talking about gaining access to new clients with the express permission and warm cooperation of the business that acquired those clients in the first place.

This process is known as setting up a host-beneficiary relationship. Company A (the host) agrees to let Company B (the beneficiary) deliver a sales message to people who are Company A's clients. Company A could even agree to encourage their clients to purchase a product or service from Company B and actually sing their praises.

Do you have a Visa, MasterCard, or American Express card? What do you see every month when your bill arrives? Right in the middle there's an offer for another product or service. That's a host-beneficiary relationship at work.

If you are the beneficiary in this arrangement, it will bring you more clients and more cash right away. Believe me, I have done it myself over two hundred times. And I've had clients do it thousands of times.

It will also help you if you are the host in the process, because your clients will respect you for helping them learn of a new value in the marketplace.

There is no strain to create powerfully profitable host-beneficiary relationships. This is all you have to do:

Step one: Ask yourself, "Who already has a strong relationship with people to whom I might be able to sell a noncompetitive but related product or service?"

Step two: Once you've got names on paper, contact those noncompeting businesses and ask them to introduce your product or service to their audience. Supply them with plenty of information on what you sell, and some testimonials attesting to its high quality.

You should locate companies that have clients logically predisposed to your product or service. (For example, a real estate company might have clients interested in carpet cleaner; a stockbroker might have clients interested in a financial planner.) Negotiate with those companies to sell your product or service to their clients. Each company should give an endorsement to your product or service, and in return they should receive a certain percentage of the profits from all sales. Or offer other forms of compensation like donations to their favorite charity or help with their accounting expenses.

Approaching the Host

You get other companies to promote you or your company by employing a simple, graphic, and overwhelmingly appealing proposition.

Ask the potential host company's president if he would like to make $10,000, $20,000, $30,000, or more almost instantly—for absolutely no effort, no risk, and no investment.

Virtually no profit-oriented businessman could turn that down, at least not without inquiring to know more.

Once you have the company's attention, point out the following facts:

1. Your product or service is absolutely noncompetitive to the host's product or service. In the case where you approach a competitor, point out to them that any ancillary profits will result from reworking their list, after they

have drawn all the profits they can from their products. This may be especially appealing to companies who own large one-time-purchaser lists.

2. It's not going to take away or supplant any income or profits the host would ordinarily realize.

3. It augments their profits.

4. They don't have to lift a finger or spend a dime. If they do wish to participate, that's even better.

5. You'll create all the marketing material—subject totally to their approval, of course. You can offer to pay all the printing, postage, and other costs—or avail them of the opportunity to joint-venture with you (correspondingly, their profit share should be commensurate with their capital and time commitment).

6. You'll indemnify and hold them harmless—plus you'll unconditionally guarantee every item or service sold.

7. The host company can have all orders and/or services routed through them for verification.

8. Point out that particularly in those situations where the host is far removed or totally tangential to your business, it's purely bonus income for them.

Appease any fears that the potential host may have by addressing those fears immediately and confidently. Most often, the potential host won't understand the concept and how it will work for them. Educate them about yourself, your company, and quantify the potential profits which would result from a relationship.

It sounds very simple and it is. However, there are usually a few details that come up and I will explain them for you.

First of all, it's usually necessary—when you're the beneficiary—to offer the other company's clients special inducements. For instance, in order to really gain the clients' trust, you may have to give a longer guarantee, or more options, or a lower initial investment. This overcomes their natural sales resistance and it helps make the host company look good in the eyes of its clients because it's offering them a special deal.

In deals like this, the parties negotiate the payoff. There are no hard-and-fast rules for who gets what. Usually the beneficiary company pays the marketing costs and gets repaid off the top. Frequently the marketing cost is quite nominal. Both sides share in the remainder of the revenue. In other cases the two sides might split the marketing expenses and split the revenue equally.

Not all the splits are fifty-fifty. It depends on the offer. Sometimes it makes sense for the beneficiary company to forgo any profit on the front end because it can get a lot of repeat business from the clients. The beneficiary may give the host company all the profit on the front end and nothing or very little thereafter, because the beneficiary plans to make all his money on the residual sales to those clients.

If you want to be the host you just reverse the situation. Find companies with products or services that your clients would want to buy, and then you negotiate a host-beneficiary deal where you give your endorsement to their products or services in exchange for a percentage of the profits. Again, the parties negotiate how revenues and expenses will be split.

A Different Host-Beneficiary Approach

If the company or the professional you contact has an ongoing selling relationship with their clients, then your approach to the host-beneficiary relationship should be a little different.

You should focus on the fact that you are not going to take a dime away from the host. Show the host that there's no conflict whatsoever, that there's only a complementing connection, between what they do and who they do it for and what you will do.

And make your offer economically appealing enough to get the host excited. Show them that because you expect the advertising and marketing costs to be lower and the response rate and the average sale to be higher, you feel very comfortable offering to share what may seem a very generous, but to you a very justifiable, amount of all new purchases resulting from their endorsement. Then tell the host what the arrangement would be, and that there are options. It can be a share of the profit. It can be so much per client. It can be so much per prospect, lead, or inquiry. It could be a fixed fee for doing it. Or any combination of these options.

Once you've told them what the financial consideration to them is, denominate it into terms the host can get enthusiastic about. What does this mean? It means using what is called future pacing. Project ahead and show your prospective host what the money you pay them or the stream of income it will generate for them could be worth.

For example, if you were a moving company, and I was talking about sharing 12 percent of my landscape fees with you, I would say: "Let me tell you what I think that means, Mr. Moving Company. Worst case, if my projections are correct"—that's a key phrase to use: "if my projections are correct"—"I expect to be giving you a check for $47,000 six months from now."

That alone—focusing on that lump-sum figure—gets people excited. But then I recommend you take the process to a higher level of leverage. Show them what they can buy with that money and with subsequent money. For example, you might say, "And if it works out, you can expect a check similar to that every six months forever." Then you say, "What could you do, Mr.

Mover, with a $47,000 check twice a year for life?" And you don't ask them to think, you tell them. "Well, I suppose you could pay off some of the debt your moving company has. Or you could run ads every month in every newspaper in town. Or you could hire two new salespeople. Or you could expand your facilities. Or you could . . ."

It's important that you instill in the mind of the prospective host or endorser the fact that he or she is going to get most of the benefit from the proposition. Tell them this is a wonderful way for them to perform a market test to see how much leverage they really have with their clients. If you're right, they can do this with other companies, and you'll even assist them if it works out. If it doesn't, the loss will be yours because you'll be the one who will have funded the program and extended all the effort. They will benefit either way. And then you give them indemnification. You give them a written warranty that you will only do great work, and that if there is any problem, you'll make it right.

Remember I said you could use this concept to virtually eliminate the exorbitant costs of "prospecting" and only spend your time and money on people who are ready to buy. For example, assume you're spending $12,000 to bring in one hundred clients, and you gross $20,000 in sales from those one hundred clients. Your profit is $8,000. What if somebody were to give you one hundred new clients from whom you would gross $20,000? These clients wouldn't cost you any more. Would you be willing to pay that person $10,000 for those clients? Why not? That person just saved you $12,000 in marketing expenses. You're still $2,000 ahead.

That's what I mean by eliminating your marketing expenses. No, you're not going to get your clients for free. But you can significantly reduce your marketing expense if you negotiate this type of deal. Furthermore, this kind of relationship is usually not a one-time deal. The host will be constantly bringing in new clients for you to play off, so you both benefit from a perpetual stream of income.

What both of you are leveraging takes on significant value. The beneficiary company leverages off what the host company has built up—the years of existence . . . the hundreds of thousands or millions of dollars worth of advertising . . . the scores of salespeople and employees . . . the hundreds of thousands or millions of dollars worth of capital invested in equipment, offices, furnishings, and inventory . . . all that the host company has invested in over the years.

You get the benefit of all of this investment for no more than a share of the profits. That's why I always encourage people who are contemplating being the beneficiary to offer the host the maximum front-end revenue and residual profits because it's worth a tremendous amount of money to play off all the beneficiary's previous investments.

However, when there are residual sales, you, as the host, want to get the largest percentage of the profit. For example, you could go to a company and tell them that you'll allow them to market their product or service to your clients. You'll give them an endorsement and pay all or half of the up-front marketing costs, and you won't take any percentage of the profits on the first sale. All you want is 25 or 50 percent of the profit from all the residual sales that company makes to your clients.

This is an enticing offer to the beneficiary company because it allows them to access a whole new group of clients with little or no up-front marketing expenses. They'll acquire clients they probably wouldn't have been able to get, and all it costs them is a certain percentage of the profits from future sales.

Benefits to the Host

What are some of the benefits to you as the host? You are making money you otherwise wouldn't have made. You're generating outside streams of cash flow without any cost of sales or overhead. And you're able to recoup the investment you've already made in your clients and prospects and all the other assets you've built up in your company over the years.

These new profit centers will allow you to revalue the marginal net worth of your clients and prospects, thereby enabling you to allocate more money for advertising and marketing. You'll know that every time you bring in a new client, you're not only going to make $100 from your own product or service, but you're also going to make $1,000 because of the host-beneficiary deals you've got lined up. With that in mind, you could probably afford to triple your current advertising budget or increase some other aspect of your marketing effort.

By putting together different combinations of businesses that are synergistic, you open up vast areas of unrealized profit for both sides. For instance, if you're the beneficiary, you can show the host company how to make easy money just by endorsing your company. And you get to play off of all the assets that the host company has built up over the years—and do it for next to nothing.

If you're the host, it's the other way around. You make the easy money just for endorsing someone else. You get to recoup the investment you've made in all of your business's assets. And you get a perpetual stream of income from your percentage of the beneficiary company's future sales to your clients. It's a wonderful relationship no matter what side you're on.

Special treatment is critical to the whole dynamic of a host-beneficiary relationship. Why? Because it's critically important that the client feel that the host—the recommender, the endorser of the product or service—has gone to the mat and negotiated a below-market price or an above-market benefit, bonus, or guarantee that gives them extra value. It's important that anybody you get to endorse you distinguishes their clients as being special, important, and unique.

You've got to show somebody that by teaming with you they have an opportunity to bring a great benefit, a great advantage, and a great result to their clients that they've never thought about. You've got to do that with sincerity.

Developing a host-beneficiary relationship means going beyond the conventional sales and marketing routines and tapping into related products or services that your clients need. It means offering your product or service to somebody else's clients in a related field.

Here's an example.

If you are in a business where you have a good product or service, but you're having a hard time making a profit because you've got to spend so much on advertising, this is a wonderful way to generate an ongoing stream of profitable business. You won't have to spend $10,000 to get $8,000 worth of sales. You'll know that every dollar coming in your door has a guaranteed profit attached to it because you didn't have to pay any up-front marketing cost.

Here's what you should be thinking right now: "How can I add somebody else's product—even a competitor's product—to my business and make more money than I'm making on my own?" Or: "I can't add anything to my business, but I can take my product to other businesses and take advantage of their assets." Almost every business can go both ways. You can bring all sorts of things to your business and you can take your business to all sorts of other people. I call it the two-way-valve effect.

Moreover, if you don't have a business but you'd like to start one without any overhead, this is a great way to do it. All you have to do is be the middleman between the host and the beneficiary and tie up the rights both ways. You go to as many businesses as possible and say, "I want to market your product for you by having other businesses in related fields sell it for you. All I want is 25 percent of the profit." And then you go to the other business (in this case, the host) and say, "I want to bring products to you that you can market and all I want is 25 percent of the profit I make for you." This way, you're putting the deals together and profiting both ways. By doing this, you can put yourself into business immediately.

What I'm trying to teach you is a new way of seeing things— a new perspective. Unfortunately, most of us are prone to inertia and are risk-averse. Everyone is worried about failing, or they think there's a risk I haven't mentioned. "Oh, it's going to ruin my business," they say. What they don't realize is that people respect a business that can ethically recommend its competitors. It's like the scene from *Miracle on 34th Street* where Macy's was telling people to go to Gimbel's if Macy's didn't have what the client wanted. The clients loved Macy's for that. United Airlines' web site does just that and actually profits whether they sell their own tickets or their competitor's.

This host-beneficiary concept works three ways: You're the host and you're bringing other business to you. You're the beneficiary and you're taking your products to someone else's business. You're a person who doesn't have any assets but you want to leverage somebody else's assets. If you understand the leverage, it's incredible. You can do it all without really investing any money yourself. Amazing, but true.

Negotiating the Deal

Some advice on negotiating a host-beneficiary relationship and how to answer some of their possible questions.

Objection one: "How do I know it's not going to take away my clients?"

Your answer: "First of all, we'll do a test to see if it works. We test it on a small percentage of your clients, not all of them. Then we'll compare the revenue from this test against the revenue you're making from the rest of the clients who were not approached in the test.

"We just want to augment your business, never supplant any part of it. We'll take as long as is necessary to get accurate results, and we'll be as conservative and as analytical as you want so we can prove to you that it's only going to make you money."

Objection two: "I want control. I don't like you having control of my clients."

Your answer: "To assure you that you'll have control over the quality of our product, you can check us out as thoroughly as you want and you can impose any kind of controls or standards that you want. We'll even create the kind of product or service that you feel most comfortable with. We can repackage it to be anything you want. If you want it to have a longer guarantee, a lower price, a higher price . . . it doesn't matter. We can do whatever you want."

Objection three: "How do I know I'll get paid?"

Your answer: "Simple. You control the money and I'll collect from you. I'll trust you even if you don't trust me. Or, if you prefer, we'll have a separate account with a separate bank of your choice and we'll give the bank escrow instructions. Every time I deposit a dollar, and if 20 percent of sales is real profit, ten cents out of every dollar is automatically transferred into your account. There's no risk that you won't get paid."

When you're negotiating the details of the deal with the other party, I recommend that you be conservative and completely honest with one another. The greatest wealth this kind of program creates is in the residual effect of enduring relationships.

If you cheat somebody by including nonexistent costs, it makes the return even more marginal and the other party may eventually decide he or she doesn't want to keep doing it. You're better off making it obscenely profitable for the other person so he or she will continue the relationship.

Another important point: When you cut the deal with the host, try your hardest to get a guarantee that when the test does a certain amount of business, your relationship with the host is automatically renewed on an exclusive basis for a set time period.

If you do, then the host can't bring in a competitor or do it himself. You want to be duly rewarded for showing him how to make all this money, so try to get an "automatic renewal and exclusivity" agreement.

On the other hand, when you're the host, you don't want to get involved in a perpetual or exclusive relationship. You want the flexibility to work with other beneficiaries. So if you approach a beneficiary company and they want a perpetual exclusive, try not to give it to them.

By the way, depending on the amount of ingenuity, you don't have to split fifty-fifty. The average split can be anything the market will bear. Above all, optimize and leverage all that you do, including every dollar you spend, every client you bring in, and every resource you have.

When you're the beneficiary the worst thing you can do is to have a short-term deal where your brilliance brings something to somebody and then they dump you after they see how well it works. On the other hand, if you're the host company, you don't want to show a beneficiary company a good idea and you not profit from your effort. Tie the beneficiary up. If you are the beneficiary, avoid the issue altogether.

It may turn out that you could make more money letting all your competitors use your concept if it's an exceptional idea. To secure half the profit, you want all that business to go through you. The bottom line is, you want to tie it all up in the beginning. You want to get all the important concessions squared away at that point, and you want to have a binding, long-term contract to protect yourself.

Now, nobody in his or her right mind is going to give you a perpetual contract. So I recommend making it provisional. As long as the initial market test does a minimum amount of business, the relationship is automatically renewed for a finite period of time.

When I did a lot of work in the financial-newsletter field, I often acquired the rights to do inserts in the various newsletters. The first time I did it, I tied up a minimum performance renewal, which automatically gave me a two-year relationship with my client. As a trade-off, I had to give them a percentage of gross sales—not the usual profit split that I normally do.

One time I did inserts on a fifty-fifty deal. Another time the client didn't want to pay me out of profits, so I gave them all the profits and they gave me their mailing list for my unlimited use. So sometimes you've got to go around and around to get these considerations.

Sometimes the people are going to drive a hard bargain and you won't be able to make the profit split you want. Keep in mind that if you can find a way to make the deal profitable, you should be willing to trade the profit for some other considerations that make you money. In other words, be flexible.

And don't lose track of the fact that if I gave you $100,000 for no effort on your part, would you give me back $90,000? Well, in theory, everyone would say yes. But in reality, most people get offended for having to "pay" you so much. Just because you can't get exactly what you want doesn't mean it's not a good deal. If you get something and it doesn't cost you any time or resources, you are a fool not to make a deal. But most people don't see that.

For instance, if you want 50 percent of the profit and the guy says he's only going to give you 20 percent—and you do everything in your power but you can't get more than 20 percent—that 20 percent is still more than you had when you started. And if it doesn't cost you anything—if it's pure profit with no expense—what do you have to lose?

But here's the biggest reason you shouldn't be too choosy when you're negotiating the test deal:

You need validation!

When you put together a host-beneficiary relationship for the very first time, it's an abstract concept. It can be hard to sell. But once you've done a test and it works, then you've got validity. You've got an empirical example. And that's easy to sell.

So if your idea can be replicated—meaning you can do it with more than one company and in more than one area—you should go for almost any deal you can get when you're trying to validate your concept.

By the way, be sure to get all the documentation you can from your test. It's crucial so you can prove your concept to other people. Sometimes the host company is apprehensive about entrusting their client names to you. What do you do then? Personally, I always warrant in writing that, under penalty of punitive damages, I will not make their names available to anyone else and I will not use them for other than the express purpose designated in our agreement.

Endorsements

When you get an endorsement, you eliminate all the steps of trust development that are necessary for a business in the marketplace. It is immediate and efficient, and the cost of accessing clients is a fraction of what it would be in the outside market. But the yield is many times more than it would otherwise be.

Financier Jay Gould was well known on Wall Street. Once when Gould was attending his local church, the minister asked the financier how to invest $30,000. Gould advised him confidentially to buy shares in Missouri Pacific. The stock did rise for a while, but then failed to maintain its speculative fever and collapsed. The minister, who held on for too long, was all but wiped out. He poured out his woes to Gould, and the financier there and then wrote out a check to cover his entire losses. Then the minister confessed that, despite Gould's request to the contrary, he had given the tip to buy Missouri Pacific to many other members of the congregation. "Oh, I guessed that," Gould replied, "they were the ones I was after."

More Examples

What if you're the beneficiary company? Well, let's say you sell a very inexpensive photocopier and you know that many people can't afford an expensive copier like Xerox. Yet Xerox brings in 1,000 prospects for every 10 to whom they sell, and they just basically abandon the other 990. You should go to a distributor of Xerox and say, "Look, you're spending $10,000 on the 990 people you don't convert. You're just wasting your money. How would you like to get back not just the $10,000 you waste on them, but a $10,000 profit on top of that so you could quadruple your advertising allowance? I'll make you a deal that's irresistible."

And then you propose to them two things: First, you'd like to get them to sell your photocopier when they can't sell their own. But if they won't do that, you want them to give you the leads they're finished with. In return you give them a share of the profit from every sale you make. It's so logical, but no one does it.

The same thing applies in spades to car dealers. I once addressed car dealers and said, "You spend $10,000 a month in advertising to bring clients onto your lot. You sell to 5 percent of them. You know that of the 95 percent you don't sell to, 20 to 50 percent are serious buyers and they're going to buy from someone else.

"Why let them leave your lot without a car? If you can't sell them one of your cars, why not say, 'Okay, I understand you want to buy a Toyota and I sell Mazdas. I think you're foolish, but if you're going to buy a Toyota anyhow, I can get you a good deal on a Toyota because I have very good relations with the Toyota dealer. I can make a deal with you right now and you won't even have to go anywhere else. Just tell me what you want and I'll give you the best price. If you buy it from me, you'll save at least $1,000.' "

I then asked these car dealers, "How many more sales do you think you would make if you had a program like this? Quite a few, right? So why not make them? Conversely, you could also go to other dealerships and try to get them to sell your cars. You

WITH A LITTLE HELP FROM MY FRIENDS

say, 'Look, if you know someone's not going to buy, why let them off the lot when you could still make $500? You can actually reclaim your lost marketing expense. All you have to do is sell my car as a backup when you can't sell yours. I do it, and it works great.' "

If you're in landscaping, look at who deals with your intended prospect one, two, or three transactions before they are ready to buy from you. Once you identify who those generic companies are—contractors, real estate agencies, painters, movers—then move to more specific identification. Turn to either the Yellow Pages or a business directory and locate every builder or every contractor or every real estate company or every moving company in whatever geographic or industry segment to which you currently are marketing. And then contact them. When you do, you might tell them this:

I am a highly respected landscaper in our community. I would like very much to forge a joint venture with you. The reason I'd like to do it is that I realize that you have spent an enormous amount of time, effort, emotion, energy, and expense building goodwill with your clients. Those clients—when they're done transacting business with you—may have nothing else to bring you in the way of new business for many, many years. But there is a way—an ethical, valuable, worthwhile way—you could reclaim the time, effort, and expense that you invested in that relationship and do your client an incredible service.

A landscaping firm persuaded a real estate firm to introduce its shrub- and tree-planting service to recent home-buying clients. The landscaper reaped orders galore as a result. Sales rose 40 percent.

A swimming-pool distributor persuaded a house-painting company to introduce its "early season above-ground pool installation discount" to people who had recently had their houses painted. Again, there was a strong response.

An attorney who handles heavy-duty tax cases wrote a letter to his clients, and in the postscript told them they might want to look over a checklist of tax-filing hints given him by a new tax-preparation service. The tax preparer got all kinds of new business as a result of that link-up.

One of my clients is a hard-asset company, which means they sell gold and silver to investors. I went to diamond companies because their clients are also hard-asset investors. I got the diamond companies to endorse my hard-asset client, and then we did special promotions to the diamond companies' clients. Those clients were already predisposed to hard-asset investments and they trusted my client's company because of the diamond company's endorsement. (Needless to say, the diamond company was paid a percentage of the profits for allowing us to use the endorsement.)

This concept was so profitable that we decided to turn the table and set my client up as the host instead of the beneficiary. After my client had saturated its clients with all the gold and silver they wanted, we sought out other firms that sold something which the hard-asset company's clients could buy (a newsletter or books about precious metals). Then the hard-asset company endorsed that product in special mailing promotions to its clients from the other company.

An interesting example that you might be familiar with is one being done right now by many supermarkets. Right there in the supermarket there are other businesses operating in a host-beneficiary relationship. There might be a delicatessen, a bakery, a flower shop, a seafood shop; even banks are putting small branch banks right there next to the dog food. They're all separately owned businesses that are playing off of the super-market's enormous assets (such as location, traffic, and advertising). It makes perfect sense and it's working beautifully.

In my neighborhood there's a young man whose mother owns a garden shop in the area. They have two thousand or three thousand clients. Of those clients, 80 percent of the business comes from five hundred people. I spent some time teaching this young man how to tap into some of the back-end business opportunities that are inherent in his business. So now he's going to those five hundred people who are spending lots of money and suggesting other services they can buy from him.

For instance, he's going to coordinate such services as swimming-pool cleaning and ordinary gardening and landscape maintenance, and then put it all together as a package deal. He'll pay the laborers their regular fees and then mark that up to the client as his compensation for bringing all these services together and making sure all the jobs get done right.

He'll basically be the middleman or broker, playing off of the business his mother's garden shop has already generated and adding value to it by bringing in other services. As middleman he estimated he would make close to $200,000 a year, about the same as the garden shop would make that year.

A small video store didn't do much marketing. However, they did have twenty-five hundred clients. So I questioned them one day about the kind of host-beneficiary relations they could have. "What do all people who rent videos have or need?"

Video Store: "Uh, they all have video players."

Me: "And what do we know about video players?"

V.S.: "Well, they need to be cleaned and reconditioned about once every twelve to eighteen months."

Me: "What's the average age of a video player?"

V.S.: "Probably two and a half years."

Me:"How many do you think have been cleaned and maintained?"

V.S: "About 4 percent."

Me: "Do people know whom to take their video players to for cleaning?"

V.S.: "No."

Me: "Is it an inconvenience?"

V.S.: "Yes."

Me: "What do people normally do?"

V.S.: "Wait until it breaks down."

Me: "And what does it cost when it breaks down?"

V.S.: "About four times as much, which means they've got to buy a new one."

Me: "Okay, then what's the point of a cleaning and reconditioning service? The point is how to quadruple the life of your video player, right?"

V.S.: "Yes."

Me: "Do you know VCR cleaning shops that are good?"

V.S.: "Yes, we refer people to them all the time."

Me: "Do you make anything from referring people to the repair shop?"

V.S.: "No."

Me: "What do you think about this. You've got twenty-five hundred clients, probably 80 percent of which need their VCRs reconditioned. What does it cost to have one reconditioned?"

"Around $50."

"Okay, let's say you charge $100 and you had a deal where the clients just brought their video players to you and you gave them a *free* loaner while theirs was being cleaned, and you even gave them two or more tapes, or free tapes until their player was returned. Then you sent it out to the repair shop and they charged you $50; you would end up making $50 on each sale. And if you got 50 percent of your clients to do this, you'd make $50,000—which is about what you make per year on the business alone."

That was the first thing I suggested they do. Secondly, I told them they could make deals with companies that sell expensive sets of video movies. I said, "The company could pay the cost of mailing their offer to your clients, and you could get 50 percent of the profits. They would get business they never had before, and you would get more income.

"Now, if that works, you could take the same direct-mail package and the same offer and sell it to a hundred other video stores throughout the state or around the country.

"That way you can continue to make money off the project long after you've exhausted the profit potential within your own client base."

I recommended that a Realtor advertising vacation homes in out-of-state Sunday newspapers contact everyone else advertising out-of-state vacation homes and get the names of inquiries who did not convert. I advised a carpet company to tie in with local Realtors. The Realtors gave them the names of their clients who had recently purchased a new home. An endorsed mailing from the Realtor recommending the carpet company pulled very well. I advised an upscale remodeling company to contact fence companies, security services, and swimming-pool companies. The clients from those other companies were most likely to be interested in expensive remodeling.

Every asset that your company has must be fully maximized if you expect to succeed and compete in the future. One of the most powerful assets your company has (and it won't be found on a balance sheet) is your client base. To rephrase an old adage, "The client is always right . . . for your business and mine."

We engineered a million-dollar profit for one of our clients by contacting a software firm that specialized in contact management software. Contact management software, by the way, is software that helps companies who have salespeople manage the contacts and keep communicating on a frequent basis with prospects and clients. It's a very big part of the selling system today.

We went to the company that sold that contact software and got them to recommend to all their software clients that they attend sales-training programs my client provided.

Thousands of companies attended these seminars—paying $1,000 to $5,000—and none of them would have been there if it weren't for the recommendation of the host, who they trusted and whose direction to action they followed.

An attorney we worked with generated $3 million worth of fee income one year by following my lead and going to a financial institution, in this case a savings and loan, and persuading them that it was in their clients' best interest to set up trusts. It was in the banks' best interest to help those clients set up trusts because once the trusts were established, the bank could then sell those clients investments on insurance products and other financial instruments to fund those trusts.

Consequently, the bank had enormous motivation in recommending the attorney to speak for the bank at seminars the bank organized, funded, promoted, and recommended to all their clients and which drew hundreds of people each time the bank promoted them.

The attorney built a client base of four thousand just through this host-beneficiary process.

A financial planner who specialized in succession planning for owners of tightly controlled, privately owned businesses, went to a major bank in New York. He offered that bank the same kind of arrangement the attorney offered the savings and loan—seminars for the bank clients who owned tightly controlled, privately held businesses. The bank accomplished three wonderful things.

Number one: They put together an environment where they could meet intimately and privately with their top clients in a very stimulating session.

Number two: By helping those clients set up methods that would reduce the estate taxes the family would have to pay when a death occurred, the appreciative clients turned to the bank for other banking services. So, everybody won on the transaction.

Number three: The bank extended their role and their value in the eyes of those clients by being a provider of additional benefits and services.

When the bank introduced the financial planner to their clients, they were giving their clients an enormous amount of value and expertise at no charge. The bank funded a luncheon seminar during which the financial planner shared with their clients thousands and thousands of dollars worth of his expertise at no charge whatsoever to the attending clients.

When you start thinking about how many different ways you can engineer lucrative host-beneficiary relationships, you won't want to sit on the sidelines observing. You'll start organizing your action plan, contact potential candidates, and get into the game yourself. You'll be amazed at how the relationships you establish can turn into the ultimate distribution network.

Action Steps

Start by making a list of products and services that complement, precede, or follow your product or service.

Then make a list of businesses that sell those products or services.

continues to next page

If you are employed in a career, your list should be of people or organizations that are, or have access to, the key decision makers in your life.

Next, contact those individuals or businesses and propose setting up a host-beneficiary relationship.

Don't expect anyone to say yes immediately. Think of this as a process. Don't try to slam-dunk a deal in just one communication, be it in person or by phone. A letter should precede and prepare a potential host-beneficiary partner for your call or visit.

After your initial letter, follow up with a call, then, if possible, a visit. Set up a logical, systematic progression of letter, call, visit, letter, call, visit, etc.

Compile numbers, facts, and logical reasoning, and present the irresistible factors that make saying yes to your proposal the only ultimate decision your potential partner can make.

Start out with the sincere belief that it's only a matter of time before those you're contacting become your strategic partners and start contributing to your wealth and success. Don't wait until an agreement is signed to start contributing value to this relationship. Share ideas and give advice and recommendations each time you communicate.

While two to four relationships may not seem like a lot, even a small number of host-beneficiary relationships can produce impressive results. If you choose your partners wisely, you could actually improve business by 50 to 100 percent.

11

Someone You Should Meet

I'D BET A LOT OF MONEY THAT A SURPRISINGLY LARGE PORTION of your new clients actually come from direct or indirect referrals right now. (You might think of it as "word of mouth.") But I would also bet that you've never put a formal and aggressive referral system into place.

You need to. You've invested far too much in your business and clients. You provide far too important a value and benefit to allow all of the friends, coworkers, family members, and colleagues of your current clients to be denied access to you.

Most businesses spend all of their time, effort, and money on conventional, externally focused advertising, marketing, or selling programs when a fraction of that time and money would get them many times the results if they developed a formalized internal referral system.

Let's examine the psychology behind such systems before I tell you exactly how to use referrals; then let's see how other clients of mine have applied referrals to their enterprises.

The psychology: You have a moral and business obligation to

extend the same superior level of results or benefits you provide to each and every one of your clients, to everyone they hold dear.

If you show you care about your clients and how your product or service makes a difference in their lives, businesses, or careers, they will eagerly refer a constant flow of quality clients to you. All you have to do is show your clients what to do.

In this chapter you will learn how to create and implement a cost-free, formal client-referral system that will bring you an immediate increase in clients and income.

What's my rationale for saying this? It all stems from a fundamental belief I hold about what you do.

Most people in business think of the generic aspects of what they do . . . they sell shoes or real estate or stocks or insurance or industrial parts. Refuse to allow yourself to become a commodity. Instead, focus on your contribution to your clients' lives or business and the ultimate impact that results.

Start looking at your enterprise in the same proud light.

If you sell computers, focus on the fact that because an enterprise bought one of your computers, now that business is being run more effectively and efficiently. The owner or management of that business has probably been able to reduce overhead, processing time, and waste by dramatic amounts, thanks to your computer becoming the nerve center. What used to take three people to do may now take only one, and your computer made it all possible.

Focus on the incredible contribution or benefit your product or service made possible. Never focus just on the generic commodity value of what your product or service does.

The same goes for the industrial-parts business. Focus on the contribution you make to the completed manufactured product, and to the fact that this product performs for years, or for thousands of service hours, without failure or interruption, in some or in great part because of what you do.

Whatever your product or service, the moment you alter the way you see yourself and your contribution, everything in your business or profession changes for the better. This could not be more applicable for referrals.

Change Can Be Dramatic

When you change your sense of self-worth, you also alter the way you look at your relationships with clients. No longer do you, or should you, see them as mere purchasers of your wares or services. Instead, look at each and every client as a dear and valued friend. A lifetime friend, because that is precisely what your clients are to you: dear and valued friends.

After all, they've befriended you and your enterprise; they've trusted you with critical and intimate buying decisions that impacted and affected their very security, well-being, comfort, happiness, or prosperity. They trust you. They depend upon you.

Once you accept that premise, you will immediately understand the point I am about to make, and it ties directly back to referrals.

You wouldn't allow anyone who was important to one of your valued, dear friends to make a bad purchasing decision if you could possibly keep it from happening.

If your mother, brother, boss, or secretary was about to spend money on anything important, and you knew that, left on their own, they'd probably make a mistake or choose less than they deserved to give themselves, you would intercede.

Do the same for your valued clients. If you know that people important to your clients are making decisions on their own about the product or service area you specialize in, and they aren't getting the very best outcome they could get, you must intercede. You have to do it not so much for yourself as for your valued client you care deeply about.

Anyone important to your clients has by nature got to become important to you. That means you must, for your client's best interest, extend yourself at every level to make your services or products available to anyone in their lives who might need your advice or help.

And that means you must encourage and develop referrals as often as possible.

With that said, look at every active and inactive client you deal with as a potential source of dozens of referrals and new, valued friendships for you over his or her lifetime. But it's up to you to stimulate those referrals.

A psychiatrist I've advised made his business boom by following just one piece of advice: He told the people who referred patients to him (the bulk of his business) to tell anyone they referred that they wouldn't have to pay for the first session. The psychiatrist ate that cost himself, but more than made it up in new business because so many patients urged friends and family to try him out.

A client of mine with a landscaping service company increased his business by 33 percent in one year using referrals. He gives his vendors a finder's fee of 20 percent of what the referrals spend for deep-root feeding and pruning services. This averages out annually to a nice $300 referral fee per client.

Putting a Referral System in Place

Look at how many referrals you get accidentally right now. Then multiply that number by ten. Then double it. And then redouble it.

Potentially, that's the increase in business you could be looking at producing. A formal ongoing client-referral system will bring you an immediate increase in clients and profit.

A referral-generated client normally spends more money, buys more often, and is more profitable and loyal than any other category of business you could go after. And referrals are easy to get. Referrals beget referrals. They are self-perpetuating.

How to Do It

Step one: Every time clients deal with you in person, through your sales staff, or by letter, E-mail, or on the phone, diplomatically ask them for client referrals. But first you must set the stage.

Tell your clients that you realize you enjoy doing business with them and they probably associate with other people like themselves who mirror their values and quality.

Tell them you'd like to extend to them the opportunity of referring their valued and trusted associates to you.

Then help the client see a clear picture of who in their lives could benefit most effectively, and naturally, from your services or products.

Tell them what kind of person or business it might be, where they are, what they are probably doing—and why they'd be benefited. Show them what that person or entity would be doing or buying right now so that the picture is vivid. Then extend a totally risk-free, totally obligation-free sales offer.

Step two: Willingly offer to confer with, review, advise, or at least talk or meet with anyone important to that client. Offer to consult their referral or let them sample or get a demonstration of your product or service in action without expectation of purchase, so your client sees you as a valuable expert with whom they can put their friends or colleagues in touch.

If you do this every day to every client you talk to, sell to, write to, or visit—and you also get your key team members to do it, for just five working days to start—you can't help but get dozens or even hundreds of new clients. I have seen business literally triple in six months when people followed an aggressive client-referral process.

Referral Systems Are the Key to Optimization and Exponential Growth

Why do you want referrals?

You want referrals because this is the least expensive, has the least risk, and has the highest leverage and highest potential payoff of any way to acquire new clients. An additional benefit is that the client who comes from referrals is much less likely to price-shop or to have buyer's remorse.

The law of consistency is such that if clients recommend you to someone else, they have committed themselves also.

Why do you want a formal referral system?

You want a formal referral system so that you consistently get referrals no matter what else is going on because it is a formalized, sequential process.

Why do you want multiple systems?

Because this is the best way to attract new clients. If you want to optimize any business, then you will have at least four to five different referral systems. Plus, after reviewing the templates and the referral-system examples that follow, you will see how easy, simple, and effective it is to set up multiple referral systems.

The best approach to optimizing any business is to determine four or five new referral systems you will test immediately.

The initial information you would ideally want to know before you go to the referral-system template is discussed below.

1. Who are your ideal prospects? (The ideal prospects are the clients you would like to have more of.)
2. What is the benefit (or benefits) your ideal prospect wants and needs?
3. What benefit or result does your competitor(s) provide? What things does he do better than you and worse than you?
4. What benefit or result do you provide? What things are better and worse than what your competitor(s) provides?
5. What is the ideal prospect's biggest problem that is not being met? How could you help him solve it?

Referral-System Template

Use this guide to help you and your clients recognize and refer more clients to you.

1. What are the demographics of your ideal prospects?
   a) Income
   b) Financial worth
   c) Age
   d) Gender
   e) Ethnic group
   f) Neighborhood
   g) Geographic region

h) Type of business
i) Marital status
j) Religion
k) Hobbies
l) Political views
m) Membership in associations or groups
n) Type of automobile
o) Subscriptions to magazines, cable, or newspapers
p) Educational background
q) Type of investments (home owner, savings account, stocks, bonds, etc.)
r) Physical health
s) Mental health
t) Health interests (alternate health, vitamins, vegetarian, etc.)
u) Smoker or nonsmoker
v) Alcohol use (social drinker, etc.)
w) Vacations
x) Buying preferences (retail—upscale or discount; direct mail; magazines; phone; etc.)
y) Position
z) Any other demographic group that applies to your business

2. Who can refer these prospects to you?

For each of the following groups include both existing and former contacts. For example, you would consider existing and former vendors, clients, employees, competitors, etc. Or you could consider combinations such as former employees of competitors.

a) Vendors
b) Clients
c) Employees

    d) Competitors

    e) Relatives

    f) Prospects

    g) Prospects who did not convert

    h) Neighbors and friends

    i) Church members

    j) Association members (fraternal, social, industry, charity, or interest-based)

    k) Other businesses and professionals whom your prospects trust in your area

    l) Other businesses and professionals whom your prospects trust outside your area

    m) Leaders or celebrities whom your prospects admire, respect, and/or trust

    n) Magazine editors, writers for publications

    o) Special interest groups (cigars, travel, music, whale watching, etc.)

    p) The individuals or companies with which prospects do business before, during, and after the prospect does business with you (in other words, companies or individuals who have the clients you want)

    q) Governmental regulatory agencies

3. Set the stage for getting referrals.

    a) First make sure you have a good or valuable product or service. If not, improve it.

    b) Revere what you do.

    c) Position yourself as different from your competitors.

    d) Show interest in your current clients by asking them about themselves.

    e) Explain that even if the referral does not buy, you will provide a valuable service for them by letting them know what they should look for, what they should avoid, what they should expect, what they might over-look, and anything else which could negatively or positively affect the referral.

f) Give them both logical and emotional reasons they should give you referrals. Explain that you get much or most of your business by referral. Because you do get referrals, you are able to invest your money and your time in providing a better product or service.

g) Offer to give them an incentive for the referral. (In the case of some professionals who cannot ethically take pay for referrals, you can do things to help them grow their business, donate money to their favorite charities, etc. In some cases you will need to make sure that any compensation is not based on a per-referrals, per-leads, per-buyers, or additional-profit basis.)

h) Offer to give their clients a product or service for free or at a discount and tell them that this is something that the person referring you to them has bought them.

i) Offer to give the referral a special incentive. These special incentives could be bonuses, money-back guarantees, additional service, a discount, or anything else that has perceived value to the referral.

j) Have your client call or directly contact the referral.

k) Do something in advance of asking for the referral for the person from whom you want to get referrals. This will induce the law of reciprocity. This could be a birthday card, buying them lunch, giving them a referral, giving them a report or book, or anything else that has perceived value.

l) Keep in frequent contact with the people who have

provided referrals in the past. Acknowledge the people who have provided referrals who become clients. Get back with the person who provided referrals to you and let them know what happened.

m) Ask for referrals when clients are most receptive. This could be when they have just bought your product or service. This could be when you have done something great for them such as given them a large refund, a good sale, paid off a claim, or fulfilled your promised service or obligation. This could be when something special has happened in their lives such as a marriage, the birth of a child, a promotion, a special honor, being elected to a special office, retirement, or a transfer.

n) Don't be bashful; *ask* for those referrals.

o) Thank your clients for referrals.

4. Help your clients locate the referrals for you. Ask them, "Who do you know who _____?" (Fill in the blank for as many different groups of people and scenarios as possible to jog their memory.)

Group one: people they normally interface with

a) Vendors (and former)

b) Clients (and former)

c) Employees (and former)

d) Competitors (and former)

e) Relatives

f) Prospects

g) Prospects who did not convert

h) Neighbors

i) Church members

j) Association members (fraternal, social, industry, charity, interest-based)

k) Other businesses and professionals whom your prospects trust in your area

l) Other businesses and professionals whom your prospects trust outside your area

m) Leaders or celebrities whom your prospects admire, respect, and/or trust

n) Magazine editors, writers for publications

o) Special-interest groups (cigars, travel, music, whale watching, etc.)

p) Friends

q) Go through their Rolodex or personal telephone listing directory and get them to tell you about each person.

r) Listing of businesses they expect to use

Group two: people they think about because of an event

a) Someone who comes into their office

b) Someone they meet in professional circles

c) Someone who has retired (or is planning to)

d) Someone who has gotten married (or is planning to)

e) Someone who has had a child (or is planning to)

f) Someone who has gotten divorced (or is planning to)

g) Someone who has bought something (such as a house, a car, pet, boat, home entertainment center, computer, business, building, or investment)

h) Someone who has sold something (such as a house, car, boat, home entertainment center, computer, business, building, or investment)

i) Someone who wants to buy or sell something

j) Someone who has just moved

k) Someone who has just remodeled his or her house (or is planning to)

l) Someone whose children have grown up and moved out or are planning to

m) Someone who has had a death in the family
n) Others they can suggest to you based on their knowledge of their activities

Referral-System Examples

A specialty catering business creates meals that meet the needs of people with food allergies. They have developed a series of new products that they have also put into stores. Their clients are asked to refer friends who then either subscribe to the meal service or ask for the products at the store. The products in the store carry ads for the meal service and the meal service touts the products. The growth through referrals has been overwhelming.

It's entirely possible that client demand at the stores is driving the stores and therefore the distributors to carry the products, another benefit of the referrals.

An insurance and investments company created earthquake insurance in California after the Northridge quake caused a moratorium on this type of insurance. Investors get a graph showing how the investment has increased by 950 percent in the last fifteen years, and they are then asked to show this graph to people like themselves who are investment oriented. The graph made the difference, and sales were ten times higher in the months after the earthquake.

A land sales company was selling homesites in a specific new development. People would pick a homesite, but before they could write the check, they had to give five referrals. They sold 113 lots in 120 days, and sold seventy-four referrals over the phone.

The owners and management of a manufacturer of cellular-phone broadcast antennas built a $40 million business on referrals. They wanted to sell to the top twenty companies, but the buyers threw them out. They went to their clients (the local carriers) to discover the voids the top twenty companies were leaving open. It turned out every carrier wanted the same things. They configured and delivered what the buyers all had asked for, and each thought it was a custom system done just for them. They told the prospects they were a little company and needed to sell to all their locations and "Could you give me a list?" When my client got there the new clients had already called ahead because they were selling/referring "their" product.

A health club's new clients are 80 percent from referrals. When new people are introduced, the emphasis is on service and results. When they sign up, the club gets them to commit to consistently come into the club and use it—then they get them to promise to refer their friends so they can help them out, too. After the new clients get the results they were after, the club asks them to write a letter of recommendation. Fifty out of a hundred people do it.

A mortgage business that's in the top 1 percent in the country makes it clear that they expect to get referrals if their performance lives up to their promise. It's very important that they deliver what they promise. Some Realtors didn't give them good referrals, so they told those Realtors they might have to stop doing business with them. Then they told them what they needed to do and got them to realize the company's value to them. Respect who you are and explain why it makes sense to do business that way. Referrals will follow.

A stockbroker felt that, in his business, people were reluctant to give referrals because they feared that the friend they recommended would lose money. He overcame resistance by telling them his job is to find clients the best investments. If he has to keep looking for clients he can't spend as much time at finding you great investments. What would you rather he do? The quality of referrals was phenomenal and the closing ratio extremely high.

A walk-in medical center offered tours to school kids; now the schools send kids to them for physicals. They also built relationships with fire, police, and rescue departments. If they were busy with a bad accident, they would send the walking wounded to the medical center.

An insurance and benefits consulting group caters to a very narrow market segment, people who are fifty-five to seventy years old with a $3 million or better net worth. They can't just say, "Who do you know?" They research landowners, grouped by county. They also ask CPAs and attorneys in town for leads. When someone comes in, they get out the list for the county that client lives in. They go down the list, and if it turns out the client knows someone on the list, he or she will say, "Oh, yes, I know so-and-so, you can use my name." It works like a dream.

The lesson here is that when people are asked for referrals, they don't always know whom you want. If you give them a list of qualified prospects and they know somebody on the list, they are much more likely to give you high-quality referrals. Or if you don't have a list, explain to your client the details of the type of referral you want.

A European skin-care business offers free facials in ads and promotions. For every ten who come in for a free facial, many will buy products or programs. On average every free facial is worth $75 to them. When people buy a program, which is six facials, they get four referral cards. For every one of their referrals who buys a program, they get another free facial.

A heating and air-conditioning company scripted the referral process. They show clients referral letters and ask if they would be willing to write one if everything they promise is true. When a referral does business with the company and when the sale is closed, they tell the new client, "You get another $50 off the price we've already agreed to because you were referred to us by so-and-so. When you get us a referral, we'll give you a check for $50, and your referral in turn will get the same $50 off in the way you just did." It works very well.

A shooting range gives away special business cards to their members. On the back it says, "Free Range Time." They ask their members to put their initials on the cards when they give them out. They encourage clients to give out three or four at a time because people like to come with friends or family. They allow members to bring up to twenty-four guests a year at no charge. Probably 30 percent of these guests become members, and a great many of those who don't will return as clients on a pay-as-you-go basis.

A sales rep for AT&T is a member of the chamber of commerce in his area. People there know he's really helped other members, and they automatically give him referrals. He closes about 75 percent. (Organizations like Lions Clubs, Rotary clubs, and charity groups are excellent vehicles to good referrals.)

A photographer photographs about three hundred high-school seniors in an eight-week period every year. When they call in to initially book, he educates them about the whole process, but he also recommends that they bring in their friends at the same time. They photograph as many as seven or eight kids at a time, and each kid gets a free eleven-by-fourteen-inch photo of the group. It takes nothing away from their individual sales, but the eleven-by-fourteens normally list for $94. They cost $6, but they develop goodwill and get many of those kids into the studio.

An investment broker does business with institutional investors. How does he reach the CEO? How does he get to the top person? By going to retired senior executives, former regulators, or anyone who has had contact with the current decision makers. They get excited because the broker pays them 10 percent of the gross and shows them the contract they can sign. Now he's got referral people bringing in more referral people who are friends of theirs. About 20 percent of his business comes from referrals each year.

A car dealer gains referrals through helium-filled balloons. Balloon packages are delivered to clients who buy a new car. People ask about the balloons because there's no advertising on them. The client then volunteers a great buying experience, generating referrals. Within nine months, business from referred clients increased 58 percent.

An orthodontist's referrals all come from general dentists. He invites them every six months to his office for a "lunch and learn." They come with their entire staff and he shows them around and gives them a nice lunch. He has always extended professional courtesy to the doctors, their families, and their staffs, but now he tells them that. During lunch he explains all that he can do for them (and their patients) in orthodontic care. The results have been incredible.

A hair-transplant doctor sends a letter offering a limited number of free grafts to the client base. If a client brings a friend he'll receive thirty free grafts. From six hundred letters he got one hundred new clients, and the cost was pennies. Each new client is worth $30,000 over the long term.

A large apartment complex gives people a $100 credit toward their monthly rent for each person they refer and who moves into the complex. And they'll go sequentially all the way up to $900 a month. After you reach $900, they'll give you $900 toward next month's rent for each additional person you refer to them.

They expanded this concept to include a lifetime referral fee.

If you live in one of their properties and then you move out—assuming they didn't evict you—they'll pay you a referral fee of $150 cash, per referral who moves in, for as long as you live. This has worked very, very well for them.

On the back of their business-reply envelopes, an audiotape and CD publisher asks for referrals: "If you know of anyone else who would benefit from our products, please give us their name and address and we'll send them our catalog." They get thousands of referrals this way.

An optometrist sends a very simple thank-you note which he handwrites to patients who have referred other patients to him. If you have "Dr." in front of your name, laypeople aren't expecting to be acknowledged by you, much less thanked. When you do, it creates a large impression on people.

What the doctor discovered from handwriting the notes himself is that he was sending them to the same people over and over again. If you were sending out a computer-generated form letter, I doubt it would have the same impact.

A client from Boston told me that anytime he referred someone to his dentist, the dentist sent him a written thank-you note and a lottery ticket. He said he'll never forget that, and he continues to refer people to his dentist.

I have a client who is a public speaker. Ninety percent of his business is referral-generated. He speaks for all kinds of groups and associations. He has found that the best way for him to continuously generate referrals is for him to keep himself constantly in the mind and awareness of his clients. In order to do that he has a very comprehensive listing of all the issues and interests his clients have and he continually finds and sends to those clients valuable and important information, books, articles, reports, tapes, interviews, and videos on subjects of keen interest to them.

His strategy is very simple. He understands that if he thinks about the interests and needs and well-being of his past clients at a higher and more continuous level than anybody else, he's going to be constantly on top of their awareness. So when they're with people, when they're socializing, when they're playing golf, when they're having dinner with friends or colleagues—if the opportunity presents itself and someone ever mentions or discusses any area where my client has any suitability—his clients are automatically predisposed to refer my client.

The effort it takes to set up a formal referral system is more than worth the small amount of time you invest. Remember that referrals will be one of your best and most loyal categories of clients.

Referrals are your first line of business-growth "offense." They are easy to generate no matter what business you're in. They are a much more enjoyable category of people to talk to, work with, or sell to. Setting up a formalized referral system is also about the easiest business-building lever you'll ever construct for your company or career.

Action Steps

START LOOKING AT YOUR CLIENTS AS DEAR AND VALUED friends. Think about how many other friends, family, coworkers, clients, and colleagues they associate with that they can refer to you. Review the template on pages 193–199. Make a list of all the factors that you know apply to your clients. Then pick out one or two example referral processes from this chapter that you can use directly or with slight variation. Pick the best prospects for referrals from your client list based on your relationship with them, their level of past purchases, or their degree of satisfaction. See how many referrals you receive within the next five, fifteen, thirty, and forty-five days. Adjust and perfect your system so you're comfortable with it. Then once it proves out, incorporate it throughout your operation—and continually use it. Then start experimenting and implementing more systems. You'll be introduced to dozens, hundreds, even thousands, of new clients you can serve, protect, and contribute value to for years to come. Referral-generated clients buy more often, buy more each time, stay with you longer, negotiate less, appreciate you more, and refer their own contacts with a high degree of frequency. All you need to do is start working a regular referral system and process, and the clients will start flowing in.

12

The Prodigal Client

THE EASIEST POSSIBLE WAY TO INCREASE YOUR CLIENT BASE is laughably obvious, but hardly anyone does it. You can instantly increase your number of clients by regaining your inactive clients.

Every business or profession I've ever looked at, and I'm confident yours is no different, has an overlooked aspect to it that almost nobody focuses upon. That factor is attrition. Attrition is the opposite of retaining or continuing buying relationships with clients. Attrition is the number of clients who stop doing business with you or your enterprise. They're inactive clients. They are people who move out of the area or who for whatever reasons stop dealing with your company. Most people I work with don't even have a clue what their level of attrition actually is.

Until and unless you first identify how many of your old clients are no longer actively dealing with your company or your practice, you can't begin to immediately improve on that figure. By just knowing the percentage and by also knowing exactly who those clients or prospects are who no longer actively do business with you, you've gone a long way to reducing your attrition rate. And the opposite of attrition is client retention.

If you lose 20 percent of your clients a year, you have to add 30 percent more clients just to get a 10 percent increase in sales. Every business or profession has clients who leave them or stop buying. But you can sharply reduce or even eliminate most of this lost business from happening. Follow these easy lost client preventative-maintenance steps, and your business will soar even if you never increase your new-client-generation activities. Once you stop the leakage, the natural flow of new business and referrals from existing activities will build because you're no longer forced to make up for lost ground just to break even. This same philosophy applies to quality people you have lost as an employer or manager. Plug the hole and the bucket will fill up fast.

In this chapter you will learn how to instantly increase your client base and income by reactivating past or lost clients and relationships.

So your goal first and foremost is to identify and understand that whatever business or practice you're engaged in, you have some level of client attrition. You want to figure out what that level is and who those specific clients are who aren't doing business with you right now. Then you want to recognize the reasons clients stop doing business with you or your company.

Most people stop buying from you for one of three reasons:
1. Something totally unrelated to you happened in their life or business that caused them to temporarily stop dealing with you. They intended to come back, but they've just

never gotten around to taking action and doing business with you again.

2. They had a problem or unsatisfying last purchase experience with you that they probably didn't even tell you about. So they're turned off to you or your company.

3. Their situation has changed to the point where they no longer can benefit from whatever product or service you sell.

Let's explore these three reasons in greater detail.

Your mind is bombarded each and every day with hundreds of thousands of messages that vie for your attention, time, or money. So is everyone else's.

Out of sight, out of mind. A trite phrase, but very true. Once you stop dealing regularly with a company, or a professional, no matter how good or valuable the product or service was to you, you tend to forget about the product or service.

Have you ever let a magazine subscription accidentally expire and never quite gotten around to resubscribing, even though you thoroughly enjoyed that magazine's contents?

My wife and I used to go to a nutritionist every two weeks, and we loved it. But once relatives came to visit for three weeks, we stopped going and never went back.

I'd like to go to the nutritionist again, but on my own, I don't. Why? If I had to explain it, I'd say because I don't value the service enough to take action on my own. Yet, if that nutritionist contacted me, if she came over or called me up or even wrote me a nice little note, I'm certain I'd start back up in a second.

My point?

It's this. Over one-half of the client attrition I see is the result of loyal, satisfied clients who only intended to temporarily stop doing business but never quite got around to starting back up again.

I strongly suspect that a large portion of your inactive clients are these same kinds of well-intentioned but forgetful people, too.

You have the wonderful and noble opportunity of assisting your past clients to restart their buying relationship with you again.

When you do this you actually help those clients put more value and benefit into their life or business. Don't forget that whatever product or service you sell has worth, value, and benefit to those people, and they have been disadvantaged for all the time they have not been dealing with you. By helping them to start dealing with your company or practice again, you help them gain more advantage and benefit for themselves.

So, you see, you actually have a responsibility, an obligation, to reconnect them to the original reason they did business with you, and to help them start enjoying those benefits once again.

I'll show you the easiest way to do that.

But first, let's consider the second most frequent reason clients stop buying from you.

They become dissatisfied or unhappy with you or your company.

Here are some interesting statistics regarding unhappy clients from a study done by the Research Institute of America for the White House Office of Consumer Affairs.

- The average business will hear nothing from 96 percent of unhappy clients who experience rude or discourteous treatment.
- Ninety percent of clients who are dissatisfied with the service they receive will not come back or buy again.
- And to make matters worse, each of those unhappy clients will tell his or her experience to at least nine other people. Thirteen percent of those unhappy former clients will relate their stories to more than twenty people.

- For every complaint received, the average company has twenty-six clients with problems, six of which are "serious."
- Only 4 percent of unhappy clients bother to complain. For every complaint you hear, twenty-four others go uncommunicated to the company—but not to other prospects or clients.
- Of the clients who register a complaint, up to 70 percent will do business with the organization again if their complaint is resolved. That figure goes up to 95 percent if the client feels the problem was resolved quickly.
- Sixty-eight percent of clients who stop doing business with a company do so because of company indifference. It takes twelve positive incidents to make up for one negative incident in the eyes of clients.

The best way to address this problem is to never lose a client in the first place by embracing and living the concept of the Strategy of Preeminence. However, when you do lose a client due to a negative encounter, all is not lost. In fact, it can be one of the best opportunities to reconnect and bond with the former client.

Perhaps your business was unusually busy, or shorthanded, and one of your employees became short or curt with a client— particularly a fussy client.

Maybe that client had a lot of unnecessary concerns or questions, and you or your staff didn't have time to deal with him or her.

Maybe the client needed special attention or help and didn't feel he or she got it.

Maybe you promised, or at least the client felt you promised, to do something additional after the sale—and it was never taken care of properly.

Maybe there was a billing problem that aggravated the client. Or he or she went home, or back to his or her business, and realized that what you sold him or her may have not been the best product or service for his or her needs.

Maybe they just didn't feel important, appreciated, valued, or acknowledged by you and your organization.

I could go on for pages listing overlooked reasons why clients stopped doing business with you. But the important thing to recognize is that rarely did you intentionally offend, dissatisfy, or fail to acknowledge that client.

In fact, I'd bet serious money that up until this very moment you didn't even think about the possibility that you—or your organization—could be the reason clients stopped buying.

Out of the thousands of business owners and professionals I talk to, only a handful have ever thought about this before. So I'm reasonably certain none of your competitors have ever thought about it either.

The moment you recognize that 80 percent of all lost clients didn't leave for an irreparable reason, you can almost instantly take action and get many—even most—of those clients back. And when they do come back, the good news is that they tend to become your best, most frequent, and most loyal clients.

They also tend to turn into your best single source of referrals.

If a client stopped purchasing for reason number three (because their situation has changed to the point where they no longer can benefit from whatever product or service you sell), they obviously still have enormous stored respect, goodwill, and connection to your firm. By merely contacting them and honestly expressing your concern about their well-being, you position yourself perfectly. If they tell you they no longer can use your product or service, ask them to recommend you to friends, family members, and associates who can benefit from what you do. They're usually delighted to do so, but never thought about it on their own.

Find out what change has occurred in that client's circumstances. If it's an improvement, be happy for them. Congratulate them and celebrate with them. If it's a reversal or decline in circumstances, be empathetic with them—and, above all, genuinely care. Show deep, heartfelt emotional connection to them. This is the secret to great referrals. Care about them. Not just about yourself.

This simple action—contacting people who can't use you anymore, and nobly asking for referrals, has increased the sales of client companies I work with by as much as 50 percent within months. As they say, "your results may vary," but results will definitely be surprisingly positive.

Reinstating Your Lost Clients

So, what do you do to get all these people buying from your business or practice again?

All you do is contact them. But contact them sincerely and humbly.

For example, make an appointment to go visit them at their businesses or homes. Or call them, if a visit is impractical. Or write to them. If you can't personally do this, the next best thing is to get your salespeople and client-service representatives to contact old, inactive clients for you.

Here's what you do and say when you talk to them.

First, tell them the truth—that they haven't been buying products or services from your firm for quite a while and you sense something is wrong. Make certain you communicate this in a way that absolutely conveys your genuine concern for their well-being.

And you should be concerned for their well-being. Why? Because if they have a problem or difficulty, they can't continue receiving the benefits and value your product or service can provide them. So their lives are less enriched. You can help improve that situation for them.

After you caringly express concern for the lack of contact and transactions your firm has had with them, sincerely ask them the question, "Is anything wrong?" Follow that up—before the client responds—by adding, "Have we done something wrong? Did we offend you? Because if we did, it certainly wasn't intentional. Is everything all right with your business, job, family, health, etc.?"

Your point of focus should be on them—and their well-being. Obviously, something has happened to cause them to stop purchasing, and you want to find out exactly and truthfully what that something is—and how to fix it.

This simple-sounding approach is almost magical in its effect on inactive clients. But be sincere in your effort to regain lost clients. An insincere effort will do more harm than good.

A perfect example of insincerity causing harm is the story of the airline passenger who found a roach in his salad. Arriving at his hotel that evening, he immediately wrote an angry letter to the airline to register his complaint. By the time he returned to his office from the business trip, a reply from the airline had arrived.

The letter said, "Dear Sir: Your letter caused us great concern. We have never before received such a complaint and pledge we will do everything within our power to insure such an incident will never happen again. It might interest you to know that the employees serving you have been reprimanded and the entire plane is being fumigated. Your concern has not fallen on deaf ears."

Needless to say, the man was impressed. Until he noticed an

interoffice memo inadvertently stuck to the back of his letter, with this message: "Send this character the 'Roach Letter.' "

Unlike that example, a sincere effort to correct a problem has the effect of bonding you closer to the client than you probably ever were before. Also, it instantly neutralizes any anger or negative feelings they may have felt toward you.

Clients expect and deserve a sincere and personal response to their complaints. Flippant, rehearsed, or apathetic responses only serve to aggravate an already bad situation.

Most of your inactive clients will fall into the first two categories referred to earlier. Either they stopped buying "temporarily" and never quite got around to starting up again. Or they had a problem they felt was not satisfactorily dealt with.

If they've gotten derailed, unintentionally, and just forgot to start dealing with you again, they'll actually feel slightly embarrassed by, but appreciative for, the call. And normally they'll start buying again from you within a few days or weeks.

If they had a problem the last time they purchased from you, they'll probably tell you about that. At this point, you have the perfect opportunity to acknowledge them and their value and importance to your business, to apologize for the problem, to assure them that the problem was not intentional—nor were you even aware it occurred or existed, and to do something really special and noble to make it up to them.

Depending upon the business or profession you're in, making up for their dissatisfaction may mean you fix the problem now. Or you replace something. Or you give them some free goods or services to make it up. Or you offer them something bigger or better, at a great price.

The important point to focus on is to do whatever it takes to make them happy and aware that their well-being and satisfaction is of the utmost importance to you. Don't do it conditionally. Don't do it only if they buy something from you again.

Sounds simple, doesn't it? And you know what? It is. Do this in the next thirty days and I guarantee you that you'll bring back a significant number of old clients.

The Added Bonus

There's also a wonderful bonus benefit you get by doing this. Feedback.

You can't help but learn all kinds of ways to improve your business. Old clients will tell you exactly what they like and dislike about you, your company, your people, your products, or your service. They'll tell you exactly how to improve your service and client satisfaction. They'll tell you what benefits or advantages they got from you. And they'll guide you to areas of your operation where you can be more helpful for all of your clients.

Whom to Contact First

I'm assuming you know exactly who most, if not all, your inactive clients are.

If you don't have that information, go through your files and records and examine who hasn't been buying from your business in a while. Collect all those names, addresses, and phone numbers and organize them on the basis of recency and frequency. In other words, pick out the old clients who used to buy the largest amount of your product or service, or who used to buy the most often, and contact them first.

A lot of times in the process of doing this reactivating, you'll talk to people who left you for a competitor. But what frequently happens is that the competitor doesn't treat them as well, or benefit them as greatly, as you did in the past. Yet inertia holds these people back from returning to you on their own. When you contact them, you're giving these old clients "permission" to come back and buy from you once again.

Total up the number of inactive clients you've identified. Often the number and amount of combined lost business just sitting there waiting to be reclaimed is astonishing.

Understand this. If you can cut your attrition rate in half, it's just like adding that number of new clients to your business or your practice. So if you've been losing 20 percent of your clients every year and you start with a client base of one thousand clients, you've been losing two hundred clients a year. And if you cut your attrition rate in half, that's like adding one hundred new clients every year. In ten years you'll double just by reducing attrition. That's a powerful thought to contemplate. Do nothing else but reduce the amount of attrition, and every ten years you double the size of your business.

By taking the time to contact all of your inactive clients and communicate with them, you have the effect of impacting and impressing these inactive clients at a level you can't even fathom.

Just by contacting and communicating with every inactive client or prospect you have, a wonderful thing occurs. You can bank on the fact that certainly 20 percent and probably more like 50 or 60 percent of all of those inactive clients will almost immediately start repurchasing or repatronizing your business or your practice again. And, once they start repurchasing from you, there is a high probability they will actually become the most loyal and profitable clients you have.

So the first thing you're going to do is identify all the inactive clients you've got and you're going to contact them. If you have the time and the occasion, you're going to do it in person. If that's not practical, you're going to do it by phone. If that's not practical, you're going to have salespeople, a secretary, or an assistant do it. If that's not practical, you'll do it by letter.

How Some Got Their Clients Back

A retail store I consult sends a $20 no-strings-attached voucher to any client who does not purchase something from them within a nine-month period. Few people can turn down a $20 buying opportunity for free, and fewer only spend $20. If they spend at least $40 (the average purchase of reactivated clients for this retail store is $60), my client makes half and breaks even on that first renewed purchase, which is great because we've found that out of every ten inactive clients we win back with the coupons, four continue their repurchasing for years.

An attorney I advise wrote to all of his inactive clients and offered a free two-and-one-half-hour consultation, just to make sure they weren't overlooking some necessary legal steps or exposing themselves to a legal hazard. More than half of his old clients took him up on the offer, and about half of that number later became paying clients again.

A heating and air-conditioning company I helped called and offered free tune-ups to people who hadn't used them in at least a year. Forty percent of the old clients contacted took advantage of the offer, and about 65 percent of those people became active, paying clients again.

A restaurant my wife and I used to frequent, but stopped going to, sent us a request to be their guests for lunch any day of the week. We used the gift certificate, liked the food and service, and went back there many times that year—in fact, we still frequent the restaurant. But you know what? If they hadn't asked us to come back, we probably wouldn't have gone back.

Anyone can perform nobly when things are going great. But how you perform when you seemingly have nothing to gain impacts people a lot more.

Michael Basch, one of the founders of Federal Express, told me that FedEx always tries to make the ordinary extraordinary. And whenever they have a problem, they immediately respond to it.

For example: A client's critical package got lost. FedEx paid that client on the spot a penalty payment. They found the package and paid to put it on a major carrier and hired a courier to deliver it to the intended recipient. They apologized verbally and with a letter to the client, and they did the absolute same for the recipient. This explains why even when FedEx screws up, they rarely lose a client. You'll regain tons of lost clients, too, if you follow their wonderful example.

Let me share a sad story of how a dry cleaner I know is losing $6,000 a year in business from me—$6,000 he could have had back immediately, if he'd done the right thing.

I had a problem with a dry cleaner. He gave my wife someone else's shirts and I took them with me on a trip to Australia. I was shocked when I went to put them on. What he gave my wife were not my shirts, but a bunch of worn-out, old cotton buttondowns. The ironic part, however, was that these shirts were my size.

Rather than get mad at the guy, I just wore those shirts. I didn't want to spend $3,000 on new clothes and make him reimburse me.

When I came back, all he did was not charge me for the shirts I never received. (But my wife had already paid for the wrong shirts, so it was no big deal.)

I thought his attitude was bad, so I stopped going there. But the place I went to was even worse.

But I seem to have too much pride to go back to my original dry cleaner. And he's too product-driven, instead of client-driven, to call me up, apologize, and do the right thing to get me back. So I spend $6,000 on dry cleaning somewhere else in total dissatisfaction. He loses $6,000. No one wins—and that's my point. Everyone can win when you acknowledge that you care about the client.

Ways to Win Back Old Friends

A newsletter publisher I've worked with sends out five different letters to people whose subscriptions have lapsed. A different letter is mailed every seven days, starting approximately at the time someone's subscription expires. Each letter makes my client money, meaning that each letter pulls back a lot of people who either never got around to resubscribing or were ambivalent but easily persuaded by one of the different letters. Each letter hits people from a different hot-button perspective. One assumed the subscriber had procrastinated too long. Another offered him or her a discount for the next year. A third letter offered a bonus inducement worth as much as the entire newsletter subscription.

What are some of the more dramatic nontraditional approaches that succeed in winning back lost clients?

One is sending unsolicited gifts to people—gifts that transcend the limitations for whatever the basis for that relationship was. Include a letter explaining how you thought this gift would really help them in their life. At the same time make them an offer that isn't mandatory.

Many of my clients have reclaimed their lost clients and added tens or hundreds of thousands of easy profit dollars to their bank accounts.

A chiropractor I've worked with has his assistant call any

patients who haven't scheduled at least a routine checkup in eight months, and ask what's wrong. The assistant says, "The doctor is concerned about you and has asked me to call you to see if everything is okay." About 60 percent of the people contacted schedule an appointment within two weeks.

Eighty percent of clients who leave you don't leave for a reason that can't be rectified. And you can regain the vast majority of these clients at a fraction of the cost of acquiring new clients. And much like referral clients, they tend to be one of your best, most frequent, and most loyal client groups.

The Lost-Cause Client

If the client definitely won't come back to you, do you just drop the client and the effort cold?

My response is to thank him or her for helping me identify weaknesses in my product or service that I can fix or eliminate. And in doing so massively increase my future success or income.

This client helped me improve my product or service, and I want to reward and respect the client for that.

This attitude and approach is so dramatically different, unexpected, and impactful, it frequently turns the tide and breaks through to the lost client and actually wins him or her back.

Even if it doesn't, it has a wonderful residual benefit. People can't stop telling other people when someone does something beneficial for them—particularly when they had nothing to gain.

So ironically, you can actually use this mind-set and strategy to get totally dissatisfied past clients enthusiastically referring new clients to you.

This is not, by the way, manipulative. Quite the opposite. It's reciprocal. You owe any dissatisfied clients satisfaction. If this gives it to them, you're doing something worthwhile for them.

Remember, if you cut your attrition in half it's just like boosting your sales and profitability by the same amount.

Get going immediately on plugging up the hole in your business or career dike.

By the way, if you work for someone else, your hole or attrition might be losing good, loyal, skilled people (turnover) or not recruiting and hiring the best people you can.

Action Steps

Start a policy of communicating regularly and intimately with as many active clients as possible (if not all of them). This will help avoid the misunderstandings, unintentional interruptions in business, and lack of attention that open the door to competition.

Make a plan to contact as many inactive clients as possible. Preferably call upon them yourself in person or by phone. If impractical, get your assistant, staff, or management team to help you. If it's a job that's too big or time-consuming for you or them, send heartfelt, empathetic, and totally respectful letters, faxes, or E-mails. Then follow up with everyone. If you have to choose, start with the most recent inactives. How do you decide they're no longer active buyers or clients? There'll be an average buying pattern of time periods, dollar purchases, or product mixes. Anyone who used to follow such a pattern but no longer does has become (or is fast becoming) inactive. Your job (and financial opportunity) is to turn that situation around.

When you talk to or get contacts from the inactive clients, you'll need to do one of three things:

continues to next page

Many will start quickly buying and referring again because they never purposely intended to stop. So reward them for your lack of initiative in the past—do something special and preferential for them as a "welcome back" reward or gesture of appreciation.

For those inactive clients who express dissatisfaction with a past experience with your company, do the right thing—whatever that may be. Do something special at no charge or little charge. Express respect and sensitivity for their position. Give them a great deal on a subsequent purchase or do something distinctive that has nothing whatsoever to do with your product or service. You could send them a certificate for dinner, or tickets to the theater or ball game, or a book that's subject-appropriate or . . . use your imagination.

A great approach to remember when dealing with any inactive, dissatisfied client is: ". . . even if you only take advantage of our make-good offer but never do business with us again, it's important to us that your last transaction with our company be a positive and satisfying experience. So please give us this chance to see that that happens for you."

Do this and almost no one can continue to hold a grudge. And even the few who still do will have to "grudgingly" tell their friends about the gracious gesture your company extended to make up for the problem. Ironically, this approach will often generate referrals from the very people who left you and never intended on returning.

continues to next page

Finally, when you make contact with past clients who are inactive because they have no further need or use for your product or service, don't write them off. Instead, thank them for all their past loyalty and patronage. Then diplomatically look to them for quality referrals. They'll be only too happy to accommodate you if you really communicate appreciation from the heart.

13

Your Ten-Thousand-Person Sales Department

How would you like to have ten thousand or more tireless men or women working around the clock, each and every day? Your own sales force, capable of calling on the maximum number of the absolutely most qualified prospects for your product or service.

What if I told you that you could get those ten thousand or more tireless salesmen or saleswomen to work for you without pay, without ever getting tired, without ever calling in sick, without ever going to work for the competition, without ever asking for any benefits—and without ever forgetting to make any selling point or any closing argument?

Well, that ability is available to you instantly by recognizing and utilizing the powerful tool that is direct mail.

By *direct mail* I don't mean those inexpensive flyers that show up in your mailbox. I use the words *direct mail* as an umbrella that encompasses all categories of powerful written material people in business can use to communicate with prospects and clients. From casual letters to sales letters to brochures to formal written proposals. And the material might be sent via regular mail, E-mail, or fax. For ease of reading, I will frequently use the words *direct mail,* but hear the entire spectrum of specific and often very sophisticated applications.

Any business or businessperson can use these forms of direct mail in a multitude of ways.

The effective use of direct mail can develop and penetrate new markets, niches, and opportunities. More so than any other form of influence or persuasion-based communication you currently use, direct mail offers overlooked, undervalued, and little-known applications that can easily boost your success in business as well as your career. You can make a more powerful case, reach people you'd never get on the phone, make a perfect presentation every time, command attention and respect, and stimulate interest prior to every meeting with a client or prospect.

In this chapter you will learn how to effectively use direct mail in lieu of thousands of salespeople. And to use business letters to generate new clients and increased sales.

Sales letters can be used to generate new clients.

A sales letter can be used to develop a stream of prospects—prospects you then go out and visit, prospects you send further information or samples to, prospects who come to you, prospects you have to call, prospects you turn over to independent agents and manufacturer's reps.

Direct mail can also be used to penetrate or access markets

or prospects too small or distant to allow your customary form of selling or marketing to be effective.

You can use direct mail to precede a call or a visit a salesman or saleswoman would make. You can use direct mail to follow up after a call, close many people, or at least advance them to the next stage of sales closure. You can use direct mail as a mechanism to add as many satellite offices as you want.

Most conventional salespeople rarely get an audience with a qualified prospect the first time they call. Certainly, if they did, the odds of them getting the prospect's undivided attention for ten to fifteen minutes in the privacy of their home on an evening or weekend is almost incomprehensible. But you can do that as many times a day as you like if you rent mailing lists of people whose names include at-home addresses or if the information that you put into your sales effort is compelling enough that the recipient wants to take it home to read it attentively.

It can cost you $100 or more to make a cold sales call. Many cold calls take weeks or months to set up. Yet it costs you less than $1 (often only pennies) to contact your target audience through the mail or computer.

Sales letters often let you make a more compelling argument than you might normally make on the phone or in person. Because you don't have to fight off the resistance of secretaries to get through to your prospect and make a complete presentation.

With a sales letter, that's never the case. If you get the letter opened and you get it on the desk or in the hands of the intended recipient, you've got the complete message from beginning to end. You've got every question answered, every issue addressed, every problem solved, every reservation overcome, every application made, and every call to action expressed.

Sales letters are the most powerful prelude to telephone marketing efforts. I have seen many situations where, by sending a sales letter out ahead of a phone call, the effectiveness of the call itself was increased by 1,000 percent.

Let me state this a little differently to convey the true potency of direct mail.

How would you like to get ten times the business that you're getting now for no more investment? You can do that just by predisposing or preparing your market by getting ten times the number of people to say, "Yes, I'll take that," or "Yes, I'll come in," or "Yes, send it out," or "Yes, come out and make a presentation." That's what you can do by sending out a sales letter.

Why? Because when people call cold or visit cold, they're introducing an idea for the first time. It has to settle in. It has to be embraced. There are a lot of negative issues you have to overcome. When you make that the job of the sales letter, it does all of the dirty work for you.

Your sales letter prepares the audience. It predisposes. It breaks the ice. It sets the stage. It's not uncommon for the letter to be a profit center in its own right. But if all it does is break even and set the stage for you or your salespeople, that would be a victory in itself.

I've seen companies use modified direct mail to generate hundreds of thousands of profitable sales through prospect generation. There are lots of companies that have thought about creating a telephone marketing division, but feared going to market cold. Cold-calling by telephone is not the most powerful or profitable or productive option you have in your marketing arsenal. However, if you use telephone selling behind a sales letter to prospects who either write in, mail in, or call in, the whole dynamic of the situation changes to your profound advantage.

Direct Mail Will Work for Anybody

People sometimes say, "Jay, I'm not a retailer or a mail-order company—I don't see how in the world I could possibly use direct mail."

Nonsense. You can use some form of direct mail and you should use it, because if you don't think you can use it, then chances are your competitors aren't using it either. And if you use it you'll have the field to yourself.

Let me give you some examples that will help puncture the myth that says, "I can't use direct mail":

A packaging company I worked with started sending letters to their old, inactive clients. They were able to recapture 40 percent of them.

A company that sold annuities door-to-door built a $60-million-a-year business with a combination of letters and endorsements from financial newsletters.

An aerospace manufacturing company got a list of every airline and airline manufacturer worldwide, then mailed out sales letters. Result: four hundred new clients.

In the last decade or so, a set of "rules" has been established in the direct-mail industry that provides guidelines on how to write a good letter, how to call the buyer to action, and so on. Marketing courses, books, and seminars have made these rules widespread. As a result, many direct mailings have become similar in content and appearance.

I advise against doing anything drastically different. These rules have become widely used because they work. Testing has proven which techniques work and which don't.

However, there is still room for doing things innovatively to make your direct mailing stand out. Just keep your creativity balanced and within the realms of good taste. It's okay to experiment, but do so cautiously. Carefully consider any changes.

You can use direct mail to prospect nationally or locally and to target narrow audiences, like doctors, lawyers, plumbers, new mothers, right- or left-wing political donors, people who own BMWs or airplanes, accountants, schoolteachers, maintenance engineers, or . . . you name it.

You can use direct mail immediately after a sales or service call to reduce or eliminate refunds or complaints.

You can use direct mail to solicit or work special segments of your client base where it would not be practical to mass-solicit. For example, you may have ten thousand clients, but only five hundred are high-ticket buyers interested in high-end products or services. It's not feasible to mail a letter to all ten thousand clients about your new stock of expensive sweaters or your high-minimum-investment mutual fund when you want the message to go to only five hundred primary prospects. Segmenting mailing lists allows you to focus your offer on the right prospects.

You can use direct mail to promote store traffic by letting potential clients know who, what, and where you are.

You can use direct mail to introduce your product, service, or business to specific new areas of the marketing community when your business expands.

You can use direct mail (instead of display advertising) to generate a list of favorably disposed prospects. Then you can have salespeople solicit them, cutting your sales expense by half.

You can use direct mail to identify and attract any client,

prospect, or industry market. You can use direct mail to revitalize former clients or prospects.

You can use direct mail to recruit salespeople, executives, and specialized personnel anywhere in the country by zeroing in on targeted lists of specialized professions.

You can use direct mail whenever your company is stuck with overstocked, slow-moving, imperfect, or undesirable inventory or with excess labor capacity you need to put to use. You can use direct mail to add a mail- or telephone-order division to your operations.

You can use direct mail to test quickly and accurately all sorts of sales, pricing, conceptual, and packaging propositions. Test results will tell you how to expand the application of the tested concept to TV, radio, print, outside sales calls, and telemarketing.

You can use direct mail to promote high-ticket, high-profile products when you don't want to tie up your money in inventory. By utilizing direct mail to presell special-order items, you not only get prepaid orders for positive cash flow; you also can prebook enough advance orders to enable you to negotiate a better price from the supplier. And that's just for starters.

Once you've mastered direct mail, you possess a potent marketing tool that can stretch your marketing abilities many times over.

Everybody's Doing It

Direct mail has grown into a multibillion-dollar industry. The major players who've discovered the gold mine of opportunity include magazine and newsletter publishers, catalog companies, department stores, and music and book clubs.

The next time you come home and find a stack of so-called junk mail in your mailbox, don't pitch it into your round file. Take a few moments to read a letter or two.

People don't keep mailing these letters because they don't work. They mail hundreds of millions because they *do* work. You, too, can tap this potential marketing technique. All you need is a basic understanding.

With conventional advertising (like TV or display ads) it's hard to identify and correlate results. But direct mail provides the tools to measure your results to the penny. You can test and compare all sorts of marketing possibilities.

Direct mail is one of the least expensive and most effective ways for you to tell your full sales story to your clients and prospects. I know you have thrown away a lot of direct-mail literature and wondered just how such advertising could possibly pay off. The successful direct-mail advertiser knows that a huge percentage of the people who receive a letter from them will probably do just as you have done: throw it out. But if the letter is properly crafted and intelligently tested to a small segment of the list before being aggressively rolled out, it will indeed get sales from an impressive number of people.

In my own mailing experiences, we are perfectly satisfied if ninety-five out of one hundred people receiving our cold prospect mailing don't open it, so long as half of the remaining five reply. Let's look at the math.

1. At a price of approximately forty cents a letter, it costs about $400 to mail out one thousand letters.
2. If only 2 percent (twenty people) respond with an average sale of $100, the gross is $2,000 for the $400 spent.
3. Deduct 50 percent of gross for selling expenses and the $400 for mailing and advertising, then subtract 10 percent of the remaining for general and administrative expenses.
4. A mere 2 percent response can still net almost $600 sheer profit for every one thousand letters mailed out.

If mailing a million letters gives the same percentage response (and it will), you can make a killing. Even half of that yield would still be pretty impressive. These returns are possible with the right lists and the right offer.

A Paper Salesperson at the Client's Convenience

Let's assume you are in the manufacturing business. You make and sell products directly or through salespeople. You are succeeding modestly, but you crave larger profits.

An intelligently crafted direct-mail offer can present your prospect with all your products or services, or you can focus special attention on a single product. At their convenience, your prospects can review and reflect on your selling proposition. Your prospect has plenty of time to evaluate and reflect on your proposition.

New Business

You obviously don't have all the business or clients you would like to have. Direct mail can help develop new clients and accounts.

You haven't acquired all the clients you want for a number of reasons:

It isn't profitable or economical to solicit them through salespeople or via ads in magazines, newspapers, radio, or TV.

It costs too much time and sales power to convert prospects to clients.

You don't have a cost-effective way to identify the best prospects or to get the prospects to identify themselves.

Direct mail overcomes all these obstacles and is a dynamic adjunct to your sales efforts. For just pennies per piece, you can unleash an army of paper salespeople all over the city, marketing area, or industry you want to penetrate. And, in a surprisingly large number of cases, direct mail does better dollar-for-dollar than salespeople.

By now you're ready to put direct mail to work. What should you do?

First and foremost, identify the most probable audience for the most appealing and attractive single product or service you offer. When you have identified the audience, go out and rent five thousand or one thousand—or the smallest meaningful quantity of—names from that list that you can afford and can access. (See chapter 14 for detailed information about renting target lists.)

Once you identify the lists of the most probable people or organizations or businesses to target, what do you do with them? Do you mail them? Do you call them? Do you mail them and call them? Do you mail them an offer for a purchase? Do you mail them an offer to send for more information? Do you mail them an offer to send for a free evaluation? Do you invite them to participate in a seminar? Do you invite them to send for a free report? Do you invite them to come to your booth at a trade show? Do you invite them to come to your office or facility? Do you invite them to spend some time on the phone?

The answer is yes! You think up what combinations work best for your particular business or professional situation, and you test. You test the best embodiments, the best possibilities, to see which ones produce the best possible, the largest, the most qualified, the most unhedged, response—and that's the one you continue with.

Construct your offer. Depending on the product or service you sell, you should find the least expensive way to get the maximum number of people to raise their hand and say, "Yes, I am interested." What this means can differ by product or service line. But try to get them to send for a free sample. Or to visit. Or to call. If that's not practical, then you emphasize the lowest-priced, easiest-to-understand, and most beneficial result your product or service offers.

The Letter or E-mail

Write the sales letter. Understand always: A sales letter is nothing more than a conversation between two friends. One person gaining knowledge from another—transferring understanding and information.

The sales letter or E-mail is the sales presentation that piques interest and convinces the prospect to buy, call, write, or come in. Its objective is the same as your salesperson's to convey your product or service image through examples, promises, and benefits.

The Components of a Sales Letter

And every written communication is really selling some position.

Here are specific components your sales letter or E-mail should contain:

It must get the reader's attention with a powerful headline.

The letter must show clear and distinct advantages in the body copy.

The letter has to prove or validate your claim of benefits or advantages through factual examples—comparisons, analysis, testimonials, or credentials.

The letter must persuade the reader to reach out and seize the advantage you promise.

The letter must motivate the reader to act, respond, order, write, come in, or send back the coupon.

If your business is successful, it's probably because you know how to sell. You can adapt those live techniques to direct mail. If you currently use radio, TV, or print, it's a simple transition to direct mail. If you use salespeople, translating your oral sales presentation to written form should be easy.

You already know the hot buttons, buzzwords, and strongest propositions for your product or service. Translate them into the printed page. Create a personal letter that conveys your sincerity and the image that you wish to project. As much as possible, the letter should replicate a one-on-one, intimate conversation.

Headlines Are the Key

The headline (or first line) is the ad for the letter. It grabs readers and gets them to read more. Offer the reader a desirable reward for reading the letter. Tell him how he can gain, save, profit, achieve, or accomplish something through your product or service. Or show how the product or service will increase mental, physical, financial, social, spiritual, or intellectual well-being, satisfaction, or fulfillment. Show the reader how to avoid, reduce, or eliminate problems, risks, difficulties, worries, or fears by using your product or service. In short, what's the big benefit or advantage to him.

The Body of a Sales Letter

After the salutation, the body of the letter shows people the advantages of your product. The reader wants to know: "What will the product or service do for me?"

Begin by clearly disclosing a single powerful advantage. Then show more progressive advantages throughout the letter. When you write the body copy, you are wearing two hats. You want to sell, but you must also put yourself in the shoes of the reader.

Write the entire letter from the client's side. The consumer wants to know the same things we covered in our discussion of headlines. Body copy is the same as headlines, only more specific and detailed. Show in words and concrete imagery what he can gain or save or achieve by using your product or service: How will it benefit him?

You must then validate your claim. Facts, and plenty of them, solidify reader conviction and legitimize your offer. People need and want facts as rational reasons for making emotional buying decisions. Facts, comparisons, and proof build belief and make the readers feel their buying decision is wise. Belief is a by-product of emotion. Never forget that the heart dictates to the head. Your reader wants to believe your letter.

Before writing a compelling direct-mail or E-mail letter, spend time thinking about it. Dissect your product or proposition and find fresh new ideas and insights that turn your readers on. Analyze the claims of your competitors and you'll often come up with novel, creative, and convincing arguments for your own product or service. If you carefully analyze your sales records, client profiles, and service records, you can generate ideas that readers will really eat up.

View your product as if seeing it for the very first time. This is important because your letter will be the first exposure many readers have to your product or service.

Just the Facts, Ma'am

When you present the facts, begin with a statement of basic truth, known and accepted by the reader. By introducing known facts, you create believability for later statements. As you present more facts, your reader will unconsciously say, "The first statements were true, so the others must be."

Facts and statements that may impress your reader include:

- Specifics about construction, material, and workmanship.
- Facts about the reputation and the standing of your business: your facilities, research, location, or night and weekend hours.
- Details about employees' experience, credentials, and skills; how many people you employ, by job category; their specializations.
- Special delivery or production processes which your competitors don't have. Also, processes everyone uses but that your competitors have not promoted—even standard operating procedures.
- Usage of data, records, and documents or case studies. People love to see data, even if they can't evaluate it.
- Names of prestigious past or present clients and their endorsements.

Always use specifics instead of generalizations when citing facts.

Explain clearly and carefully all the sound business reasons why you can offer such a wondrous deal. For example, if you can produce widgets for one-third the cost of your competitors, explain the precise dynamics.

Close That Deal—Make That Sale

Now get your reader to act.

If your headline is great, your body copy loaded with compelling facts, your proof solid, and your advantage appealing, it still won't be profitable unless you ask the reader to act now.

Many good sales letters end flat, by not telling the recipient to act. This wastes the momentum you established.

Action-inducing techniques should be direct. Tell the reader exactly what to do:

- "Pick up the phone and call me or our client-service order lines."
- "Go to our closest location."
- "Don't let another day go by without sending in for this free information. Return the postage-paid reply envelope today."
- "Send your order before the sale ends. Mail it today."

You get the idea. E-mail me back, or go to my Web site.

Amplify the appeal of the request for action with risk transferal: Tell the reader the risk is all on you. Show him he has zero risk or obligation.

I often use these devices to provoke action:

- I ask the reader to respond immediately to a specific offer totally at my risk.
- I limit the time and restrict the quantity of the offer, and clearly explain why.
- I explain in detail the loss of sampling opportunities or free bonuses the reader will lose by failing to respond in time.
- I provide a better-than-risk-free guarantee that makes it just short of ludicrous not to take me up on my proposition.
- I tell the reader precisely and in progressive steps exactly how to respond.

How Long a Letter?

Should your letter or E-mail be long or short? Make it long enough to tell a complete, informative, and interesting story. People think others won't read long, multipage letters. That couldn't be further from the truth. You'll read any number of pages if a letter captures your interest. Make your sales letter long enough to tell a complete story and to thoroughly address all the necessary components.

Don't shortcut to save space. Edit ruthlessly for waste or boring content (this is particularly true with E-mail), but never jettison fascinating facts, forceful reasons, or specific information that adds to your compelling story.

If you had a salesperson calling on a client, would you tell that person to stop the presentation after thirty seconds to save time? Of course not. You want that salesperson to take as much time as necessary to make a compelling case. That also applies to sales letters.

My most successful sales letters have been eight, ten, twelve, even sixteen, pages long. But every paragraph was informative, and every section advanced the case. If you have a hobby or profession, how much will you read on that subject? A page? A chapter? A book? The answer is: a lot. Provided it is interesting. If your sales letters are interesting, people will gladly read them.

The Fact-Filled Brochure

Your sales letter should be warm, human, sincere, honest, personal, and one-on-one.

Your brochure or your company product or service report should be technical. It showcases the attractions, components, advantages, or positive benefits of the product or service. Your brochure should be written in terse one-sentence or one-paragraph statements that list important facts and benefits. Reprint or excerpt your best testimonials, endorsements, and recommendations.

Begin your brochure or report with a headline that summarizes the contents:

- Here is a quick review of reasons why you should take advantage of this offer.
- Here are the reasons why we are enthusiastic about our special offer.
- Some important facts you should know about our product or service.
- Here are the reasons our product or service will benefit you.
- Facts, figures, and testimonials that confirm the case for buying our product or service.

Before you list all the data in your brochure or report, write tight sentences or paragraphs that set the stage for each cluster of facts and figures. When listing performance characteristics, for example, preface the list with something like:

"You probably are interested in hard facts. These performance characteristics distinguish our widget from our competitors'." Then provide the list. When listing or reprinting testimonials, preface them with an introductory statement like this:

"We are biased in favor of our product. You'd probably like to know what users say about it, so here are unsolicited testimonials we've received. You can have any of their addresses and phone numbers if you'd like to contact them." Then print your testimonials or endorsements.

At the end of your brochure, summarize and repeat a call to action. For example:

"These are some compelling reasons to purchase or at least try our product or service risk-free. Take us up on our money-back offer. Come in. Or send in the . . . Or call in and let us send you . . ."

Also, clearly and prominently restate your guarantee as powerfully as possible, and summarize the entire proposition. It's absolutely essential. Never, ever, use a brochure in the mail without an accompanying sales letter to amplify and dimensionalize it.

To Coupon or Not to Coupon?

A coupon-oriented direct-mail offer can track your responses. Write a powerful one-paragraph statement of affirmation, repeating the offer and the appeal as if the reader were stating it aloud:

"*Yes!!* I agree!! Your proposition is irresistible and your product appears superior. Also, your bonuses are so darned attractive it's hard to refuse. But your 100 percent money-back guarantee, keep-all-the-bonuses, better-than-risk-free proposition is the real reason I am replying.

"I will take you up on the exact guarantee and try the product or service, but only for the next sixty days. If it doesn't perform or if I don't benefit just as you promised, I will send it back and expect a full and immediate refund. And I'll get to keep all those desirable bonuses for my trouble.

"On that basis only, here is my order."

If you are seeking leads or inquiries, say something like:

"Your case is indeed compelling. I don't know if your product is for me, but I want to learn more. So send me the kit or have a representative call and answer my questions. Better yet, do both.

"But only on the condition that I am under absolutely no obligation and no risk whatsoever."

Go from there to name, address, city, state, zip, phone, and E-mail address. Always get information for follow-up. It'll make you a lot of money.

On the back of your brochure, place a summary and a composite of statements from other people who've already done what you're now asking this new respondent to do.

Then put together a simple but declarative response device—either a card they send back or an order form they can return. And put together a means for them to return it. Either a self-addressed envelope, a self-addressed postcard, or an envelope they put the response mechanism as well as their check or their charge-card information in.

Always focus on specificity—demonstrating performance attributes and credibility at the highest level.

For example, does your response device, or order card, summarize your offer in a specific way for the client? "Yes, I do want to learn how to cut ten strokes off my golf game." Or "Yes, I am a hard-nosed, bottom-line manufacturer who wants to learn how to cut 10 percent out of my waste." Or "Yes, I do care about getting more performance and loyalty out of my staff. Send me your free report."

Whatever the offer is, take the risk out of it for the client. "I understand I get this report without risk." Or "I understand that even though it normally costs $1,000 for the analysis, I will get it free." Or "I understand that even though I am sending you my check, neither you nor I will consider the purchase binding for thirty-five days until after I've had it, tested it, put it to work, and either proved or disproved it."

All those items have to be there, along with name, address, city, state, daytime phone number, E-mail address, and ordering provisions. If it's ordered by check, make sure there's a box for "check." If it's charge-card information that's being sent, make provisions for charge-card information: what the card number is, expiration date, and a signature.

All those elements have to be there. A device to cradle and

contain and hold that response has to be included, too: a response envelope or—if you don't have critical information and charge-card information, or other confidential information isn't being sought—just a response postcard.

Or it might be a little postcard that is put into a "favor of your reply" envelope. But it needs all those components. All of those must appear. All of those should be contained if you want the maximum profitable outcome from your mailing.

If you're using regular mail instead of E-mail, you have to consider the outside packaging which holds the components— the envelope. It needs to be enticing enough that it won't be considered just another piece of "junk mail" and end up in the recipient's trash.

Accordingly, there are a multitude of decisions to be made about the carrier envelope—size, color, postage (meter versus live postage), paper stock and color, whether it should include a teaser (copy printed on the outside that will entice the recipient to open it), and so on.

Teaser Copy

Many opt not to use teaser copy because it immediately distinguishes your package as "junk mail." However, teaser copy may also lure the reader into opening an otherwise nondescript envelope. Weigh your decision in the matter of teaser copy thoroughly, and choose your copy carefully.

The carrier envelope can present a sales message that does the same job as an ad headline. The job of the envelope is to get the letter opened. Crafted properly, the envelope can prevent the recipient from throwing away the letter. This envelope can promise a powerful benefit inside and get the letter opened and read.

Take a tested headline (possibly one from your most productive display ad) and put it boldly on the lower left corner of your envelope. Or boil down the first few words from your most effective sales pitch and put them on the outside or back of your envelope. Remember, space is limited.

Also, postal restrictions limit your message to a certain portion of one side of the front and back of the envelope. Check with your local postmaster for current limitations. You must be ruthless in condensing down to the most powerful words that will cause the reader to become curious.

On the other hand, the envelope may be plain (white or colored), resembling a personal letter—with no hint as to its contents. By disguising your direct mail to look like personal correspondence, it can get by the secretary and avoid the circular file.

Some people put distinctive language on the upper left corner of their carrier envelopes, like "Executive Offices," "President," "Research Department," or "Treasurer." Experiment and find what works best for you.

I've used both teaser copy and plain white envelopes. Both worked well, but for different purposes. Test to see which approach yields the most profitable response.

Keep a written record and a file of carrier envelopes that got your attention. Remember, the envelope must get opened in order for the enclosed letter to be read. Once this all-important task is done, the envelope's job is over.

Direct-Mail Successes

Here's how a few people I've worked with have used direct mail specifically in their business activities.

A really inventive-minded client I worked with in Seattle had a medical diagnostics laboratory. He sold diagnostics services to physicians all over Washington State.

When I told him how much more he could be doing by using direct mail, he surprised me. He took the easiest, simplest application and parlayed a $500 investment into $900,000 worth of first-year new clients and business.

How did he do it?

He took a new diagnostic service his company came out with. He summarized the service on the front of the postcard and he made a very irresistible offer. He identified the thousand doctors in his marketing area he was not doing business with for that service. He made each one of them a very powerful but very simple offer on the back side of his postcard. And seventy responded to his first mailing.

A $500 investment generated not only $900,000 in sales, but $900,000 more in repeat sales.

He remailed that postcard three or four times. He built the business into the millions and he was able to sell his business to a division of Revlon in New York.

A company I advise found direct mail to be the most effective selling mechanism they had available to them when they were trying to reach secretaries of chief executive officers in order to sell them legal forms.

They found out that they could rent lists of secretaries by going to certain publications where secretaries were the prime subscribers. They mailed letters that talked one-on-one to each secretary, acknowledging the buying power the secretaries wielded on behalf of their bosses.

They made a specific offer that they extended to these secretaries through these letters and they used risk reversal to make it irresistibly appealing for the secretary to send for the legal forms for their business.

By changing their selling method from just field salespeople to very targeted direct-mail letters, they tripled their business and reduced their selling expenses by about 40 percent.

I have a client in the Northeast, who was the largest and most successful single representative in the country for a major insurance company. He has significantly increased his income by using highly targeted direct-mail letters to business owners around New York State.

He sent them a simple letter, offering them a free preview analysis and giving them the opportunity to respond discreetly, without risk and without obligation, to see how much of a difference certain financial services might make in their future and in their retirement years.

That simple approach, executed beautifully, has created a seven-figure-a-year income for my client, who never leaves his office. Almost all his business is transacted by telephone, E-mail, and overnight mail.

A mortgage broker went from making $90,000 a year and spending 90 percent of his time driving all over Los Angeles County to the point where he was able to stay in his office 95 percent of his day and just send out highly placed letters, every day of every week, every month of every year. These letters went to targeted home owners who were in a perfect position to refinance, and he was able to generate a $250,000-a-year income. Without ever knocking on any doors. Without ever cold-calling on any prospects.

A nationally prominent swimming-pool company built a massive multimillion-dollar business of new swimming-pool installations just by identifying affluent home owners who did not have swimming pools. The company sent them fun, nonthreatening, full-color, very rich-looking postcards that offered them a wonderful benefit and a bonus if they would call up or send the card in to get a free consultation of how a swimming pool might fit into their home and what the resulting cost might be.

That simple process alone, done strategically and continuously, built a $40 million swimming-pool installation business.

A Realtor sends out twenty-five hundred pieces every month to sellers who are on the fence. The "free" piece is an informative newsletter. He also sells his database to allied companies who could benefit businesswise from people who move. For example, home insurance companies and moving companies. This pays for his mailing. His profits are up about a third.

A financial planner sent two-dollar bills with his mailings. He found others were doing the same, so he thought he'd up the ante to $10 based upon the lifetime value of his clients (approximately $7,800).

Remember the Diet Pepsi commercials on TV with Ray Charles, *Auh, huh*? Well, it didn't do anything for Diet Pepsi sales. A new marketer for the soft drink came in and identified the demographics of the people that drink soft drinks, direct-mailed affinity soft-drinkers by zip code, and gave them a valuable coupon to switch for one week. It worked fantastically, but a senior executive who didn't like direct mail canceled the program.

A Word About E-mail

Many people use E-mail with great success. It's fast, easy, and usually very efficient. However, I am not convinced that E-mail is right for every business situation, and it should be given special thought in selling and marketing. It's true that E-mail can present the same written presentation as a letter, but it can be eliminated by the push of a button. It takes some extra effort on the reader's part to make a hard copy. And for the most part, it looks the same as every other E-mail on the screen.

Frequently people won't even open E-mail from unfamiliar sources because it may contain a virus that could wipe out their entire hard drive.

For many people, E-mail is an excellent vehicle to contact prospects and clients. But make sure it's right for your situation before you rely on it. (More about computers, web sites, and the Internet in chapter 16.) Whatever you do, whenever using E-mail make certain it contains and conveys tremendous content value and more than justifies the intrusion into someone's digital life the transmission incurs. We just did a fabulously successful E-mail test that produced over a 50 percent response. How? By giving value then delivering far more value when the recipient responded to our request.

Action Steps

Make a complete list of every business contact you make—in person; by phone; when people call you, your order department, or your client-service or technical people; accounts payable and receivable; etc. Each is a perfect opportunity to add one or a series of direct-mail letters to the sales process you currently use.

Then list every critical situation or opportunity in your business where a preceding or follow-up direct-mail or direct-response letter could result in a more positive outcome.

Next, remember that continuous contact and communication with the client has been proven to have a significant positive impact on order size, frequency of purchase, loyalty of clients, referrals generated, etc.

Now rank your various lists on a priority and frequency-of-occurrence basis. Once you've done that, start writing some powerful, purposeful, and profitable letters. If you don't have the time or talent, find a salesperson in your organization who can write. Or sit down with someone you respect and just naturally talk out what you'd like to say to someone—a spontaneous flow of thoughts from your heart. Record this conversation and then transcribe the session. You'll be surprised at what a good letter you've created once it's edited.

Once you're focused, and some letters are written, try them out in small test-run quantities or applications and see what a difference it makes.

Also, the same applies in career situations when you need to impact someone in another department, in upper management, or a board member. It applies to civic activities and community work as well.

14

Fish Where the Big Fish Are

WHEN INFAMOUS BANK ROBBER WILLY SUTTON WAS ASKED why he robbed banks, he replied, "Because that's where the money is."

It costs you an enormous amount of effort, human capital, and money to travel, send out samples, or bring someone to your facility or office in order to get them to the point of saying, "Yes, I want to be a client." You can't afford to waste time and money on people who aren't sincerely interested. You need to target higher-quality prospects rather than a higher quantity. Quantity does not matter in lead generation. Quality and convertibility are what's important. In other words, go where the money is.

One of the biggest wastes of time and opportunity that I see is people who do not qualify the prospects they target. Instead of going after primary prospects, they go after suspects. The difference between a suspect and a prospect is quality. A suspect is anyone who maybe, possibly, somehow could or might—squint your eyes—someday have the capacity to buy your product or service. A prospect is someone who is qualified today. They need your product or service. They have the capacity to pay for it. They have the ability to make a decision now. They are prime, qualified targets for what you do.

Why use a shotgun if you can use a rifle with absolute precision? Focus your efforts and attention on the markets, prospects, and activities that offer you the highest probability of a payoff and you'll always do better. But most people don't stop and question whether there's a better way, an accessible and qualified decision maker or source they can reach easier and more effectively. When you do realize there are ways to focus on prospects who are more likely to be interested in your product or service, you will experience greater results with less effort, time, and money expended.

In this chapter you will learn how to focus your time and money on targeting the most likely prospects in order to achieve the most cost-effective and profitable results.

Simple Enough for Kids

Winter in cold-weather areas of the country offers an excellent chance for kids to make extra cash. And the ones who target high-quality prospects make the most money. After a heavy snowstorm, the kids would get their shovels and start knocking on doors, offering to clear the snow from a home owner's driveway for a modest fee. The rate of closing sales was only about one in three. The kids who figured out how to target the most likely prospect, however, closed four of five sales at no reduced fees.

Who were these more-qualified sales targets? The adults who

had declined the original offer to have their driveway cleared, decided to do it themselves, and were now halfway through the project, very tired, and in fear of an imminent heart attack.

Ads in magazines or newspapers, brochures or letters, telephone calls, radio or TV spots, should offer very specific qualifying propositions so that when the men, women, or companies respond, they are qualifying themselves. They are saying, "Yes, I want to do business with you because I have an interest in your product or service or I want to get that result."

For example, a bank should never run ads just saying how wonderful it is. The banks should run ads offering a booklet that says, "How to Finance a New Home or Refinance an Existing One and Save $15,000 or More over the Life of Your Mortgage." That example only appeals to people who are seriously interested in either making a financing or refinancing decision with a bank. They are quality prospects.

When you send letters, don't make them general. Always make them refer to some product, service, or process the recipient of that letter can take advantage of and would have a very strong interest in acquiring.

Where Do You Find High-Quality Prospects?

There are mailing-list directories available to you of almost any target audience you want to reach.

You can rent lists, not just by name, but by title and job specification (and many times by phone number). A list broker can provide you with lists of predisposed buyers, or you can consult such publications as the *Thomas Register*, or the *Standard Rate and Data Service Directory* (SRDS). These lists, combined with properly written letters and effective telemarketing, will result in quality prospects and much higher and more effective closings.

Computers and Mailing Lists

Marketing by mail has exploded because it is the fastest-growing, most-profitable and most easily traceable means of marketing, thanks in part to the sophistication of computer programming and the availability of highly specialized mailing lists, categorized by every imaginable classification. Readily available are compiled lists that categorize virtually everyone: attorneys, golfers, company presidents, personnel managers, fleet managers, computer experts, swimming-pool owners, dog owners, horse owners, gardeners, tennis-club members, or what make, model, and year of car people own, and on and on and on.

That's merely the beginning of the ways you can microscopically focus on prospects for any business product. Want to know who subscribes to any of a thousand different magazines, journals, newspapers, and newsletters? No problem: You can readily rent the subscribers of all but a tiny handful of publications. Wish you could tap into the people who bought merchandise from the Sharper Image? Hey, that client list can be rented. So, too, can the client lists of nearly five thousand other mail-order firms.

Likewise, you can rent lists of voters, donors, churchgoers, or any demographic designation you can dream up. Thanks to computers, you can eliminate the possibility of duplicating names, even if you rent a hundred lists. You can avoid wasting your money mailing to people who hate "junk mail." You can personalize every letter by name, address, and salutation. Many lists can be rented with all kinds of additional data included, such as phone numbers.

The List Is the Most Important Factor

No one will buy your product or service if they're not interested in it. You should concentrate your sales efforts on people who have a history of buying your type of product or service, or who are logically predisposed to what you're offering.

There are two types of mailing lists:

1. Compiled
2. Direct response

A compiled list is a categorical list of people who have similar things in common. Owners of certain kinds of automobiles. People who live in certain kinds of affluent areas. People of certain age groups. People of other types of similarities like political affiliation. Or educational affiliation. Or professional distinction.

Direct-response lists, on the other hand, include people or businesses who've actually responded to previous solicitation. They have either purchased or inquired or attended or participated in some way in some very specialized product or service or activity that demonstrates that they have a commitment toward the area of interest you're trying to sell into.

Someone who is a direct-response-generated name might be a subscriber to a specific publication. Or an attendee at a specific seminar. Or a purchaser of a specific type of book or a report or tape set. Or a purchaser of a specific type of product or catalog. Or a member of a specific type of nonprofit organization. And on and on and on.

So I suggest that the very first thing you do is get your hands on a *Standard Rate and Data Service Directory* (SRDS). They are not inexpensive. A year's subscription costs about $400 (800-851-SRDS). So you'd save money going to a well-stocked business library and using an SRDS from their reference division. You could peruse through all the categories that seem best related to the area of business activity or need that your product or service typically fills. It's an experience of a lifetime to go through these pages and see the descriptions of all the different companies that have identified all the different people and organizations, by all the different categories and definitions, that you can directly profit from.

What other sources are there? Well, if you are in an industrial business—if you are selling to an industrial market—you can get companies listed by SIC code by getting the *Thomas Register*. You can contact Dun and Bradstreet, which has compiled some of the most powerfully defined lists of target audiences ever seen. You can also go to virtually any trade magazine, any consumer magazine, any specialized magazine, or any association and get them to make their membership or subscriber list available to you by all kinds of different qualifications. Name. Address. Home address. Title. Size of organization. And so on.

Here's what I mean:

A company selling sophisticated wealth-preservation plans for upper-income individuals rents lists of subscribers to *Yachting* magazine and *Polo* magazine, Rolls-Royce owners, and American Express platinum cardholders.

A security alarm company acquires weekly lists of people whose homes or businesses have been broken into.

Let Your Search Continue

Use all the wonderful free resources the Internet now makes readily available, too. Just log onto your favorite search engine and go for a digital spin.

Ask yourself, "What other industry would normally be selling to my clients?" When you understand what those industries are, then go a little deeper. Go to the next level of definition. Define and identify exactly who those people are. By defining and identifying who they are, you'll know exactly who to write or call and ask for. Then call them and ask if they would be willing to make their clients or prospects available to you, either for a fee or for a percentage of the business that results (or the leads that result).

Or offer a trade—where you'll trade them access to your prospects and your client lists. After all, if they're not competitive, and you are complementary, you both have everything to gain by working together.

What other ways will help you identify your best possible target audience and acquire the best possible target audience list?

You can actually go to your own direct competitors and make them an audacious proposition. Ask them for a list of their inactive clients—their unconverted leads. Offer to give them a substantial share of either the initial sales or the ongoing sales resulting from any mailings you do to these old, tired names.

You can go to competitors who aren't doing well (or who are phasing out of areas you're trying to be more expansive in) and work out deals where they turn over the business to you for an equitable ongoing share of the profit.

A lot of people don't make money in certain segments of a business that you might make all your money in. By making a deal and offering to take over their business and their client names and working that list, you can make them more money and get them out of unprofitable and inappropriate areas where they don't want to commit their time and money.

Don't Overlook the Value of Your Own List

When you compile your own client/inquire list, you're sitting on a valuable source of additional income to your company. Just as you would like to get ahold of other companies' lists, so can you expect a wide range of companies to be interested in your client list. And they'll pay to rent those names from you. And renting them is far more profitable than just throwing them out a window. Here's what I mean.

Among the tons of paper thrown from office buildings during a New York ticker-tape parade for the 1984 Olympic medal winners were hundreds of listings of Bear, Stearns and Company's client accounts and transactions. Dozens of competing pin-striped brokers scrambled around the street and sidewalk, snatching up client leads. One broker walked away with a hundred sheets listing Bear, Stearns accounts, complete with names, addresses, dollar volume, and portfolio details. "Frankly, we are embarrassed," a Bear, Stearns managing partner told the press. "I haven't caught the person who did it, but if I did and we were in an Islamic country, we would probably punish him suitably."

Compiling Your Own List

So how do you build a client list?

Let's say you have a retail store. First, you make certain that whenever you have a credit-card purchase, you start asking for your client's name, address, city, state, zip code—and phone number. Do it naturally and matter-of-factly, and no one will refuse to give you that information.

As you capture this information, transfer it to a databased software program on your computer. There are many good programs to choose from. When transacting straight cash sales, go through the same process. Try prefacing this information request by telling the client you will also put them on the preferred-client mailing and announcement list (put strong emphasis on the word *announcement*). Tell the client you mail out advance notification of special purchases and sales. Tell them you give preferred clients advance access, along with additional discounts and/or bonuses. Few people will turn down the chance to earn or receive preferential future pricing access or bonuses. It's important, however, to follow through and make formal and systematized announcements once you compile the list.

If you're at all uncomfortable with this approach, consider how the great mail-order operators who also run retail facilities do it. Companies like Radio Shack, Victoria's Secret, and the Sharper Image know and respect the importance and necessity of capturing a client or prospect name, and they methodically ask for and receive them from every client.

You must do that, too.

If you're paid by check, pick up the name and other vital information from that check. The same goes for a driver's license—and ask whether or not the address on that license is the current and correct one.

Let's say that you run a service station. It's not different for you, really. Collect names, addresses, and phone numbers wherever and whenever possible. Reward people for becoming or gaining "preferred-client" status. You might be able to sell a coupon book of services at a discount as you gather names and addresses.

Come up with valuable and appealing rewards or distinctions for frequent purchases and repurchases—or for purchasing larger quantities.

All things being equal, a client who comes in and fills up with super unleaded once every week is worth four times as much to you as one who fills up only once a month. So reward and encourage them—first for getting their name on your special or preferred-client list—and next, for their frequency of repurchase.

Do not limit your capturing of names merely to people who buy. Separately collect and retain a mailing list of prospects, leads, and inquirers. A surprisingly large number of prospects and leads can be turned into very profitable clients just by regular and strategic communication with them.

Your goal is to identify all your active and inactive clients, to know who and where they are, and then to communicate with them and frequently reward them—attracting them to gain greater benefit when they fulfill their needs and desires through your enterprise.

I want you to commit to collecting, acquiring, and keeping every client and prospect on a mailing list, and working that list properly. Keep segmented lists of clients by their purchasing habits. Remember, you make the rules. If you see a client-list technique that works for another industry, try it.

E-Alert!

Whenever possible, also secure your client's E-mail address and permission to communicate information and offers of value and importance to him. Find other businesses and Web site owners who have significant E-mail addresses of their clients and permission to communicate with them and work out host-beneficiary relationships to E-mail or E-mail link to you Web site, too.

One of the biggest overlooked uses of E-mail is to drive people to call your offices or order or client service lines.

Once You Have a List, Now What?

Even if the rental income from letting other direct-marketers use your mailing list does little more than pay the computer service bill for the year, you're still ahead of the game. After all, you have to computerize your mailing list anyway. The only additional costs you'll incur in order to rent your mailing list to others are the running charges involved in producing the list and the commission to the list manager or broker for placing the rental order.

Lists are marketed through mailing-list brokers. There are five different categories of list people:

List owner: somebody like yourself or your company who owns a mailing list that has been built for marketing their own products and services.

List broker: a middleman who represents the list owner to sell rentals of the list for a 20 percent commission.

List user: the company that rents somebody else's mailing list for the purpose of sending out its promotional mailings.

List manager: a firm that undertakes the promotion and sale of your mailing list to other brokers. The firm may be involved in computer services and can also handle the computerization and maintenance of your list. It may also function as list broker and list compiler on a fee or percentage basis.

List compiler: a firm that builds mailing lists from raw sources. Its sources can be mail-order response, business directories, or telephone books. This company owns the list that it may market itself or it may market through list brokers—or both.

How do you generate income from your mailing list? You can rent your list. Exchange lists. Joint-venture lists. Reverse host-beneficiary or work out insert deals you put into your own marketing or packages. You can simply create a mailing piece giving details about your list, mail it to the list brokers (whose names are readily available out of *Direct Mail List Rates and Data*) and sit back and wait for the orders to come in. The broker will bill the renter on your behalf, and when he receives payment from his client he will remit it to you less a commission of 20 percent.

The broker takes no liability for collection of the bill. When he gets paid, you get paid. If he doesn't get paid, it is your problem. Thus, it is important that you exercise credit approval on his client and do not hesitate to ask for cash up front if you doubt the credit worth of his client. Most brokers are reputable and will remit to you after they've been paid. *Caution:* List brokers are frequently slow in paying for rentals. They blame it on the fact that their client didn't pay them, but we have documented dozens of cases where the broker has taken weeks after he has been paid by his client to remit to the list owner.

Another way to rent your client or prospect list is to put it in the hands of a mailing-list manager. Either you can furnish him with the list and he'll do all the work for you or you can simply send him raw data (inquiries, orders, etc.) and he'll computerize and maintain your list for you. Obviously, he'll charge you for his computer time. If you send him your disc, he'll charge you the running costs for producing labels. Or you can retain your lists and he'll send you orders that you can produce and ship.

If you don't have time to devote to selling your mailing lists, you can put the list into the hands of a list manager. The list manager normally gets 10 percent in addition to what the broker already gets (20 percent) plus charges for his computer time at his cost or on a fixed schedule of fees.

The list manager takes the headaches out of running your list business—he handles all selling effort, inquiries, the furnishing of accounts, the producing of orders, billing, and collecting. You won't get paid much earlier from the list manager (in fact, probably an additional few days will be added for the processing in his office), but you'll be able to break into the list business much more rapidly.

Most mailing lists are rented for one-time use. Most rentals begin as test mailings for five thousand or ten thousand names. Continuations will result if the test works. It takes a full year to generate a good list-rental business, so most managers will insist on a two-year exclusive contract to handle the list.

A turnover of six to ten times per year on your list is good. If you pay the broker 20 percent, the manager 10 percent, and your running costs are 20 percent, that leaves you 50 percent profit on the list rental income—that is pure profit to most mail marketers.

How Some Have Targeted Prospects

I have a friend who is in sales. He used to work for one of the nation's foremost copier companies. He had a territory in southern California, but the way he worked his territory was inefficient and unproductive.

In essence, what he was doing was taking every suspect in his territory and treating them all as if they were prospects. By that I mean he would just take a section of his territory and from morning to night call cold on office after office and store after store. Almost indiscriminately. His results were at best mediocre.

I asked him, "Does your company have information or data that would tell you what kind of industries or businesses or professions tend to be higher than normal prospects for copiers? In other words, there must be certain kinds of businesses or professional practices that have about ten times the probability of needing one or more copiers or going through copiers faster and more frequently than others."

He did some research and it became evident that there were several industries that were on average ten times better prospects than all the rest.

And I said, "Well, it seems to me that we ought to first of all isolate who those primary prospects are. Get a list of who and where those kinds of companies are in your territory, and call on them first before you call on the less likely prospects."

He agreed, of course.

We got a qualified mailing list of the names, the addresses, the phone numbers, and the key decision makers at those businesses.

He was able to call ahead, make appointments, and organize his day. And guess what? He started working about half the hours and his commissions tripled.

Why?

Because he used his time and his efforts more effectively and efficiently.

That's what happens when you identify and use qualified mailing lists. And the uses for these lists are not limited just to mailing. You can use the mailing list for calling ahead, for tele-marketing, for calling after a mailing.

I have a client who's become the foremost real estate workout attorney on the West Coast. Let me tell you what a workout attorney does. He works with either the owners of the property or the financial institutions who end up taking properties back when people go bankrupt or go into foreclosure. And he works with one or both sides, helping them make the transaction work, whatever *work* means for them.

About two years ago this attorney decided he was going to become the top authority in an emerging field.

No one really had a lot of expertise, himself included. But he decided he was going to position himself as the foremost author-ity. So he acquired a number of lists of financial-institution workout specialists. He approached them very systematically by mailing them an invitation every month to an event he con-ducted on their specific workout situation: hotel workouts or apartment workouts or shopping-center workouts, etc.

Each and every month he also sent a mailing designed to give

to pay the significant asking price of the property, but also to show they could afford the $50,000 per year maintenance costs. Anyone who failed to meet those qualifications was not allowed to view the home.

A company selling very expensive hydroponic plant-growing systems goes to what some would consider extreme measures to make sure that they deal with only high-interest prospects. First it charges prospective purchasers of their system $29 for a video that demonstrates and explains the system. Then it requires serious prospects to fly to Ohio, at their own expense, to see if the system is right for them. Two out of three people who fly there, buy.

A high-end woman's retail shop does daily luncheon fashion shows at exclusive Beverly Hills restaurants.

The first expedition to Antarctica got their party by running this qualifying ad in the *New York Times*: "Wanted. Courageous adventurers for dangerous, four-month expedition to Antarctica. Pay, terrible. Hard, exhausting work. Probability of success: unlikely. But fame and glory to those who make it back." They had more than enough highly qualified applicants. And the expedition was a success.

One Last Example

At one of my training programs a few years back I had speaking for me a prominent and respected expert in advertising. He was trying to make a very powerful point which parallels what we're talking about in this chapter.

He asked the audience a really interesting question. He said, "Let's presume we're going to go into the restaurant business and each one of us can choose the one advantage we could have over everyone else. We're going to go into Los Angeles and you get to pick the first advantage before I do. What are you going to pick?"

And he went around the room and let every participant choose the one factor they thought would give them the greatest success.

When he was done he said, "Fine. Now let me tell you the one factor I want. I want a starving crowd."

The lesson: The right list will connect you with your starving crowd.

Action Steps

Sit down with your client files and salespeople (if you have them) and make certain you have a complete, comprehensive list of all your clients.

Separate your clients by their various buying patterns or interests. Determine which clients buy what category of products or services and which ones buy larger units of sale and buy more frequently. Identify people or businesses that purchase more of specific categories of products and services or far more specialized applications.

Note if there are similarities among various buying groups that point to opportunity trends. For example, if you discover that your biggest buyers are all doctors, or chemical manufacturers, you'd be able to target more of these groups as primary prospects.

See if there are geographical trends, demographic indications, or general age, family, business type and/or size factors that correlate to specific buying patterns.

continues to next page

When you recognize what these patterns are, you can use that knowledge to fashion propositions geared more to that segment.

It only makes sense that you'd want to deal differently and spend more time or communicate more extensively with clients who buy more and buy more often than ones who don't. Yet few businesses do this. The only way you can start is by finding them, then acting on the information you're sitting on.

Once you start analyzing and interpreting your data, it will lead you to significant opportunities. Because now you can start targeting precise lists of the highest probability and viability prospects—people or businesses who most mirror the patterns and characteristics of the clients you already serve. Don't forget to include the Internet and E-mail in any strategy and action plan you develop.

15

Watson, Come Here, I Need You

VIRTUALLY EVERYONE IN ANY BUSINESS SITUATION USES THE telephone to sell. This is true whether you own a small retail shop or are the CEO of a worldwide corporation. The term for using the telephone for business marketing and selling is *telemarketing*.

If you use it correctly, telemarketing can produce explosively profitable results for almost any business or professional practice. Yet, if you or others mismanage your telephone efforts, it will waste tons of your precious cash and jeopardize relationships with your best prospects and clients.

To avoid the potential downside, remember these basic telemarketing rules:

Start the Process by Mail

Telemarketing works best when you prepare the way for it with a letter or advertisement that causes prospects to write to you for more information (or perhaps for a free report that you're offering).

Once you know who is interested enough to at least return a coupon, request a free report, send an E-mail or a general letter of inquiry, you have prequalified your prospects. You or your salespeople won't be calling blindly, or simply dialing category names lifted from the Yellow Pages.

A premailing isn't critical when you want to set up calls to existing clients, but it never hurts to let existing clients know in advance that you will be calling them. The courtesy will be appreciated, if nothing else. I have seen courtesy play a decisive role in closing many sales.

Telemarketing is probably one of the most underutilized maximizing tools available to you or your team. It has many powerful ways to add sales, profits, impact, reach, connection, or penetration to your business activities.

In this chapter you will learn how to use the telephone to increase sales and profits. And what to avoid so telemarketing doesn't do more harm than good.

Test Before You Telemarket

Don't jump into telemarketing with both feet until you've tested it on a small scale and determined that you stand at least a fair chance of turning a good profit.

If you decide to set up a larger telemarketing operation than you or your staff can handle, contact a telemarketing firm that has worked in your specific field, and have them conduct either a per-order or hourly rate test for you that covers anywhere from fifty to one hundred hours of calling. Some will do this for free.

If you choose the hourly rate approach, you can expect to pay the telemarketers somewhere around $40 an hour, on average. That's the bad news. The good news is that the telemarketing agencies will handle everything for you, including preparation of the script.

Per-order telemarketing firms, on the other hand, are only paid for the orders they produce. That arrangement might look attractive to you at first glance, but it sometimes makes them more aggressive when trying to close a sale—something that may or may not offend your prospects or present clients.

To protect yourself, always closely review the script that's used by telemarketers. And insist on being able to monitor some of their calls.

Price Your Offer Right

The item or service you telemarket should be priced high enough to pay your telemarketers' wages or commissions and to cover all of your other related costs. A good working ratio is one-third to the telemarketers, one-third for any other expenses, and one-third to your minimum or you don't have any margin for error.

If the results from a telemarketing test show that you only broke even, or actually lost a little money, that may not be a cause for tears. Not if you understand the concept of establishing the lifetime value of your clients. A break-even figure would look pretty good to me if I knew from experience that my average new client would make numerous purchases from me over a transactional lifetime.

And, if I actually made money on my test, all the better.

Stair-Step the Telemarketing Presentation

Whether you telemarket on your own or through a telemarketing service bureau, begin conversations with prospects by asking a few broad questions that will put them at ease. (And first ask permission to ask them even broad questions.) Whatever you do, don't plunge immediately into pointed questions that could trigger a fast "no."

Once a prospect has been "favorably predisposed," you can move to your offer, but present your offer just as naturally and conversationally as you began the exchange. Never be argumentative, pushy, or demeaning.

Also, don't address the people you call by first name, and don't try any gimmicks like saying you're returning the prospect's call, or saying that one of the prospect's friends asked you to call them (a friend whose name you couldn't produce if your life depended on it).

In telemarketing, as in any other phase of business or professional practice, complete honesty and candor is always the best policy. It is a profession and you and your people should conduct yourselves accordingly.

When selling by phone, you have approximately thirty seconds to convince the prospect to listen to you. You need an opening statement that will capture the prospect's interest. This statement should convey who you are, what you want, and why the prospect should listen. Get your benefit to them across immediately.

State your name and your company's name clearly. Then state the reason you're calling. Tell the prospect how you obtained their name. (Again, if you have preceded the call by letter or advertising, the prospect may have requested information.) State an important benefit of your product or service and mention a feature that backs up that benefit. Ask for the prospect's time, then ask preliminary probing questions to help you qualify the prospect. By incorporating these elements into your opening statement in a creative manner, you can persuade the prospect to listen to your presentation.

Asking Questions in Telephone Selling

Learn to ask questions as you talk to prospects. It's the best way to sell. Keep the following points in mind as you refine your telephone skills:

1. Develop a plan. Before placing a call, be aware of exactly what it is you want to learn before the call is over.
2. Prepare a list of topics to cover. Have a specific question under each topic.
3. Ask permission. It's common courtesy to ask the client's permission to ask questions.
4. Time questions properly. Avoid making your presentation sound like an interrogation.
5. Begin with broad questions that relax the prospect and get the ball rolling. Then your questions can become more specific as the prospect reveals certain needs and concerns.
6. Build upon previous answers. Your feedback shows the prospect that you're listening.
7. Balance the number and type of questions. Though asking too few questions isn't a good practice, too many questions can make the prospect impatient for you to get to the point.
8. Don't ask manipulative questions (e.g., "Of course you would like to save 60 percent on your materials' costs, wouldn't you?"). They insult the prospect's intelligence.

9. Be relaxed and conversational. Always let the prospect finish talking. Listen carefully.

A Sample Script

Here is a brief model telemarketing script that, with some adaptation to fit your specific business, can help you or your callers establish proper tone, pace, and believability. (The script assumes that someone is calling a prospect who has already shown a threshold interest in a product or service. In other words, it's not a cold call, but a follow-up call.)

"Good morning, is Mr. Franklin there, please?"

"This is Mr. Franklin speaking."

"Mr. Franklin, this is Alex Smith at Catered Coffee International. I'm calling as a courtesy follow-up to the recent note you sent us asking for information on our coffee service. I'd love to tell you about our service and how we might be of help to your company. Is this a good time to talk?"

"Sure, why don't you go ahead."

"Before I do, Mr. Franklin, please tell me just a little bit about coffee service at your company right now, and what in particular prompted you to inquire about our service?"

"Well, we've got a lot of unhappy coffee drinkers in this place. We've been letting employees fix their own coffee in the company kitchenettes. It's generally pretty yucky stuff, and we've had a lot of cup breakage. Anyway, I was asked by our president to see what's out there in the way of catered service."

"Mr. Franklin, I'm sure we can make your coffee drinkers happy, and do it with delicious coffee that won't bust your budget—or bust any cups. But may I make a suggestion at this point?"

"Sure."

"I think I'd be doing you a much greater service if I could drop by at a time convenient to you and analyze your needs in a bit more detail. That would give me an opportunity to show you a couple of things about Catered Coffee International that are a little difficult to describe over the phone. Does that sound reasonable?"

"How much time would it take?"

"No more than thirty minutes. I could be out there later today, if you like, or perhaps I could drop by tomorrow—whatever fits comfortably into your schedule."

"All right, why don't you come by at three o'clock tomorrow afternoon."

There are several bedrock lessons here. One of them is to prime your prospects with a mailing (or a couponed ad) before you call them. A second lesson is to project respect, warmth, and believability whenever you talk by phone, or face-to-face, with a client or prospect. The third lesson is to always emphasize that you have called the prospect for their benefit—and to help them fill their needs. If you lose sight of a prospect's self-interest, no form of selling will produce results. That's why, in the model script above, Alex Smith stressed the fact that her coffee service would deliver delicious, affordable coffee without cup breakage. Alex saw that those were her prospect's greatest concerns.

Several Telemarketing Techniques

Call under the auspices of service to your clients. After somebody buys something or a service is rendered, call to be sure everything went right.

Use a sales letter or E-mail to invite people to call you. Make them a great offer through the mail. When they call in you're getting a tailor-made opportunity to sell to them.

A call to current clients can be equally successful. When you

WATSON, COME HERE, I NEED YOU

serve their needs, show an interest, and give information, you have a good chance of getting another order. "Mr. Connors, you haven't bought for a long time and we want to be sure you're not unhappy with us or if your needs might have changed. We've come out with a brand new chicken soup. We have a limited supply, but because you've been a good client, I want to call and extend an offer that you may like."

When the Prospect Calls You

After you stimulate enough interest to have a prospect call you, follow these guidelines.

1. Be an interested and knowledgeable person.
2. Communicate to the prospect that you understand their needs and problems.
3. Let them know you have solutions for them.
4. Create a mutually convenient appointment time (in person or by phone)—if now is not so—but remember, they called you, so maximize your position and opportunity.
5. When you talk—produce ideas, information, education, and expert perspectives they can learn from and respect.
6. Advise them. Don't just sell them.
7. Guide them professionally.
8. As with its counterpart, direct mail, you need to ethically lead your prospective client to action, telling them what to do, when to do it, how, when, etc.

How to Respond to a Written Expression of Interest from Your Prospect

When you send out direct mail with response devices, people are going to write or e-mail you to let you know they have an interest in your product. They may also let you know their problems, needs, and objectives. Be prepared when you call them.

Review the response device they have returned and learn their objectives. Be ready to sell them a specific product or service and be ready to answer any question they have about this product. Make sure the product or service fits them best and not just your commission or profit needs. Preparation will insure that you come across as a problem solver or benefit provider and not just a peddler.

When you call them, the phone conversation should go something like this:

"Hello, is Carol Jones in, please?"

"Yes, this is Carol."

"Carol, this is Joe White, with Kingdom Carpeting. I'm calling you because I can help you find, order, and install new carpets. You indicated that you were interested in doing this. Am I calling at a good time?"

"Yes, Joe. Thanks for calling."

"Can you tell me a little bit about what you're looking for, Carol? Then I can be sure I understand your situation."

"I'm an interior designer. I'm interested in buying several different types of carpeting for the homes I'm working on."

"I know I can help you find the carpeting you need. At this juncture it would be helpful if we could explore your objectives and your business situation in more depth. Would you be amenable to that?"

"I'm not sure, Joe. What do you mean?"

"It would be helpful to both of us to arrange a mutually convenient time when we could sit down uninterrupted, without any cost or obligation to you, and explore in greater detail your objectives and needs, and then determine how I can specifically help you to achieve them. How does your schedule look for next week?"

"Tuesday is a possibility, Joe. How much time would you need?"

"Approximately one and a half hours. How about Tuesday morning at 8:30 at my office? It's located at 100 South Main Street, downtown."

"Next Tuesday at 8:30 A.M. at your place of business would be fine."

Let's look at what is going on.

- Carol wrote in with her objectives of what she needs for her business.
- The caller established himself as someone who is genuinely interested in her problems and her objectives.
- His purpose was to get an appointment when they can mutually discuss her carpet needs. To do that she has to feel that it will benefit her. You don't sell her an appointment. You tell her what's in it for her to arrange an appointment and she will agree to meet with you.

Telephone Tips for Following Up on Leads

1. Follow up on leads promptly. Your goal is to call the prospect or client the same day you receive the inquiry. When they write or call you their interest is at its highest level. Then it becomes an increasing case of "out of sight, out of mind."
2. The purpose for your call is to help the prospect get what they need. Make that clear when you call.
3. When prospects or clients define a goal, you must help find a solution—even if that solution has little or nothing to do with you. If you don't provide them with a solution, your competition will.

Telemarketing Examples

There's a software company I work with in Tulsa, Oklahoma. They sell expensive software—$3,000 to $10,000 on hire.

They send out mailings every month to their target audience. They follow them up with telephone calls, just to make sure the people they mail got the letter, understood how the software worked, and where it offered them the best value, and to answer any questions they have.

They hadn't previously done telephone follow-up. Before I met them, they would send a letter. The letter would pull about three times the cost of the mailing and they made a meager profit.

The first year I got them to use telemarketing follow-up, their sales jumped 900 percent. That's a nine times' increase just by following up behind a letter with a phone call. They found that there were dozens and dozens of people they called every month who had received their letter and were interested but never got around to buying or trying it out. They made so much money the first year they closed down the company for two weeks and took every one of their employees to Honolulu for a paid vacation. They were that successful.

I have a client who sells drapes and blinds.

They sell $40 million worth of draperies.

They use telemarketing to follow up all the inquiries they generate. They get hundreds of inquiries every week. Those prospects are sent a booklet that helps people decorate their homes more effectively.

That booklet answers questions and shows them the multitude of different ways they can use blinds and draperies to make their homes more attractive.

After the booklet is received, my client calls them on the phone. They answer their questions, serve them in an advisory role, function as an interior decorator by telephone, and close 45 percent of the people they contact.

Of the approximately $40 million in sales they do each year, $30 million would not happen if they didn't add telephone follow-up after they sent the booklets out.

A car dealer that I worked with used telephone follow-up to contact all his clients who bought new cars but did not buy the extended-warranty plan.

He would call them two weeks later and tell them they were still eligible, retroactively, if they wanted to add extended warranty to their sales package.

He found that 35 percent of the people he called took advantage of the warranty offer.

It added enormous profit to each of those transactions.

A cosmetologist had a very successful specialty practice for affluent clients. She called referrals all over her state and had women flocking in to see her from as far away as three hundred miles. Simply because she called them at the request of her existing clients.

She would talk to them and ask questions about how they viewed their appearance and what kind of cosmetic questions and problems they had. Then she would offer them advice that they could perform themselves, but she offered to work with them, one time free, if they wanted to come to her salon.

Hundreds of people from miles away drove to her salon because she was such an engaging and authoritative consultant over the telephone.

You can use telemarketing to find out why people don't buy from you and to convert them.

I worked with a chain of expensive leather furniture stores around the country. They found that three-quarters of the people who came into their showrooms did not buy initially.

Why?

Because they sold custom furniture. It's expensive furniture. It's large furniture. It's extremely dramatic furniture. You just don't look at it and say, "I'll take it." You look at it. You go back. You think about it. You measure. You look at it again.

They were spending a fortune to bring prospects into their showrooms, and those prospects did not convert. They installed a telephone follow-up system so that their prospects weren't called just one time. Rather, they called them five times over a six-week period. Never trying to sell to them. Always trying to advise them. Always trying to help them. Always trying to answer questions and give them the best professional advice possible.

As a result, they added $350,000 a month—not a year, but a month—to the bottom line of that business. Just by helping their prospects make their ultimate decisions more intelligently.

I have another client who uses telemarketing to offer his higher-level clients, the ones who buy the most often, preferential values on products and services he doesn't normally offer, sell, or stock in his stores.

By calling people and prebooking sales, he can make much greater profits because he never has to stock any items. He only purchases products after a client has preauthorized him to do so over the telephone.

So, he doesn't have to put anything in inventory and worry about it not selling.

Another client, an executive for a major advertising agency, wanted to talk with the CEO of a company about to look for a new agency. My client wanted his agency to be in the running, but he was having trouble getting in touch with the CEO in question. Our solution was to have the agency buy a cellular phone with hundreds of airtime minutes prepaid. (A couple of hundred dollars.) The phone was then delivered by messenger to the CEO. The messenger immediately called the agency to confirm the delivery. My client then dialed the cell-phone number. The CEO answered and the advertising executive got a valuable five-minute conversation with him. At this writing, only three advertising agencies are in the final review for the account, and my client's agency is one of them.

A telephone conversation with a prospect or client is the closest you can get to a one-on-one, in-person meeting. And using the telephone can cost a tiny fraction of actually traveling to that in-person meeting, both in time and money. Never underestimate the massive value of that small plastic gadget on your desk. When used properly, it's one of your greatest business allies.

Action Steps

Today no one approach or strategy can do it all for you. It takes a combined, integrated, systematic approach. Telemarketing is powerful. It's rapidly approaching direct mail as the biggest single direct-response marketing method in use. But with the advent of voice mail and the Internet and so many home-based knowledge workers being almost inaccessible, you have to respect telemarketing for what it is and accept it for what it cannot do.

Not everyone will take your call. Nor will everyone who does talk to you enthusiastically embrace what you're calling about. But properly employed telemarketing is still your most valuable and effective tool for getting more people to respond to your letters and catalogs. And to be receptive to your live visits and presentations.

continues to next page

So make a list. Start with every situation where a tele-marketing call ahead or after a specific selling or communication process would be effective. Try out your theory by calling five or ten or fifty people and see what their response is. Don't get concerned if you've never tried it before. If your interest is honorable, your motives good, and your message and information holds true value for the recipient, it'd be shameful not to call with the information.

Give it a try. You'll be pleasantly surprised by how many people enthusiastically take your call and positively respond to your position.

For those people who aren't in or who don't take your call, don't get frustrated, disappointed, or mad. Know that people are very busy. They are prevailed upon more in a day than they used to be in a week. Their time and attention is precious.

Remember that, as with every other form of persuasion-based communication you use, the focus must always be on *them*, not you. Always find the key benefit, opportunity, or advantage that's in it for them. Make that the prime reason for talking to them. Use that guidepost when stating your reason for calling to anyone who screens calls for the person you're trying to contact. If you can't talk to them for whatever reason, leave a compelling message that holds value, appeal, and desire for them.

Don't be afraid to follow up within a reasonable time. It's not offensive if you have something important to talk about. Just make sure you're respectful and mindful of people's attention span (short), time limits (many), and access (limited).

16

Big Profits.com

THE SINGLE MOST IMPORTANT FACT FOR YOU TO LEARN about selling on the Internet is this: The key to success online has almost nothing to do with the technology. The Internet is simply a powerful, but different, communication and marketing vehicle.

The second fact that you must realize is that the Internet is still in its infancy . . . but it's growing fast. Everything about the Internet is changing so quickly that valid assumptions you make today can become outdated in a heartbeat.

The third important fact is that the strategies and principles in this book will work on the Internet, but they must be applied differently. Although there are many unique aspects to the Internet, the keys to successful marketing, selling, and relationship-building are the same, whether they exist in the physical world or on the Internet.

Who Can Profit on the Internet?

Companies of all sizes are becoming very profitable selling almost every kind of product or service on-line: cars, books, gourmet food, consulting services, flowers, legal advice, sports

287

GETTING EVERYTHING YOU CAN OUT OF ALL YOU'VE GOT

equipment, cosmetics, software, real estate, airline tickets, hotel reservations, etc.

Many successful companies are not just Internet-only businesses. Many businesses have created an additional revenue source through the Internet.

There are only three things you must do to successfully sell your products or services on the Internet:

- Offer *very high-quality products* and/or services that your visitors want.
- Create *a great Web site* that sells effectively.
- Generate high-quality, qualified traffic to your site *cost-effectively*.

That's it. That's all you have to do.

You've heard the stories about the riches to be made on the Internet. The stories are true . . . some of them.

The Internet offers massive profit potential. But it is an area of business that is still finding its legs. Speed-of-light change is the norm on the Internet.

In this chapter you will learn that the solid strategies that succeed in the physical world also will prove successful in the Internet world. But there are important differences between these two worlds. You'll also learn how to avoid some of the most common mistakes made by businesses on-line.

By now I'll assume you only sell high-quality products and/or services that your potential clients want to buy.

There's a basic test to help you determine whether your product or service can work on-line. If it's high-quality and can be sold effectively via mail order or in catalogs, it will probably do very well on the Internet.

Some "experts" say that to be successful on-line you need a product that serves a global marketplace. However, many local businesses are using the Internet very effectively. So, if you're a local business (and want to remain local), the Internet can still be a great tool for growing your business.

I'll devote the rest of this chapter to creating and promoting your web site by applying the strategies and methods I have detailed in this book.

A recent study reported that about 50 percent of all commercial Web sites stated that their site is "profitable from sales at this time." Ten percent of commercial Web sites are "high-volume" producers, meaning their monthly income is $10,000 or more. Top Web sites earn more than $1 million per month. This 50 percent could be raised, just as any business success rate can, by applying the strategies and methods I have detailed in this book.

Internet Success Stories

Let's take a look at a few Internet success stories, including some companies you may never have heard about.

CDNow

Jason Olim wanted to solve a problem. He was frustrated by the skimpy selection of jazz music he found in local music stores, and was inspired after he ran into a sales clerk in a local jazz store who didn't know who Miles Davis was. So he and his brother Matthew started an Internet-based business in their parents' basement that offered about five hundred thousand music-related products (including every jazz album made in the United States) to about 1.6 million customers.

Their company, CDNow, is growing very rapidly. Before they went public in February 1998, they accomplished their growth with no inventory. The Olim twins are now worth over $100 million.

AutoByTel

Another company generated leads for local businesses worth $2.8 billion in sales . . . in its second year of business.

There is no charge to the consumer. Revenue is generated entirely from the fees paid by its network of over 2,700 local businesses in the United States and Canada.

Co-founders Peter Ellis and John Bedrosian own 19 percent and 17 percent respectively of the $350 million company.

Motley Fool

Tom and David Gardner have created a huge success with the Motley Fool, a Web site designed as an on-line forum for individual investors. The site attracts over a million visitors a month. Most of their revenue comes from selling on-line advertising.

WebMD

Jeff Arnold started WebMD, a content and health services company, and he won recognition as the "most effective start-up CEO." A mere seven months later he's a billionaire. At age twenty-nine.

FurnitureFind.com

In 1952, Robert Bookout had $600 and a burning desire to be in business for himself. Forty-seven years later, this company from southwest Michigan has created an on-line division that sells large items on the Web: mattresses, entertainment centers, living room and dining room sets, and sleeper sofas, to name just a few.

They offer name-brand furniture at good prices with free financing and free delivery. Since they don't have to pay commissions, massive warehouse fees, or sales staff wages, they've developed a model that works—and they are very successful.

eToys

eToys racked up $30 million in sales last year, leaving on-line sales at ToysRus.com in the dust. Toby Lenk, eToys' CEO, owns 7 percent of the over $4 billion company. His share is worth over $300 million.

Are these results typical? Of course not. If 50 percent of sites are profitable, that means that 50 percent are not. And most of the profitable sites are well below the billion-dollar mark.

The good news is that these successful businesses can serve as great models for your own Internet marketing. You can apply the same principles to your own business and achieve equal, and possibly even greater, success.

What Are the Others Doing Wrong?

How do you avoid becoming one of the 50 percent of on-line businesses that fail?

The biggest problems for on-line businesses come from some old (Net-wise), sometimes contradictory, and widely held misconceptions. It's very important to understand and avoid these common Internet myths if you hope to succeed on the Internet.

Most of the myths come from a poor understanding of the culture and nature of the Internet itself.

Myth: No One Is Making Any Money on the Internet.

Reality: By now you know this isn't true, but perhaps you wonder if *you* can make money on the Net. The answer is likely a resounding *yes*. If you apply the lessons you're learning in this book.

It won't happen overnight, but it can happen.

Myth: You'll "Get Rich Quick" on the Internet.

Reality: Forget it. You wouldn't believe this one off-line—Why should you believe it on the Internet?

The real danger of this myth is that you'll get discouraged when you don't see instant results, and give up too soon. Once success starts on-line, it can build very rapidly. Just give it time to get started. Keep at it.

Myth: You Can Get Millions of New Clients by Putting Up Your Web Site on the Information Superhighway!

Reality: You need to do much more than simply put up a Web site. People don't "drive by" your site and see it. You have to bring it to their attention in a way that makes them want to visit. Then you have to use proven strategies and techniques to actually make the sale.

Properly applying the marketing ideas in this book can make that a reality.

(Even if you *could* get millions of new clients overnight, are you really able to provide proper service to that many people right away?)

Myth: Internet Malls Offer the Same Benefits As Real Malls.

Reality: Same problem as above. Merchants in real-world malls benefit from the traffic of passersby. On the Internet, there are no passersby. There is no one to notice your pretty window display unless they actually visit your site.

Each "store" in an Internet mall has to do its own promoting. So what's the benefit of being in an on-line mall?

If you're determined to join an on-line mall, directly E-mail a few of the owners of sites in it before you pay for your "space." See what they have to say. You'll probably decide to put that money into promoting your own site. Use the ideas in this book, and you'll get much more traffic for your money.

Myth: You Don't Need to Own or Use a Computer to Make Your Fortune on the Internet.

Reality: This myth is often promoted by people who run Internet malls or design Web sites. Forget it. People who shop on-line also want service on-line. If you can't answer their E-mails directly, you'd better be prepared to pay someone else to do it.

A less obvious problem with this idea is that it keeps some people from finding out some of the biggest benefits of using the Internet and the savings available. You can easily save $5,000 to $50,000 a year (or more) in reduced FedEx, fax, telephone, postage, and printing costs . . . just by using E-mail.

Using the Web also allows you to provide information for your clients when they want it—even if your "brick and mortar" store is closed for the weekend.

In spite of all of the myths and hype, the Internet does offer tremendous opportunities, benefits, and advantages to anyone who has an excellent product, service, company, or business idea—as long as he's willing to invest some time to learn the Internet culture and the most effective strategies for Internet success.

Many businesses haven't taken full advantage of the tremendous opportunities the Internet offers because they're intimidated by the technology. Others haven't succeeded because they became overly seduced by the technology.

Remember, it's not the technology that counts. It's the strategy.

Here are a few of the elements of a successful Internet strategy.

Your Internet Business and Marketing Plan

Put simply, to be successful on the Internet, you need a plan.

In the case of an Internet plan, less is more. The Internet is changing so fast that your business and marketing plan must be brief and flexible to allow you to adapt quickly to new information and changing rules.

You need a plan that's easy to modify and adapt—or it won't work.

You need a plan that can be used on a day-to-day basis by company leaders as working tools to achieve maximum success.

You need a plan that provides clear answers to key business, strategy, marketing, management, and innovation questions. This approach allows you to take advantage of the "80–20 Rule": You gain at least 80 percent of the benefits of business planning with about 20 percent of the total effort.

Many successful businesses were established with short business plans. Intel's first business plan was on one page. And Sun Microsystems' was just three pages.

I've seen many business plans that were extremely precise, with huge spreadsheets based on impressive demographic data. But they were missing critically important key assumptions. Don't waste time, effort, and expense to develop a complex

Internet plan that just sits on your bookshelf, or a plan that's not flexible.

The numbers change fast, and your assumptions can become outdated just as quickly.

What should your plan include? You must:

- offer very high quality products and/or services that your visitors want.
- create a great Web site that sells effectively.
- generate high-quality, qualified traffic to your site cost-effectively.

Let's look at some of the key ingredients that will make your plan work. First, let's focus on creating a great Web site that sells effectively, and then we'll talk about how to generate high-quality, qualified traffic to your site cost-effectively.

Be Passionate about Your Business and Your Clients

This is important off-line. On the Internet, it's a matter of survival.

Why? One of the keys to Internet success is understanding the Internet culture. Part of that culture is having a Web site that's fun to visit and great to shop at. Almost every successful business on the Internet has done this.

The fact is that it's almost impossible to create this kind of experience if you're not passionate about what you're doing. You can't fake it—people can tell a mile away.

Headlines

Ninety-five percent of all Web sites use the company or product name or logo as the headline, or they say: "Welcome to the home page of XYZ."

Wrong. Product and company names are not headlines. They don't provide any benefits to your visitors. This is a big mistake.

When someone visits your Web site, you only have a few seconds to get them engaged, so they'll stay and explore. It's important to use a compelling headline to make the most of those few seconds.

A powerful headline can dramatically improve the results of a Web site. A headline is responsible for 90 percent of the success of a space ad or direct-mail letter. Although I don't know of any comprehensive research on headlines on the Web, I have personally seen that an effective headline, rather than a company name, can increase sales by over 500 percent. My best guess is that the impact could be as high as 21 times (2100 percent), which is what I've found in every other mode of marketing I've tested.

That's incredible leverage, especially since there's virtually no cost to making and testing these changes.

In fact, the absence of decent headlines on the Web is shocking to me, since successful marketers have known for more than half a century how important it is to use powerful headlines. I've seen many experienced, smart marketers in other media go brain-dead when it comes to marketing on the Web. They don't seem to translate their physical world success strategies to the Internet. They seem to forget every marketing principle that has made their own business successful. I don't want this to happen to you. Reread the chapters in this book with a view towards applying these money multipliers to your Internet activities.

An Internet Web site is the perfect vehicle to test your offers, prices, headlines, and more. The Internet, like every other aspect of your business or career, is a place where you can realize maximum results—*if you test.*

If you currently have a Web site with your business or product name as your headline (or your headline is "Welcome to the home page of XYZ"), try this:

Take what you currently have as your headline and turn it into a subhead. Put it below the replacement headline. Then, develop a compelling, powerful headline that targets your market and provides a statement of a specific benefit to your visitors just for visiting. Think about why they should stay and explore your Web site and tell them "what's in it for them."

Do this for just a week or two. You'll soon create better headlines that produce better results.

The World's Cheapest Printing Press

Think of the Internet as the world's cheapest printing press.

It allows your company to deliver your message to the world, twenty-four hours a day, but without the bill. And to as many people in the world as you want—hundreds, thousands, tens of thousands, hundreds of thousands, possibly even millions.

And there are almost no limits to what you can "publish." For example, in addition to documents with text and graphics, you can also publish audio (such as radio interviews or music), photographs, software, video, other computer files, etc.

Further, you can make changes as frequently as you want or

need. That lets these messages become dynamic, continuously more innovative, growing, almost living, documents. And these changes will cost you almost nothing to make.

Imagine making changes to your ten-thousand-page catalog every day, virtually for free. On the Web, you can.

Or, if you have technical documents and the specs change, it's effortless to make the adjustments and tell your clients around the world about them in just seconds—free.

Use the Internet to publish and give away useful samples or bonus items. Many successful Web sites employ this strategy.

You can give away free samples as an incentive to add to your client list and capture the name, address, city, state, zip code, country, phone number and/or E-mail address of new prospects.

One client gets at least one hundred people to fill out a simple form that asks for one of their special reports each day. They get one hundred new highly qualified sales leads a day—and it costs them almost nothing.

Eighty percent of the companies on the Web don't do this. And this is one of the biggest ways to turn the Internet from entertainment to a selling mechanism.

Create a Virtual Community

Let's take this concept of the world's cheapest printing press to another dimension, and really use the power of the Internet. In addition to simply providing information to your visitors, the Internet allows you to interact with them. It allows your visitors to help share the experience. In other words, you can use the Internet to create a virtual community.

This is exactly what most successful Web sites do.

eBay is a very successful on-line auction company. eBay's auctions have become almost a ritual, partly bargain-hunting and partly entertainment. In other words, eBay has created a virtual community. And this strategy has worked well for the company.

They list over 250,000 new items for sale every day, and have nearly 4 million registered users.

Creating a virtual community doesn't have to be difficult. Simply make your Web site interactive.

Here are a few suggestions:

- Let your visitors contribute to your Web site. For example, they can contribute articles, reviews, stories, paintings, or ideas. Leave it to their imaginations, and your visitors can surprise you.
- Create an editorial page, and invite visitors to contribute their viewpoints.
- Create a bulletin board where visitors can ask questions. You can answer some of the questions, but let others answer questions, too. Scripts for this sort of forum are common, and usually either free or very inexpensive.
- Ask you visitors for suggestions about how your web site should grow—and implement the best ideas.
- Create a regular poll or survey. Post the most interesting comments about the topic.
- Sponsor interesting contests.
- Allow visitors to share their success stories about how your products or service benefits them.
- Solicit experts in your field to come to your Web site and provide an article, set of tips, interview, etc.

It would be easy to fill several books the size of this one with tips about how to create a great Web site that sells. These principles will provide an excellent foundation for your site.

Use Laser-Focused, Target Marketing on the Internet

You can find people in just about any target market on the Internet. And in most cases, they've already identified themselves for you based on their demographic information or other interests, so you can target them very precisely and at almost no cost.

In fact, there are over one hundred thousand special-interest discussion groups you can join for free to find people who are your best prospective clients.

There are tens of thousands of additional specialized electronic newsletters (e-zines) that target people of almost every imaginable interest. These e-zines provide great sources for submitting articles, information, and ads to get your message to people in your target market.

But always follow the "netiquette" for each group about direct advertising: Don't blatantly advertise where advertising is not welcome. "Lurk" (which means reading the material from the group before you contribute) and read the "FAQ" (frequently asked questions) to find out what the rules are.

Here's a very powerful strategy: Publish your own e-zine. The market has become flooded with e-zines in some areas (marketing, for one), but quality content always rises to the top.

Many of the more specialized topics are still largely untouched. You can become the Expert in your field! Develop a niche e-zine (such as NUA—www.nua.com—did by becoming the leader in Internet demographic and market research); you can become the leader even in a crowded field.

Target Your Market Precisely

Let's consider another Web technique that takes advantage of being able to precisely target your audience. Say you market your products or services to three different and very specific niche markets. You can create three special Web sites—one for each of your markets. Each site can target its market precisely and provide specialized content, all at very little additional cost. And, you can easily promote your sites to only those people in specific target markets.

The result? You'll enjoy exponentially greater success than if you target all three markets with one generic Web site and marketing campaign.

Use Search Engines Properly

Another way to generate traffic to your Web site is to use search engines.

There are millions of Web sites. Because of this, perhaps the most important tools for helping people find what they are looking for are the directories and search engines. Most of these directories and search engines provide free listings to Web site owners.

Say you want to know how to get more publicity for your business. You go to one of the top search engines and you type in the key word *publicity*.

You'll get back a message that says the search engine found 574,930 pages containing the world *publicity*. These search engines list Web sites in groups of ten, and the first ten come up when you complete the search.

Viewing all 574,930 pages isn't an option. You'll look at the top few sites to find what you want. And that's what your prospects and clients will do as well.

How do you get your Web pages ranked at the top of the search engine lists?

I suggest you do not use an automated service to list your site with the search engines. Many companies offer to submit your Web site to anywhere from one hundred to twenty-five hundred search engines for a fee. But since each search engine is different (and uses different criteria to select which sites to list at the top), you could wind up listed near the bottom of every list. That's not where you want to be.

Also, don't try to "trick" the search engines. Many so-called experts promise secrets that supposedly will get you top listings. Their secrets usually involve techniques that are actually quite dangerous. Every major search engine currently has a penalty for trying to trick it. Some search engines will simply ignore your page and not list you at all. Others may ban your Web site forever. It's not worth the risk.

Devote your time to gaining great placement with the top eight search engines. Ninety percent of all searches are done through these eight. The hundreds of other search engines aren't used enough to be worth the effort.

What are the top eight search engines?

Today they are:

- Lycos   (http://www.lycos.com)
- AltaVista   (http://www.altavista.com)
- HotBot   (http://www.hotbot.com)
- Northern Light   (http://www.northernlight.com)
- Excite   (http://www.excite.com)
- InfoSeek   (http://www.infoseek.com)
- WebCrawler   (http://www.webcrawler.com)
- Yahoo!   (http://www.yahoo.com)

Spend your marketing time learning everything you need to know to do well with these search engines. It is very time consuming, but the payoff can be tremendous.

Here are a few more tips to help you succeed with the search engines:

- Focus on how your prospective clients will search for a company that offers the products or services you offer. Come up with the important keywords and phrases people would use to find your products or services. Look at the keywords your competitors use on their Web sites for ideas.
- Always use the plural of words (such as "cars" rather than "car"). Otherwise if someone searches for "cars," and you've used "car," they won't find your site.
- Include your most important keywords in your page title and in the first few paragraphs of your Web pages. Write great page titles for each separate major page of your Web site. Almost all of the search engines pay a lot of attention to page titles, so the words you use in it are very important.

  Failure to put your most important keywords in your page titles is probably the main reason people get poor results from the search engines.
- Keep it simple. Avoid using large graphics at the top of your Web pages. The search engines can't read them, so you'll reduce your position with them.
- Using the strategy of looking to other businesses and industries to find innovations for your business is equally effective when dealing with the Internet. Do a search on each of your major keywords. Observe and visit each of the top ten sites. What text is used in the title? Do you see your keyword on the page? Do you see other good keywords that might apply to your product or service? Make notes, and then make changes.

There are a number of excellent resources for winning the search engine game. For more information, visit:

NETrageous
(http://www.netrageousresults.com/searchengines/)
Search Engine Watch
(http://www.searchenginewatch.com/).

Go Global, without Leaving Home

The Internet offers the first easy and truly cost-effective way for small and medium-sized businesses to promote their products and services successfully to global markets. In fact, there is no additional cost whatsoever to reach international (English-speaking) prospects. You can automatically "publish to the world" through your Web site.

One true Internet opportunity that almost everyone leaves untapped is translating your Web site into other languages. People in other countries are hungry for good information, products, and services that are presented in their own languages.

One of the larger retailers on the Web, Cyberian Outpost, increased their sales dramatically by translating their Web site into twelve different languages. With sales now over $11 million per month, a huge part of their sales come from international clients.

If you do choose to translate your Web site into other languages, you'll be pleasantly surprised at how modest the fee is to do this (and sometimes you can even get it done for free).

How do you decide what language to translate your Web site into first? You can easily check the listing of visitors to your Web site and determine what countries they come from. Although your Web site is still only in English, you might have visitors (and subscribers) from all over the world. Translate your Web site into the language of the countries where you have the highest number of visitors. Later you can expand that list.

A Little Time, a Lot of Profit

Investing a little time to learn how to best use (then maximize the business-building benefits of) E-mail and the Web can provide handsome benefits for your business for years to come. No matter how small or large your business is, you'll easily save thousands of dollars and find yourself generating more new clients than you ever thought possible.

And with E-mail and the Web, you'll be able to provide your clients with more immediate answers to their questions, thereby increasing their satisfaction. Your Web site will give your clients twenty-four-hour-a-day access to your company, 365 days a year.

In spite of all the myths and hype, the Internet does offer tremendous opportunities and advantages to anyone who has a quality product, service, company, or business idea—as long as he's willing to invest some enjoyable time to learn today's changing Internet culture and the most effective strategies for sustaining Internet success.

Action Steps

I suggest just two action steps.

First, research the Internet world deepy before you invest your money, time, or reputation on a Web site. Learn the culture. Get comfortable with it and in it.

Second, review all the strategies I've presented in this book and focus on how each one will produce greater results when applied to doing business on the Internet.

Then get ready for the ride of your life.

17

Manhattan for $29 Worth of Beads

BARTER REPRESENTS PROBABLY THE MOST ENJOYABLE, STIMU-lating, lucrative, and rewarding business opportunity available.

Barter is not giving a country doctor a few chickens for setting your broken arm. I'm talking about simple to very sophisticated forms of leverage barter. You don't have to use cash to get what you want or need. You can turn your product or service into increased buying power and create the most lucrative profit center of all.

You can barter on a small scale. . . .

Charles Dickens didn't sell the first story he wrote for money. He bartered it for a bag of marbles. Toulouse-Lautrec would trade his paintings for food and rent.

Or you can barter from small to large. . . .

The owner of a small radio station in Florida was having difficulty making payroll. So he traded advertising to a local hardware store for fourteen hundred electric can openers, which he easily "cash converted" (sold) over the air to generate enough income to save the station.

Sensing he was onto a good thing, he began trading for goods and services, then auctioning them over the radio to the listening audience. Within sixty days the small station was in the black. The seller-on-the-air concept was further tested on the local cable-television channel. When this also proved successful, investors backed the concept into a satellite uplink and went national. The company's sales now exceed more than $1 billion a year. And it all started with fourteen hundred can openers. By the way, the company is now called the Home Shopping Network.

Trading your products or services for things your business needs or wants is called business barter. Barter gives you the amazing ability to vastly increase your purchasing power—sometimes by as much as five to ten times over. Done right, barter also gives you the effect of having almost unlimited capital. It's like having a blank check to fill in. It allows you to acquire products and services now, but pay for them much later. And the longer you take to pay, the less it ends up costing you. You can make barter a major factor in your business-growth strategy.

In this chapter you will learn how to use the concept of barter to greatly leverage your buying power and create an important new profit center.

Barter allows you to do things that you couldn't do otherwise—things you couldn't normally accomplish if you're short on cash or if you don't have unlimited buying power.

When you barter, you create purchasing power almost at will. You can, quite literally, write your own credit line (or barter scrip) to unlimited amounts. You can buy goods and services at far better discounts and on far more advantageous terms than you ever could with cash.

What businesses or services make good barter candidates? Understand this: Whatever business or profession you're in, you have the capacity to generate finished goods or services that cost you less than their market value. If you're a plastic surgeon and you do face-lifts, a face-lift may have a market value of $4,000 but may actually cost you $400 in real, hard, incremental costs. If you are a manufacturer of sofas, a sofa may sell for $5,000, but cost only $500. If you have margin, you have built-in profit.

Or let's say you go to a radio or TV station and you want to trade. But they don't want your product or service. Well that doesn't mean that you can't trade. What it means is that you might have to do what is usually called triangulation.

That means you go to a third party who has some goods or services that the radio station or television station wants to trade for. And you trade with them for your product or service.

And there's no law that says you have to trade equally. Depending upon the perceived value and the margins you operate with, you might trade higher or lower.

For example: Car dealers trade automobiles that have lower margins but higher desirability. They may trade a $20,000 automobile, and they may go to a radio station or a television station and get two or three times that face value in advertising. Why? Because the station, if it wanted a car, would have to lay out $18,000 for the $20,000 car. It's easy to trade hard goods (televisions, furniture, and other things that people want very badly) in exchange for higher multiples of soft goods (advertising, services, and so on).

I've seen people trade for the maintenance of their homes, their offices, painting, signage, advertising, automobiles, trips, training—you name it. (The only precaution is to do it appropriately from a tax standpoint—and that's something you should discuss with your accountant. Barter deals do have tax implications, but they aren't an impediment in most cases.)

Don't rule out barter simply because you're in a profession and not a hard industrial product business. A lawyer, advertising executive, or CPA might, for example, trade legal services, advertising or marketing plans, or tax preparation for office equipment, medical services, or virtually anything he or she needs or wants.

Virtually anyone can get into bartering, and the rewards can be significant.

The Appeal of Barter

By engaging in barter activities to acquire goods and services, you can:
1. Enjoy up to 80 percent cash savings on all your purchases.
2. Acquire needed items with money you've already spent.
3. Finance major purchases interest-free for years, and get the purchaser to carry the paper at a discount.

Your Barter Leverage Position

Suppose you own a company that manufactures or sells a product. As long as there is an established market for your product, you've got the basis for building a profitable barter opportunity.

Perhaps you run a mill that makes carpet, or a plant that manufactures furniture and accessories. The items you create in your factories cost you a fraction of the retail price.

So make up a list of all the goods or services you need or want for both your business and your home. You may need new office equipment: computers, dictation equipment, or new heating units. Once you've determined exactly what you need you're ready to begin bartering—and profiting.

One-to-One Barter

Start by going to the most direct and logical prospects first, and then propose a direct exchange of your goods or services for theirs.

Let's say you're trying to get office furniture and your business is air-conditioning sales and service. Go through the phone book, call every retailer of the furniture you seek, and introduce yourself and your business. Tell the owner of the furniture store that you need nearly $8,000 (or any amount) worth of furniture to decorate your home. Tell him you'd like to trade an equal dollar amount of air-conditioning equipment and service for the amount of furniture you need.

Be sure to stress that you seek to trade for retail value and not necessarily the discounted price that the furniture dealer may be selling the furniture for. Dealing on a retail or suggested retail basis is an excellent way to effect most trades. Why? The reason is very simple—markup. Most retailers have a minimum markup of 100 percent, and oftentimes up to 300 percent, at full suggested retail value.

Unfortunately for them, our ultracompetitive society usually prohibits ever achieving such lavish profit margins, and the furniture-store owner must content himself by earning a still-respectable 35, 40, or 50 percent markup. But when you come to him offering to trade $8,000 worth of air-conditioning equipment for an equal dollar value of retail furniture, at full list price, the dealer immediately sees the opportunity of making that 300 percent markup on the transaction.

Whether he needs the air-conditioning items or services right now really doesn't matter, as long as he is persuaded that he will be able to use these items or services in the near future.

No Expiration Date

Herein lies a very important secret to exchange transactions. Whenever you require something right now, and the person or company you are trying to trade with doesn't need or want to avail themselves of your firm's goods or services right away, don't let the deal slip away. Offer the prospective trader this option: Tell him he can have unlimited time to take your goods or services and that he may assign the credit you are offering him to anyone else he may designate.

Now you have created rational and persuasive reasons for him to exchange with you. If he knows he uses approximately $2,000 worth of air-conditioning services a year, if he understands he can "buy" these services for you at thirty-five cents on the dollar, and if he realizes he can pay for this air-conditioning with dollars he's already tied up in slow-moving furniture, he comes out smelling like a rose.

An astute businessperson would jump at that chance. Any person who would normally take the 2 percent early-payment discount on an invoice should jump at the chance to pick up a 66 percent discount just for entering into a trade with you. Point these things out if he still resists the idea of barter.

If he is receptive to the prospect of trading, and concedes he will need the services you are offering in the near future, but claims his money is all tied up in the inventory he needs to sell, suggest two things: Perhaps he knows someone who needs $8,000 worth of air-conditioning services that he can sell for $4,000 or more. He could get almost 100 percent profit and needed cash.

The creative possibilities of such an approach are virtually limitless. Here are some ground rules you should always follow:

1. Insist on assignability for any item or service you ever receive a credit for.
2. Never try to trade your goods or services at anything less than retail value. Remember, the higher the valuation you place on the goods or services you trade, the greater the buying advantage.

The Fine Art of Triangulation

Perhaps the single most valuable technique for the creative barterer to master is the fine art of triangulation. By becoming proficient at triangulation, the astute practitioner can make up to 50 percent more barter deals and achieve net profits that may exceed 200 percent of the traditional yields that basic trade deals produce. Triangulation is the use of three separate transactions (or more) to achieve your ultimate barter objective. And while it may seem complex in theory, it is really very simple in practice. Like many other barter practices, triangulation is simple. Triangulation becomes invaluable—and essential—whenever you cannot achieve your primary barter objective through the conventional two-party trade situation. In other words, whenever you cannot convince a barter prospect to accept your goods or services directly for his goods or services, triangulation becomes the device to save the deal.

Suppose you own a restaurant that sells food and beverages that have an average gross markup of 500 percent over your out-of-pocket costs. And you'd like to trade food-and-beverage credits for a new car. Simple enough, until you approach the local car dealer, who has absolutely no need whatsoever for $10,000 worth of your food-and-beverage credits. He may laugh you out of his showroom. Then what do you do? You probably will approach more car dealers who will probably also turn you down.

Stop for a moment and analyze the car dealer's profit-or-loss perspective. What goods or services can make or save the dealer more money? How about . . . advertising. Most dealers spend between $5,000 and $10,000 a month just on radio, TV, and newspaper. How can you use advertising to help you trade credits at your restaurant for a new car? Why, through triangulation, of course.

Approach all of the prominent radio and television stations in your market, plus the local newspapers. Offer to provide them with restaurant credits they can use to wine and dine their better clients in exchange for advertising credits, which you have the right to assign. And because we know most car dealers don't begin to have the same margin spreads as restaurants, in order to make the "triangulated trade" work, you must acquire at least twice as much advertising credit to offer the dealer.

So you trade $20,000 worth of restaurant credits to be used as the station sees fit—with no expiration date—with the provision that you can assign your newly acquired credits at any time. As long as your restaurant has a solid reputation, chances are very good that the station will go for that trade. Then, with $20,000 worth of advertising in hand, you go back to the car dealer. But now you have a different barter proposition: In essence, you offer to trade him advertising time in exchange for the car, but at the rate of $1.75 to $1.00 in his favor.

You are giving the dealer $17,500 worth of advertising for a car with a retail sticker price of $10,000. (Why not the full $20,000? I'll get to that in a moment.) You're offering the car dealer something he can definitely use—at a better discount than he can get. Chances are, he'll accept your deal. Why shouldn't he? You're giving him $17,500 worth of advertising credit—something he would have to normally pay real cash for—in return for a $10,000 automobile that probably cost him no more than $7,500 max. The car dealer, who normally makes less than 10 percent on an all-cash new-car sale, increases his profit by 233 percent.

You traded $20,000 worth of restaurant credits (which, at most, cost you one-fifth that amount or $4,000) for a car, right? You bought your car for 40 percent of retail—an unprecedented savings of 60 percent off the sticker price.

That's only the beginning; chances are good you won't have to pay off on the restaurant food and beverage credits for a long time. In essence, the radio station, television station, or newspaper winds up financing your $4,000 purchase price for months or years—at no interest to you. If it's beginning to sound unbelievable, wait. It doesn't stop there. Since your prices are bound to rise over the next few years, by the time the stations or publishers start to use all of their credits, the purchasing power has been discounted. The longer the station or publisher waits to use up their credits, the less it will cost you. By putting a three-year expiration date (or no expiration date at all) on the restaurant credits you provide, you may have actually discounted your already drastically discounted purchase price of the automobile by another 10 or 15 or 25 percent—or another $1,000. Now that brand-new $10,000 automobile has cost you as little as $3,000 in hard dollars—and it's being financed, interest-free, for three years.

Other Free Stuff

Remember that you originally traded for $20,000 in advertising, but you only used $17,500. What happens to the remaining $2,500? You could go to other merchants and sell them the advertising credit at sixty-five cents on the dollar (a 35 percent savings over what they could buy it for direct), and get $1,625 in cash. That would be enough to pay all the licensing and taxes on that new car, the first year's insurance premium, and a full tank of gas. Or you can use the advertising yourself.

I use restaurants, advertising, and cars only as an illustration. In truth, almost any conceivable combination of goods-for-services, services-for-goods, or any other variable can be used in triangulation to achieve your objective. Always identify the real personal profit hot button of the person who controls the goods or services you want, and then satisfy those needs that push the right hot button.

Don't Stop Thinking

Controlling the goods can many times be just as satisfying as owning the goods. If the car dealer won't trade outright for the actual ownership of the new car, how about the use of the car for two years. Or a new demonstrator every two or three months for two years? Or . . . well, I think you're beginning to get the idea.

And one final thought: What if you have neither the restaurant credits nor a new car to offer to trade? You could become the broker for such a series of triangulated transactions—receiving a 10 or 20 percent commission from each of the parties for your efforts.

Become a Middleman

Let's explore an even more fascinating opportunity that's seemingly hidden to most people. But which almost any of you can readily capitalize on for incredible profit. You've heard of infinite leveraging. Well, here's how to do it with barter. The trick is to use other people's money. In essence, you learn to control other people's goods or services without ever having to own or invest in anything. First, approach a number of people in varied businesses or professions and ask them if they'd be willing to trade their goods or services for other goods or services they want or need.

Tell them you'll put the deal together for them for either a commission of 30 percent of face value, payable in credits, or for a 15 percent cash commission. Nine out of ten will opt for 30 percent in credits. Next, get a written assignment of a specific credit amount that they will trade for an equal value of acceptable merchandise, stipulating the aforementioned commission arrangement. Once you've contacted a couple of dozen businesses, you're ready to trade.

Now approach various businessmen and tell them that you control a specified dollar amount of such and such an item, which you'd like to trade for an equal dollar volume of their items. Tell them that if they're interested in making such a trade, you'll do it for a commission equal to 30 percent of the face value in credits, or 15 percent in cash. Without going through all the rest of the steps, it's pretty easy to see that you can end up making 60 percent of the entire transaction without investing a cent. Nor would you have any contingent liability to provide any goods or services. You'd merely pick up your goods and services and walk away to the next deal. Always remember to pick up your credits immediately, and always stipulate that said credits are totally assignable to whomever you may designate. There are many more creative variations.

You can trade one item for another at an unequal retail dollar equivalent, if one item is more appealing than another. You persuade the owner of the less desirable product to exchange with your client on a 1 to $1^{1}/_{2}$ or 2 to 1 retail-to-retail multiple. You could end up with credits above one-to-one—plus the commission. At the very worst, you'd double your commission from one side. Picking up $900 in commissions on what started out essentially to be a $1,000 face transaction, without putting up the first investment or equity dollar, is pretty astonishing. But nevertheless, it's attainable day in and day out.

There are many ways you or your company can profit substantially using barter. You can do it for and through any business you own or control. You can do it outside any business as a middleman or deal maker. You can do it for any business for huge fees or for massive shares of the barter spoils.

Here are some of the different ways people have used barter to profit:

Saving Cash on Capital Expenditures

Say you're buying a computer. After you've negotiated the lowest price possible, you agree to the price if the seller will take a portion of that negotiated price in your product or services. Ideally, 25 to 50 percent. What will that accomplish? It just lowered the true cost of that computer to you by up to one-third, and gave you dating on the barter portion of the purchase, allowing you to pay it later, interest-free. If you become really good at trading, you can probably get a higher-percent trade—up to 100 percent. You could even trade a lesser dollar value of your more desirable goods or services for a larger dollar value of computer—and your cash savings could be 70 percent or more.

Barter Increases Your Total Sales

Since many businesses focus a lot of attention on "total gross," barter accentuates the gross while continuing to minimize the overhead—which means that the cost of producing barter instead of 100 percent dollars enables you to increase your gross sales at a fraction of what doing it with cash would be. Consequently, your bartered sales could be many times more profitable than your cash sales—or the highest-profit sales you make.

Barter Lets You Pay Operating Expenditures— Even Payroll—with Soft Dollars

This means that you could be low on (or even out of) cash and still continue to operate—and prosper and employ critically needed people using barter as your means of commerce.

You Can Print Your Own Currency, or Scrip, Which Is Usable Only at Your Place of Business

The advantages and benefits of having your own legal tender are limited only by your imagination. Here's just one example to think about: Say there is something your company really needs or wants to acquire, but you can't afford it on a cash-paying basis. Using your own currency—where the cost is based on the cost of supplying the goods and services and where you take delivery now but pay for it much, much later—you can afford to acquire that needed item.

Automatically Get Terms, Credits, and Discounts Far Better and Easier Than You Ever Could Paying Cash

You issue $5,000 credit to a printer. He gives you $5,000 worth of printing and delivers it to you immediately. You pay with your barter scrip or credits, giving the printer one to two years to use his credit with you. Until the printer actually uses those credits, you haven't paid out a thing. And since he probably will only use a portion of his credit with you at a time, its cost will be easily handled a little bit each month.

Breakage

When you trade with someone, breakage represents the barter certificates you issue that are never used. A certain percentage of all barter credits issued, if they have an expiration date (which I recommend), will not be used. A major New Orleans hotel traded $125,000 worth of radio and TV time and issued barter scrip in that amount with a one-year expiration date. Right up front the hotel got $125,000 in advertising at regular cash rates. This was advertising they had to normally pay $125,000 in real cash for.

At the end of twelve months, an audit done by the controller revealed that only $35,000 worth of the barter scrip had been redeemed within the time-limit period. The rest expired unused. The cash cost of the hotel delivering the $35,000 worth of rooms was only $5,000. The hotel had leveraged up $125,000 in advertising for 5,000 hard dollars. However, that doesn't take into consideration two overlooked (but extremely significant) factors.

Statistically, $35,000 in room trade produces $17,500 in "cash" food, beverage, and miscellaneous sales with a gross profit in excess of $8,000 for the hotel. The hotel actually was paid $3,000 net after all costs to enter into the trade ($8,000 profit less $5,000 cost to fulfill on the $35,000 worth of rooms).

All $35,000 worth of rooms were not used at one time. It was spread out over twelve months, meaning that the hotel got to pay the $5,000 over twelve months totally interest-free. In essence, they got $125,000 worth of advertising up front and got paid $3,000 plus deferred interest to do so.

Cash Conversion

Many barter items, merchandise, or services you acquire (in addition to paying bills with) can be sold or converted to cash at a fee well above the cost of acquiring them. Several years ago Chrysler Corporation traded 192 cars for airtime on a Spanish television network.

The seven-station chain sold most of the cars to their employees at a 30 percent discount under what the cars normally stickered for. The employees were overjoyed because the most the dealer would discount them was 15 percent. So they saved double. The average value of each car was $10,000, and the television network received from the sale more than $1,920,000 in real cash for unsold airtime that cost them zero (time that probably would have gone unused and, thus, produced zero revenue unless it was traded).

Forty-five of the cars were traded to a television transmitter manufacturer by the radio station in exchange for a half million dollars' worth of transmitter equipment that permitted the station to open up a new full-power UHF station in San Francisco—without using any cash. The ability to trade for this equipment enabled the San Francisco station to get on the air more than one full year earlier than originally thought. And it enabled the station to operate without draining all their cash during the start-up.

They became a runaway success before any other Spanish station ever penetrated the San Francisco market. The stations subsequently were sold for $400 million.

Create a Barter Profit Center

Some salespeople who are not effective in cash selling are extremely successful in bartering. So you might have a sleeper employee whose sales will skyrocket and will give you huge bonus margins on the products or services you sell if you trade for products and services at full rate and then turn right around and sell the merchandise you acquire to the open market at a slight discount under the going price.

For example, a prominent travel magazine traded airline credit for full pages of advertising in their magazine—pages they wouldn't normally have sold. A page sells for $15,000, so they receive $15,000 worth of first-class tickets every time they run an ad. The actual hard cost of the page of advertising to the magazine is a mere $750, or one-twentieth the rate they are charging.

The magazine has a barter liquidation department that takes the airline credits and immediately resells the tickets for eighty cents on the dollar (twenty cents less than anyone could buy the tickets for directly from the airline itself). As a barter profit center, the magazine takes ad pages that cost them $750 and turns them into $12,000 of revenue.

Does this give you any imaginative ideas of ways you could profit from operating a barter profit center of your own inside or outside your business? You can net profits of double or quadruple your costs in a few weeks. Annualized, the income a barter profit center can produce dwarfs any other division your company may operate.

Vastly Expand Your Available Advertising Budget without Using Cash

An international air courier company in competition with Federal Express hired a barter firm to pay for its upcoming television schedule. The barter company put up the cash and ran the television spots. It took credits with the air courier service as payment, which it cash converted over the next two and a half years. Only new accounts were allowed to use these credits—no existing accounts could purchase or use the credits, so no existing cash revenues were ever displaced.

The barter company made a profit in the cash conversion. The courier had two and a half years to pay for the television— without any interest charge. And many of the cash conversion barter sales (some who were Fortune 400 companies) have continued to use the air courier on a full-cash-paying basis long after their barter credits were used up.

In other words, people who were originally not clients of the air courier service developed such a habit of doing business with them through barter usage that they stayed on and paid full cash after the barter credits were used up. We estimate that the cash business which continues today exceeds $3 million a year for the courier service. So far, in the eight years since the original trade was done, nearly $24 million worth of resulting "cash continuation" business has occurred as a lucrative by-product of the initial one-time barter transaction.

Finance Rapid Growth without Cash

Carnival Cruise Lines, a Florida-based company that is now the largest cruise line in the world, started with one ship and insufficient operating capital. The line traded empty cabins for radio, television, and newspaper advertising in one hundred cities over a ten-year period. The cost of an empty cabin once the ship sails is essentially zero. Plus, the passengers may spend considerable cash in the bar, casino, and gift shop; thus the net cost to the cruise line to fill an empty cabin was literally less than zero. Stated differently, they made a massive profit off the bartered cabin being occupied instead of going out empty.

Here's the payoff to the cruise line. They used this technique to become the largest cruise line in the world, and they continuously advertised in one hundred cities for more than ten years without spending a penny of hard cash. A conservative estimate of sales generated was $100 million. And it all started with one thirty-year-old ship and heavy barter advertising.

Ability to Instantly and Continuously Generate a Steady Stream of Profits at Far above Closeout Prices

A cosmetic company traded a deodorant that was no longer being manufactured for advertising credits at full wholesale, thus getting their full market price in value for undesirable items. The advertising was used to advertise the new line. The old goods, which probably would have only brought in ten cents on the dollar as a closeout item, brought full wholesale as an advertising trade; thus the chief financial officer did not have to write down the product. The company was saved not only the book loss, but the cash loss, too. And they were able to take an item and benefit from it at full price while also saving millions of dollars in cash.

In a different twist, a major Japanese auto manufacturer had one thousand cars in the United States that they had been unable to sell. The cars were bartered through radio and TV stations in selected markets at full retail, or sticker, price. The advertising was used to introduce a new sports car that became a runaway success, which the company previously couldn't afford to run advertising for.

The bottom line: The cars were sold at full retail, millions of dollars were saved on the advertising schedule, and the new sports car became the basis of a blockbuster success for the car company because they advertised it constantly with the advertising they acquired—solely on trade.

Turning Excess Inventory into Cash without Losing Regular Business

A major international hotel corporation issues its own barter certificates in the amount of $7 million per year. Over the years the certificates have become extremely popular in the advertising community since they are used at more than fifteen hundred hotels around the world. The hotel corporation is able to trade for advertising with nearly any radio, TV, or outdoor advertising company because of the popularity and desirability of their hotels. The hotel corporation saves an estimated $10 million a year in cash through this process.

Recycle Dollars Right Back to Your Own Pockets

The city of Palm Springs ordered advertising for its tourist bureau. In order for the media (radio stations, TV networks, or magazines) to be paid for the advertising they had run, the Palm

Springs tourist bureau required that the media had to travel to Palm Springs and spend money in the city itself. In essence, the media had to spend an equal number of dollars in Palm Springs and show proof of purchase—before they got paid.

The entire multimillion-dollar budget was 100 percent recycled back into the hands and bank accounts of Palm Springs merchants. The tourist bureau didn't care if a magazine bought a car in Palm Springs, stayed at a hotel, booked travel through a Palm Springs travel agent, or ordered furniture from a furniture store as long as they did it with a Palm Springs merchant. Many shopping centers have also adopted this technique to recycle their advertising dollars back to their center merchants.

Stockholder Benefits

Many companies issue employee and stockholder benefits in barter, either for the company itself or for other barter they have acquired. They give Christmas presents, sales bonuses, client inducements—all without using cash.

Barter techniques can provide you with the ultimate edge against not only your local competition but foreign investors and competitors who don't understand or use it.

You can barter operating off your own business. You can do it playing off of other people's businesses. You can do it as a consultant. You can do it by the hour. You can do it for a share of the wealth or the trade credits. You can do it full-time or part-time. And that's just for starters.

And frankly, in a weak economy, the opportunities to profit through barter transactions are nearly limitless. Barter is not only recession-proof—it actually thrives and works better in a tight-money economy.

Action Steps

Start by making a list of all the products and services your business makes, sells, or markets. Make special note of excess or surplus goods, materials, equipment, inventory, capacity, space, technology, access, etc., your business no longer needs or doesn't fully use.

That list is on the left-hand side of the page. On the right-hand side, make a list of all key vendors you regularly buy goods or services from to see if any might be interested in directly trading with you for their products or services. Or for a portion of the cost you pay for them. Also add the names of your current suppliers' competitors, who might be even more eager to initially trade with you for product and service as a means to start a business relationship with your company.

Below that list, make a third list of companies with whom you might be able to triangulate for goods or services. See if there is any company to whom you'd like to start selling your products or services who would also trade whatever they make or sell in order to start a relationship. Then write down whom you could either sell or trade those items to for things you or your business needs or wants.

Now, go wild with possibilities. Try putting a few small, easy trades together at first to get comfortable with it. Then, with time, keep expanding your level of trading. I've seen companies make or save millions using barter. At the very least, it'll add an additional level of profit, revenue, or expanded impact to your business activities.

18

Leave a Message After the Beep

THE SINGLE MOST IMPORTANT STRATEGY YOU CAN USE TO maximize the value of all the other strategies is to communicate on a regular basis with everyone who contributes, or ever will contribute, in any way to your business success. You need to do this in order to maintain strong, positive relationships that can be a benefit to all involved. It's a simple strategy. It's powerful, it's incredibly enjoyable, and yet it's a concept that's not understood and practiced by very many of the businesses or professionals I get the opportunity of working with. So before I explain how to do it, let me explain to you why you must do it.

People are bombarded by more information today than at any other time in history. That causes you a real problem. The moment they have transacted business with you, their minds immediately revert to some other concern, issue, challenge, problem, or need, and you drift out of their mind. Your challenge and your biggest opportunity, if you're going to retain and sustain significant client transactions, is to keep those clients constantly connected to you. Keep them constantly thinking about how good you are, how valuable you are, how much you care about them and their well-being, how much they enjoy, desire, and value the products or services they acquire from you, and keep that connection alive and flowing. "Constantly" doesn't work if it's not strategic. And by *strategic* I mean it's got to be ongoing and purposeful, and it has to serve the client.

The more contact and communication you have with a person, the stronger and richer the relationship becomes. In business the secret to keeping and growing clients, as well as growing a career, is to keep continual and meaningful communication with everyone important to you. This is a simple but very powerful method for getting the very most out of your client or key contacts.

In this chapter you will learn how to maintain solid and profitable relationships with clients, colleagues, and others by employing proper and specific communication techniques.

Communicating with a client and telling him how great you are doesn't do the client a lot of good. Communicating with clients and finding out how well your product or service is performing, offering them a free checkup or a service review, offering them advice that will help them get longer or better use out of your product or service, is a great benefit to them. So you've got to make certain that whatever strategy you use to communicate constantly with your clients is one that always puts the client's interest ahead of your own.

And, while we're talking about communicating continually with your clients, look at clients as dear and valued friends. The way I look at it, I'm so lucky to have clients who are valued to me. They are old friends. I'm deeply connected with them. I care about them far beyond their capacity to spend money with me. I celebrate for them, I empathize with them, I'm there for the agony and the ecstasy.

If you share that feeling, you've got more motivation and desire to communicate, to keep in touch (just as you would with any good friend). If you look at your clients as friends whom you have the opportunity and the pleasure to stay connected with, it makes the process a lot more enjoyable, fulfilling, and ultimately more profitable.

And don't just communicate with clients. Open a dialogue with anyone and everyone who could help you reach your goals.

Develop relationships with colleagues. People in other departments. People above you. People below you. People who now might be competitors, but could someday be colleagues. Your employees. And your employer.

Call, e-mail, or write people who do what you do, who sell the product or service you sell, but in a market where you don't compete. Share with them, and find out what they're doing and where they're finding new avenues of success.

Find a mentor, someone who has been where you are and knows the pitfalls and opportunities that you are facing. This could be a person who is now retired from your industry but has vast amounts of knowledge that you could use to your benefit.

I have a dentist I taught to contact his patients continually. He calls every patient after they've had a procedure. He calls them up and checks to see how they're doing and how the procedure worked. He does it right after the work has been done. He marks on his calendar to do it again in a week. He marks on his calendar to do it again one more time about a month later. Have you ever had a dentist do that?

What do you think would happen if your dentist called you

two or three days after he had done a major filling? What do you think would happen if he called you a week later just to make sure that the pain and the discomfort were totally gone? You would be shocked. What do you think would happen if he called you thirty days later just to make absolutely positive there is no recurrence, no problem, no irritation, no inflammation? Do you think it would demonstrate that he cared about you at a level much, much, much higher than any other dentist you had ever worked with? Do you think you'd be inclined to think about him often and tell a lot of your friends? Do you think you'd be inclined to keep your appointments and not break them with this dentist? Do you think you'd be wanting to take all of your family members there and tell everybody you worked with or all your neighbors about the dentist? Of course you would, and that's what happens. This man's practice has boomed since he began this simple procedure.

And he enjoys it thoroughly because it connects him with his patients at a far deeper level. He says it's wonderful when he calls patients and they talk. They appreciate him. He gets connected to them and their families. And he says what happens is a transformation. The relationship improves and reaches a deeper level than he ever thought possible. This can easily happen in your business also.

When you do contact clients after they have done business with you, it is a perfect time to gently remind them of why they chose to do business with you in the first place—your unique selling proposition and your solid risk-reversal policy.

Reassure clients about their wise decisions, and show how the same USP that served them this time will be there to serve them in the future. Again, state your USP and your strong risk-reversal policy, telling clients why you've adopted it and why it's such an advantage to them. People rarely understand the benefits you provide them—unless you carefully educate them to appreciate your efforts on their behalf. Teach the clients why that USP and risk-reversal advantage is so much more important than the benefits offered by your competitors.

A post-purchase follow-up incorporating the essence of your USP and guarantees is vital, regardless of how frequently you back-end or resell to that client. You enhance the client's loyalty and value to your business by following up after the sale. At the very least, a follow-up call or letter drastically reduces or eliminates cancellations, returns, complaints, adjustments, and disputes. And it reassures clients of the prudence of their recent purchase from you.

I have a luxury hotel owner in the Southwest who makes it a point to not just send mundane solicitations to his past guests. Every month he sends them updates of the wonderful and delightful activities going on at his unique resort hotel. He sends pictures of how other people are celebrating and enjoying. He shares innovative ways people use his facilities to celebrate—couples coming for their fiftieth anniversaries, people who have come up with really imaginative ways to enjoy getting away with their whole families. He introduces them to people who come from afar. He makes your connection with that hotel very deep and very different from any connection you may have ever had with any other hotel you stayed at. He makes you feel welcome. He makes you feel like one of the family.

Another client I work with in Palm Springs does the same thing, and they have five times the repeat-client level of any other hotel in Palm Springs because they make you feel like you're one of their family. You're not just a charge-card deposit they process. You are an important, fascinating, unique human being that they thoroughly appreciate and enjoy, and they relish the chance to serve you. You are a guest and, as a guest, they treat you accordingly, and that treatment and that respect is conveyed by all the communications they share with you. So those are the three ways to increase your client retention rate.

An excellent example of communicating with clients is what American Express does. I get more wonderful letters, more surprise certificates and gifts, more updates, more alerts, and more communication, from them than from anybody I have a business relationship with. And guess what, that subconsciously prejudices me to want to use my American Express card over the other cards I carry. Simple. But powerful.

Let's look at how other businesses use continual communication to increase their frequency of transaction. A chiropractor that I work with sends letters out to his patients every four months. He calls patients personally twice a year. He alerts them to self-administrable screenings they can do, he tells them about new procedures he's got, and he offers them continual opportunities to come in for free services. Does it work? Well, all I can tell you is that this chiropractor has a waiting list of people standing in line figuratively to try to get an appointment with him every day because he's booked solid for weeks in advance. That was not the case when I first met him.

I have an auto dealer in Australia who started following this procedure after he met me, and he's reported that his business has improved 20 percent. They call, they send letters, they actually go out and visit their clients, they communicate constantly and strategically.

The more people you talk with, network with, develop a relationship with, the more opportunities and insights you will have. Opening one door leads to dozens of other doors. Opening dozens of doors leads to hundreds of others.

Action Steps

First, make a list of these categories:

Active clients
Inactive clients
Special-buying-category clients
Frequent-purchasing clients
Larger-average-purchase clients
Special-industry-based clients
Independent sales and distributors
Professionals
Industry trade contacts
Key suppliers
Noncompetitive businesses in your field (not competing directly with you)
Businesses that sell key products or services that complement, parallel, amplify, follow, or combine with the product or services you sell
Key executives above or under you
Key influential people you know
Add more as you think of appropriate categories

Under each listing, determine how best you or a member of your team can contact the people in each category. For example, call, visit, send a Christmas card to, take to lunch twice a year, etc. Obviously, the level and frequency of contact will depend upon how much time, people, and

continues to next page

capital you feel should be devoted to each category. Butremember, doing anything regularly is far better than merely intermittent contact or communication.

Then make a list of what has to be created, set up, and managed to make certain the objectives on your list are implemented, then sustained.

Prioritize them by importance and ease of initiation (making quarterly calls, for example, is much easier to do than a complex call-letter-visit system).

Then start doing it regularly, enthusiastically, and sys-tematically. This strategy works for business owners and employees with equal effectiveness.

19

Somewhere over the Rainbow

WHEN YOU GO ON VACATION, DO YOU PACK, DRIVE TO the airport, then take the next departing flight out no matter where it's going? Of course not. But often that's exactly how people approach their business lives.

Ninety percent of all businesspeople don't have the most basic thing they need—a goal. The few that do have a goal have the wrong goal, or one that can't possibly get them to where they want to be.

If your goal is "to make more money and become wealthy," I guarantee you'll never make more money and become wealthy.

You must have a specific goal. You cannot effectively get to where you want to be until you know exactly where that is.

In chapter 3 you were given questions to help evaluate your business strengths and weaknesses and determine where your career or business currently stands. Now it's time to think about where you want to go in your business or career.

This process is like going to an automobile club and getting a trip map. There are two questions you have to answer before the travel representative can help you. You've got to tell her where you're going to start from and where you're trying to get to. If you don't know both of those points, you're just wandering aimlessly.

So decide where you're going. Determine a specific goal. Make it an attainable goal. After reading the strategies in this book, you should have confidence in being able to reach a much higher goal than you previously thought possible. Make your goal one that causes a smile to automatically appear on your face. Leo Burnett, the brilliant Chicago advertising man, believed that, "If you reach for the moon and the stars, one thing is for certain, you won't end up with a handful of mud."

Having a reachable goal is more important to your success and financial prosperity than almost anything else you do. Once the goal is established, you need to work backward to reverse-engineer the exact steps, accomplishments, benchmarks, timelines, and methods you need to follow and set. And include appropriate, hedge, or contingency plans.

This chapter will show you what steps you need to take to reach the goals you set for yourself.

Doing It Backward Moves You Forward

Once you decide on a specific goal, you can't just squint your eyes and look up to heaven and the stars for divine inspiration. Increasing your business or income by a precise and substantial measure each and every year is a very easy thing to do when you work backward, when you reverse-engineer it.

So, you know where you are now (if you don't, reread chapter

3 and analyze your answers until you do know). And now you know where you want to go, and you know what percentage of growth you want—so you can work backward and wind up going powerfully forward.

For example:

Let's say you want to double your business in the next year. If you know you have one thousand clients and you know right now that those clients buy $100 at a time, twice a year, that's $200,000. If you want to double your business in a year, you have three paths you can follow—the three ways to increase your business that were in chapter 1. If, for example, you don't want to work on the size of the order, and you don't want to work on the number of times a client orders, what does that information tell you?

It tells you that to double your business, you've got to get one thousand additional clients.

Next step: Ask yourself, working backward, "What has to happen for me to gain one thousand more clients?" Well, let's look at what you're doing now. Whatever you're doing to get the first thousand, you've got to do twice as much. It may mean that you need two times the sales force. Or two times the telemarketing effort. It may mean that you have to run two times the number of ads, or that you have to run the ads in two times the number of publications. It may mean you have to send out two times the number of sales letters. It may mean you have to go to two times the number of trade shows. But it tells you what you have to do.

Whether you want to do that or not is your decision, but you can't decide until you first work backward. Or, instead of expending twice as much effort, spending twice as much money on salaries, on letters, on advertising, on exhibit expenses for trade shows and the like, there may be a better way.

Explore the two other ways of increasing your business.

Maybe getting a 50 percent higher unit of sale, and a third more transactions per year, would make it half as hard to double your business. All I want to do is show you that you've got to start by establishing a goal. Then, by reverse engineering, determine the specific steps you must take to reach that goal. By implementing the strategies you have learned, you will be able to take action and climb each one of those steps.

If your goal is to move up the corporate ladder and gain power, title, recognition, and the accompanying income, the concept is the same. Although this type of goal cannot be quantified as specifically as a numerical goal, the process of reverse engineering is equally valid.

Determine what level or position you want to reach in what period of time. Then determine the skills that specific position requires. Evaluate what your skills are at this point. What do you need to add to reach that required level of skills? Once you determine the voids, you can begin to fill them.

Other actions you can take to reach a higher corporate level are to voluntarily take on added responsibility in your area (or other areas). Use the Strategy of Preeminence with everyone you deal with inside and outside your corporation. Get referrals and recommendations from clients, vendors, and influential people in your company, both inside and outside your department or region.

Using the success- and income-increasing strategies you have now learned will enable you to become a business problem solver. Top management wants problem solvers, and the problem solvers are the people who get promotions, recognition, power, and corner offices.

Remember, incorporating multiple success approaches together vastly multiplies your achievements, minimizes your shortfalls, and comprises your timeline to achieving any goal.

Action Steps

Most people live in mortal fear that they aren't worthy of the limited and abstract goals they set for themselves. More of us set limited goals that simply aren't worthy of our true ability, potential, and mental capacity.

Set higher sights for yourself. But make them clear, specific, decisive, and accountable goals. Then reach those goals and keep raising the bar for yourself.

Sit down with your notepad. Clearly state each major business, financial, professional, personal, or family goal you have set.

Then, under each goal, write down the exact steps, numbers, events, processes, and actions you have to accomplish to reach those goals.

Finally, do a reality check. How well are you really progressing on each goal? Are you regularly evaluating and adjusting your performances and methods to reach the goal? If you're past your original goal, have you established new, higher goals? If you're behind your timeline or haven't diligently developed a daily, weekly, transaction-by-transaction plan, do it now. Break it down to simple non-threatening steps.

Without a clear destination and a precise road map for getting where you want to be, you'll never maximize your potential income or success.

But follow a good clear map with complete detailed travel instructions and your journey will be highly rewarding.

20

Your Never-Ending Success

THE SUCCESS- AND INCOME-INCREASING STRATEGIES YOU have now learned work. I know this for a fact. I've seen them work for over ten thousand clients in over four hundred different industries.

But don't stop with just one success.

When you apply what you have learned, don't just make one big score and stop.

I am astounded on a regular basis by many of my clients' results. They'll write and tell me that by applying one of my income-increasing strategies they had massive success, increasing their business or income by $50,000 in a month or by 100 percent in six months. The financial success isn't what astounds me—I expect that. What I can't believe is that many of them only use one of the strategies, and once they get a windfall they stop entirely. Every one of these strategies can produce significant results for you. And they produce more dramatic results when used in combination with each other and when implemented into a formalized ongoing strategy system.

If you're timid, take little steps in the beginning (you can test

341

any of these principles on a small scale with no financial or career risk). You'll see these strategies work. You'll gain confidence in them and yourself. Then you can start to take bigger steps. But don't just sit there doing nothing. Take the first step, no matter how small it may be. Take it.

A very wise man said, "Far more is accomplished through movement than was ever achieved through meditation." And while I think meditation, contemplation, and formulation are all quite essential to the success process, unless you act you'll never realize any rewards.

You now have the knowledge to embark on a wonderful adventure. Don't limit your trip. Don't stop when you make your business or life successful. That's only the first leg of the trip. Focus on bigger successes, greater possibilities, and constant, never-ending personal and business improvement.

In this chapter you will learn how to think about building levels of future success and profitable growth you never dreamed possible.

Adopt and Adapt

Don't limit yourself to the examples and applications I have given you of how to apply the strategies to your specific business situation. A standard-size book can contain only so many examples. But the number of applications that you can adopt or adapt is unlimited. And you can discover new variations everywhere you look.

All you have to do is refocus your mind to start looking at how other businesses sell, market, build, and keep their clients.

And how people and businesses do things to achieve any of the results you want. Then ask yourself how you can adapt that method or process to what you do.

In essence, you turn yourself into a success-practices investigator. Your goal is to uncover and identify what powerful marketing and selling approaches other industries have discovered that you don't know about, and then find an easy way to apply those methods to your business.

It's so much easier than you think. Just start being extremely observant of everything around you.

Keep a notebook at home, at the office, in the car. Whenever you observe a powerful marketing technique that captivates you—makes you want to respond to a product or service—jot down the concept, approach, language, sales presentation, etc., that worked, and incorporate similar or related techniques into your marketing tests.

Read every good ad you see published, then clip and save it for future reference. Note all the TV and radio commercials that convince you to buy—especially the ones that almost convince you even though you don't need the product or service.

When you get solicitations in the mail, stop throwing them away. Realize the fact that companies wouldn't keep mailing these solicitations out unless they produced profitable results— so there's probably something you can learn and apply by studying those letters. Maybe there's a good headline or great opening you could use in a letter you might send out to your own clients.

Headlines can be applied to ads, letters, sales presentations, etc. The same goes for positioning, guarantees, and benefits.

Maybe there's an incredible risk-reversal or closing approach in that letter that you can use directly.

A few years ago I made small fortunes for several clients by reading an ad (in, of all places, the *National Enquirer*) that offered expensive gems inexpensively. I had absolutely no interest whatsoever in the gems, but I had enormous fascination with the selling approach—both the positioning and actual copy—that the ad used.

I borrowed the concept and selling principles and applied them to software, pest control services, and other business— and my clients made over $3 million in one year for my trouble. But obviously it was no trouble at all. Instead, it was a pleasure to let other industries create and perfect success practices and then adopt and apply those practices to other businesses.

I want you to start doing the same, and start doing it today.

Whenever I'm anywhere shopping or watching my wife or family buy anything, I observe what is transpiring—and how it might profitably apply to my own or any of my clients' activities.

When you go to retail stores, shopping centers, car dealers, housing developments, clothing or jewelry stores—or when you talk with insurance brokers, real estate agents, or stockbrokers—observe how they engage you, how they lead or question or close. Watch the way they guide you from one price point or selection to another—always thinking and asking yourself how this might directly, or indirectly, apply to what you do. Note the conduct, personalities, and actions of retailers and service companies.

Every time something irritates you, make a note of it.

Every time something delights and pleases you, write it down.

If a concept cannot or does not seem to be directly applicable to you, don't reject it immediately. Ask yourself another question: "How might I adapt all or part of that process to what I do?"

By looking at how you can use all, part, or some derivative of a success practice you observe or experience on the receiving end as a client, you vastly increase your own growth opportunities.

Caution—Success Ahead

As your business or career grows and evolves, these strategies continue to work. You'll find new ways to use them, new applications for them. The only limit to your income is how much you believe is enough. Don't lower a false ceiling on what is truly possible for you, your company, or clients. Think of these strategies as you would water—allow them to constantly flow freely and let them seek their own level of success, which will frequently be far higher and richer than you'd normally take them to.

When you start applying these strategies, your business or career will improve. There's absolutely no question of that. Look into the future. Plan ahead.

Will you need more inventory? Will you need to add more staff? Will you be able to fill more orders with your current distribution system? Think these things through so when improvement happens you are prepared to handle it.

Be prepared for more clients, raises, or promotions, and a much, much better life.

Action Steps

Read the next chapter.

21

You Are Richer than You Think

THINK FOR A MOMENT OF WHAT YOU WOULD CHANGE IN YOUR everyday life if you could. Would you like to have more free time? Move up the corporate ladder? Would you like to travel? Design and build your dream house? Spend time at home with your kids? Coach Little League? Create a thriving business that will be there for your children and grandchildren?

All of this, and more—whatever your definition of success might be—can be yours when you apply these strategies.

In the previous chapters I introduced you to new methods and the mind-set required for you to uncover what I call secret wealth—wealth that has always been there for you to discover, but until now you weren't aware it existed.

This final chapter is intended to motivate and inspire you to the highest level of inventive and enriching creative achievement. To send you on your way knowing that you have inside of you the power to dramatically change your life today and forever. And that now you have the tools necessary to bring that power to the forefront.

But seeing is believing. So I want to show you how some of

my clients have creatively applied my methods in ways that resulted in surprisingly simple but powerful breakthrough strategies. I hope you'll get excited and moved to creative action by their stories and successes. In respect for their privacy I've used different names to protect the successful.

The strategies I have shared with you throughout this book will change your life. I guarantee that when you apply them with diligence and persistence you will enjoy success beyond anything you can imagine. The question you need to ask yourself is "What is my definition of success?" Most people have a tendency to define success in terms of their companies and/or careers. But the ultimate benefits you will derive from my strategies are the successes you'll enjoy in your *life*.

Your *Hidden* Assets

Stanley Brown was the catalog manager for a large, prominent, mail-order computer company. He'd risen to the highest level he thought he could go, and along the way he had trained a number of younger assistants who had quit to go on to prestigious, high-profile jobs.

The company had become extremely bureaucratic and had ceased to be exciting. Stan had become totally burned out with the entire corporate BS. He was commuting one and a half hours each way, each and every day. He literally hated what he was doing. He honestly got nothing fulfilling out of his work. And, worst of all, whenever Stan came up with a truly innovative idea, management rejected it, thus compounding Stan's frustration.

Wanted to Be Master of His Own Fate

One day, without any other job prospects, Stan just walked in and gave notice. He had decided he never again wanted to work for anyone. Stan wanted to be master of his own fate.

Unfortunately, Stan had no plan of action, and he'd just walked away from an $80,000-a-year position. Stan lived in a lovely idyllic community in northern California where there was seemingly little opportunity. Stan struggled for nearly eight weeks, trying all kinds of poorly founded "instantaneous-panacea" business-opportunity approaches. Then he learned my money-maximizer, business-multiplier formula.

Three Questions That Can Change Your Life

I had Stan answer these three simple questions:

1. Have you identified and valued your true expertise and inventoried your negotiable personal assets?
2. What performance skills have you demonstrated in the past that have not only abstract, but *intrinsic,* value and importance to a business—or a specific type of business?
3. What have you accomplished that people would not only respect, but also desire to learn and utilize to gain the same benefits for their companies?

At first, Stan drew a blank. So I asked him to analyze and reconstruct all of the monumental things he'd experienced, contributed to, and been part of since he'd started working. Not merely at his current job, but in every previous company he'd been involved with over his entire career.

To his surprise, Stan realized that, under his direction, the greatest mail-order catalog success in the entire industry had occurred. The owners of the company had become multimillionaires. Also, Stan was on the cutting edge of dozens of product-introduction breakthroughs that became massive successes. Further, the heads of critical departments at five of the industry's top catalog companies had been trained personally by Stan. It was at this point that Stan began to finally recognize and appreciate his own proprietary skills and understand that he had an enormous reservoir of performance-enhancement potential for creating greater success for others. And financial independence for himself.

A Simple Way to Find the Right Market for Your Skills

I asked Stan one more simple question:

Who would give their right arm to acquire the valuable expertise Stan now recognized that he possessed? He thought for a moment and realized that there were dozens of smaller, poised-for-success mail-order catalog companies that would probably be thrilled to have access to the deep expertise Stan possessed. But most of these companies couldn't possibly afford Stan's previous compensation level. And, even if they could, Stan had decided that he didn't want to work for anyone again.

I told Stan that was no problem. He didn't have to play by the rules that society wanted to impose upon him. In fact, one of the key ideas in what I call the Secret Wealth Mind-set (where you evolve to creating your own rules and using my concepts in your own original combinations and interpretations) is to always remember that *you* make the rules.

I showed Stan that by getting four to ten smaller companies to pay monthly or quarterly fees to him of $3,000 to $10,000 each, Stan could make more money advising or consulting with them than he ever could as a salaried employee. Best of all, he could successfully work only the hours, days, weeks, or months he wanted. Because he could ask to be paid for knowledge and results, not time spent.

Stan wrote a one-page announcement to the presidents of smaller but solidly profitable and progressive-minded catalog companies, presidents who wanted their companies to be as big and powerful as the one Stan had helped.

Stan offered his services on an industry-specific, exclusive basis for minimum one-year retainers, plus significant performance bonuses for the profit increases and sales improvements Stan's ideas, assistance, and advice brought them.

To Stan's surprise, nearly fifty qualified companies responded to that single announcement.

He picked out the six most interesting, enjoyable, outright fun, and financially promising applicants and took them on as long-term clients. When he talked with these companies, Stan knew that he was negotiating (and advising them) from a position of strength and total respect, which brought out the absolute best performance efforts in Stan. Truly a win-win arrangement.

Create Greater Power and Maximum Control

Now, instead of being dead-ended in a lower-rung middle-manager position in a large corporation, Stan deals only with the owners and presidents of fast-growing and exciting entre-preneurial enterprises. He received the respect he was denied in his corporate job and enjoyed the personal liberation and enormous power that comes with control of one's own career and life. Today, he's an extraordinarily happy man.

Moving from employee to lucrative self-employed consulting

work is easy if you understand the concept of secret wealth creation and you learn how to document and quantify your own underrecognized value and identify hidden money-making opportunities for others.

Sell, Rent, License

Jack George runs a family-owned lumber mill. One of the critical aspects of making lumber is kiln-drying the raw wood. How it dries determines grade quality and, thus, market value. Poorly dried wood can be worth 30 to 60 percent less per board foot than properly dried wood.

Jack had developed a sophisticated method of kiln-drying that produced a far greater percentage of premium-grade finished lumber than the industry average. With his method, Jack reduced waste and scrap by almost half. In addition, and probably most important to other lumber owners, Jack's process cut energy costs by 15 percent.

When Jack learned about my methods, he decided to sell, rent, and license his method of kiln-drying to other lumber mills outside his target marketing area. Because of the immense weight factor, lumber can only be cost-effectively shipped a maximum of three hundred miles. Ninety-five percent of the lumber mills in the country and around the world aren't considered direct competitors of Jack's mill (and will never be, unless they buy one of Jack's competitors, which he contractually protects himself against). So almost all mills are key prospects for Jack.

Jack has so far netted about $1.65 million off his little side-profit center and it's continuing to throw off about $350,000 each year. By the way, whenever Jack improves or comes up with a new twist, approach, or performance-maximizing addition to his process, he charges over one hundred lumber mills a fee of up to $25,000 to teach his updated findings to them.

What you know, do, or have successfully done is probably worth considerable money and value to other noncompetitors in your business or line of endeavor—or outside it.

An Instant Corporate Hero

Noah Calloway ran a technical-support division of a large real estate management software firm in the Pacific Northwest. It was losing $350,000 a year. By changing one simple strategy in his firm's operating philosophy, Noah turned the money-losing tech support department into a $650,000 profit center. All by offering his clients more of what they wanted and needed anyway.

As a support division for a software firm, Noah's department had to answer all kinds of difficult technical or operating questions people called in with every day. Noah's breakthrough idea came when he decided to view his department as an ongoing for-profit educational institution—not a problem-solving expense center.

He went to all his software clients and offered them long-term, prepaid, direct technical and operational consulting access to help them grow their utilization capabilities. Noah showed them how to apply his firm's software solutions more effectively in their real estate management businesses. Noah also came up with a separate service to train his clients' new employees who came in after the client had originally purchased the software, thus making the new employees much more productive much sooner.

A significant number of existing and previous clients signed up for these services. Noah set up regular, continuous offerings of special-situation application training sessions, expensive two- and three-day, off-site and on-site training programs, each designed to teach different client-user groups how to maximize current and add-on software performance.

Naturally, Noah got a raise and was an instant corporate hero. If you add to the bottom line, and your contribution is measurable and visible enough, you'll be lavishly rewarded, too. There is plenty of room to be an independent thinker in today's fast-changing radical corporate world. Problems are always opportunities for economic gain—once you figure out how to solve them and denominate the solution's financial value to someone.

Past Relationships Are Worth Millions

Miles McIntire was out of work, having previously had a key job with Xerox. He used one simple concept: finding someone else who needed a company's product worse than the company needed to sell it to them. Stated differently, someone who had more to gain than even he did by seeing his goal achieved.

Miles found a small but cutting-edge computer peripherals company with a great product but terrible representation and marketing. He went to work for them and used his previous contacts at Xerox, Siemans, and National Cash Register to get those companies to "bundle" or package the firm's peripherals into their computer sales process.

With this simple concept in mind, Miles took this little company up from $2 million to $8 million in about a year. Miles also got an equity interest in the business, free, for being able to engineer this deal. Why? Because it took no sales staff, advertising or marketing staff, expense, or promotional letters. Miles reclaimed and repositioned the valuable relationships he already had invested years in personally cultivating. The new company was making 60 percent gross profit and did so well that Miles was influential enough to get the company to move their offices from California to Sun Valley, Idaho, where Miles loved to ski every winter day.

Even if the names in your Rolodex aren't worth as much as the ones in Miles's, you must constantly think of your past business experiences carefully, looking for key relationships that could be an invaluable part of your secret wealth. If you have the right value offer to make to a business contact, it could change your business life and financial circumstances in less than a year, as it did for Miles.

Write down and create a permanent file of who all your past business contacts and relationships are and the business area and connection they control, and what would bring them the greatest profit and advantage.

A Money Hobby

Judith Johnson is a chiropractor in North Carolina. But her success story is not about her professional practice. It's about her "money hobby." A hobby that netted Judith an extra $300,000 in one winter season by using this Secret Wealth Mind-set—she identified what people thought were problems, obstacles, or negatives in their life or business, and found a profitable solution to help solve it for these people.

Judith found that the Forest Service had a terrible problem with falling pine needles in the forest areas near her home. So many would collect and build up on the floor of the forests that when fall came, and the needles dried out, they posed a horrible fire risk. The Forest Service actually paid trash-hauling companies to collect and haul these pine needles away. Judith knew that pine-needles-turned-mulch made the finest fertilizer around. That gave her an exciting idea.

She went to the Forest Service and underbid (by half) the job of hauling the pine needles away. She then found a trucking firm that delivered furniture to the cities the pine forests were closest to. She negotiated a fabulous discount trucking rate with them because they normally came back to North Carolina empty. So the pine-needle load Judith gave them to haul was "found money" for the trucking company. The low fee Judith got from the Forest Service for hauling the needles away more than paid the cost of the trucking expense.

Judith next found a huge retail lot that was owned by an out-of-business mobile-home sales company. It was empty. Judith made a strictly contingency (performance only) deal to pay the owner a small share of her sales to use the lot to sell bushels of pine needles to gardeners in the area to use as fertilizer. She paid people minimum wage, plus a sales bonus, to run and manage the lot.

The little enterprise made Judith nearly $300,000 extra a season as her fun "little" money hobby. It had nothing to do with her profession. It had nothing to do with anything else she did. It was a pure case of making money as a hobby by learning to apply the Secret Wealth Mind-set of my maximizing and multiplying process. If you understand the principles of uncovering secret wealth, you won't ever have to worry about fun and rewarding income opportunities again—they literally are everywhere.

Make the Most out of What You've Got

I end this chapter, and this book, by talking to you about something I call the optimum personal, business, and career strategy. What's this mean? It means that you must refuse to get less out of an effort, less out of an opportunity, less out of a day, less out of a dollar, less out of a relationship, than the maximum that activity or action has the capacity to give you. It means that you don't do things just to be doing them. That you insist on playing life to the fullest. But playing it based on your sense of value.

You have to figure out who it is you are and what it is you want. That's critical because most people I meet don't have a clue of where they're going in life and what they want life to give them. Any success, any fulfillment, any joy, any prosperity, any goodness, they get is almost accidental.

Life has the capacity to give you, in your career or business, and especially in your personal life, everything you ever want and then some. Multiples of that, in fact. But you can't have any of it if you don't know where you are going. And what you want out of the experience. You need to ask, "Who am I? What do I want? What makes me happy? What doesn't? Where is my strength, where is my weakness? Where can I make the greatest contribution in my life, in my job, in my business, in my relationships?"

To some people, money making may be a real thrill. You may only want to make enough money to have the time to enjoy it. You may not care about material things. Other people may want all the material things. I am not passing judgment. What I'm saying is you can't have what you want until you first know what it is. And you can't know what it is until you really first realize what success means to you.

I met a man who shuttled me around an airport one time who had to be absolutely one of the happiest people I've ever met. He had a girlfriend. He had no material interests. They had a nice apartment in a clean part of town. They worked very hard all day, but they didn't want their business problems to come home with them. After five o'clock is when they really enjoyed life at the highest level. That's great for some people. Other people love the excitement of business and make it an integral part of their personal life. They are one in the same.

Your first priority is to identify what you want and then make sure you take the path that's going to give you that. There's nothing sadder than to see someone get to be seventy-five or eighty years old and look back regrettably because they pursued the wrong target.

For you, I want every day to be a day of joy and enrichment that advances you to the maximum along the success path you want to pursue. On whatever you define as enjoyment and enrichment.

Are you richer than you think? I think you are. You're many times richer than you think, and I wrote this book to share with you some of the simplest but most powerful ways you'll ever come across to maximize your life, your career, your business, and your relationships. At the very least, I hope the process and the tools we've covered will help you achieve everything you've ever wanted or will want. I hope you'll take what I've shown you to a much higher level of application and enrichment than even I have. That's what I'm expecting. Because that's the reason I'm sharing this powerful performance information with you. With that stated, let the game you decide to play finally begin.

One Last Thought

I WOULD LOVE TO HEAR ALL THE SUCCESSFUL WAYS YOU FIND TO apply my strategies to your life. Please send me your results and breakthroughs. I collect and study all kinds of success stories, large or small, financial or otherwise. When I get yours, I'll send you back a free tape on "breakthrough thinking" I created. I'll also include a special report on my personal technique for creating ideas. I just developed it to help you stimulate a continuous flow of breakthrough ideas and innovative thinking for your business, career, and life.

Warmly,
Jay Abraham

Abraham Publishing Group, Inc.
P.O. Box 3289
Rolling Hills Estates, CA 90274

Apgi@abrabam.com
(800) 635-6298

For a catalog of our products, programs, and performance enhancement services, call (310)265-1840 or E-mail at apgi@pacball.net.

We have a "super site" Internet resource center that provides valuable (and highly actionable) cutting-edge ideas, strategies, and tactics you can download to help maximize and multiply your personal and business results. It's a content-rich source for answers and solutions to the issues and challenges you face. Log on to www.abraham.com.

Read On, Discover, and Prosper

FOR YOUR PROGRESS, I'M ENCLOSING AN ADDENDUM OF RECommended reading. This is trimmed down so it will conveniently start you thinking, focusing, and pursuing the questions and answers you need to maximize your performance and opportunities in business and in your career for the rest of your life. Enjoy and prosper!

Recommended Reading
My Top Ten Strategic Business Classics

Carnegie, Dale. *How to Win Friends And Influence People.*
Simon and Schuster Reissue, 1998.
Essential Message: The only way on earth to influence people is to show them how to get what they want.

Covey, Stephen, Ph.D. *The Seven Habits of Highly Effective People.* Macmillian, 1997.
Teaches us to engage in a continuous process of self-renewal based on the immutable laws that govern human growth and progress.

Deming, W. Edwards. *Out of Crisis.* M.I.T. Press, 1986.
Everything can be broken down to its core processes. Then they can be measured, quantified *and improved*.

Drucker, Peter F. *Managing in a Time of Great Change.* Dutton, 1995. Plume, 1997.
The book to read first. The successful entrepreneur always searches for change, responds to it, exploits it as an opportunity.

Hill, Napoleon. *Think and Grow Rich!* Ballantine Books, 1937; Revised 1960; copyright renewed 1988.
Summarizes the key success factors of the world's top achievers. It teaches that thoughts held in the mind tend to translate themselves into their physical equivalent.

Hopkins, Claude C. *My Life in Advertising* and *Scientific Advertising.* NTC Contemporary Publishing Company, 1995.
Topics include effective selling, the keys to impactful communication, and pre-emptive positioning—and insight on how to apply each principle for maximum results.

Mackay, Harvey. *Swim with the Sharks Without Being Eaten Alive.* Fawcett, 1996.
He teaches that most problems in business or life can be solved if you can teach yourself to look beyond the transaction—and care about the people involved.

Ogilvy, David. *Confessions of an Ad Man.* Atheneum, 1963.
Teaching ethics through advertising is quite a feat, but he managed to do exactly that. And in the process, he challenges you to achieve a higher level of thinking and personal performance.

Peters, Tom. *Thriving on Chaos.* HarperCollins, 1988.
Perhaps the ultimate example of innovative and breakthrough thinking. The winners of tomorrow will regard

362

chaos as a source of market advantage, not as a problem to be feared.

Young, James Webb. *A Technique for Producing Ideas.* NTC Business Books, 1975.
This book is nearly 50 years old and takes about 45 minutes to read. Yet, its simplified, disciplined process for innovative thinking is just as effective and valuable as the day it was first published.

Acknowledgments

NO ONE EVER SUCCEEDS WITHOUT THE HELP OF OTHERS. Thank you:

To Terry Hart, friend and talented writing accomplice, for helping explain myself to me throughout the creation of this book. Your counterperspective made a dramatic difference.

To all the fascinating, complexly driven "paradigm pioneers," whose breakthrough strategies and innovative thinking made all my accomplishments and "connections" possible.

To Socrates, for daring to probe, question, and correlate.

To the Science of Optimization, for teaching me how easy it was to maximize and multiply everything I did.

To human beings, for their wonderful, diverse perspectives, experiences, interests, and needs, without which we'd have no opportunities to tap . . . or problems to solve.

And . . . to the remarkable individuals whose combined efforts made this book a reality. Heartfelt thanks to: Barbara Lowenstein, my dedicated agent, Truman Talley, my publisher, Jill Sieracki, Matt Baldacci, John Murphy, Jeff Capshew, and all the other dedicated people at St. Martin's Press.

ACKNOWLEDGMENTS

Honorable Mention

Audri Lanford, one of my dear colleagues, has not yet written a book but probably will very soon. She is my internet collaborative source and a respected internet marketing expert. Contact her by E-mail at agl@netrageous.com.

Index

INDEX

Attrition *(continued)*
 and changed situation, 30–31, 211,
  214–15
 and dissatisfaction, 30, 212–14
 and forgetfulness, 30, 210–12, 217
 lowering rate of, 210, 219, 224
Auction business, 298–99
AutoByTel, 290
Automobile business, 108, 121,
  180–81, 205, 283, 290, 309,
  314–16, 321, 325, 333
 leases, 42
 malls, 42
 risk reversal in, 115, 116
Average sale, 169
Avis, 19–20

Back-end sales, 5, 8, 59, 69–77, 94,
  183. *See also* Repeat clients
Barter, 307–27
 and advertising, 314–16, 320–26
 appeal of, 310
 assigning credit, 312–14, 318
 benefits of, 308–9, 326
 brokering, 316
 as commerce, 319
 commission in, 316–18
 currency for, 319–20, 325
 defined, 308
 discount in, 309–12, 315, 318–19
 and employee and stockholder
  benefits, 326
 and expiration date, 312–15
 for goods and services, 309–12
 as interest-free loan, 315, 318–21,
  323
 middleman in, 317–18
 one-to-one, 311–12
 and operating expenditures, 329
 for portion of price, 318
 profit center, 322–23
 on retail value basis, 311–13, 325
 and taxes, 310
 triangulation, 309, 313–16, 327
 on unequal retail value basis, 318
 and unused credit, 320–21
 value of, 308–9
Basch, Michael, 221
Bear, Stearns, 260
Beauty salons, 98–99
Bedrosian, John, 290
Beneficiary-host relationship.
  See Host-beneficiary relationship
Better-than-risk-free guarantee
  (BTRF), 105–8

Birdseye, Clarence, 43
Blinds and curtains business, 134–35
Blockbuster Video, 116
Book-of-the-Month Club, 71
Bookout, Robert, 290–91
Book sales, 127
Breaking even, to acquire clients,
  69–77
Breakthrough(s), 34–48, 358
 accidentally-discovered, 41
 by amateurs, 42–44
 approaches to, 13
 born-again, 41–42
 creating, 46
 and curiosity, 44–45
 defined, 37
 maximizing, 46–47
 objectives, 46–47
 and open-mindedness, 40–41
 opportunity-focused, 39–40
 vs. measured pace, 35–36
Broadcast antenna business, 201–2
"Broad choice," 80
Brochures, 31, 78, 79, 228
 creating, 242–44, 255
Burger King, 28
Burnett, Leo, 337
Business
 increasing, 4–5, 338–39
 limiting, 118
 observing other, 36, 303, 342–45
 positives and negatives, evaluating,
  49–55
Business Breakthroughs, 126
Business-improvement business, 106–7

Carnival Cruise Lines, 324
Car-wash business, 127–28
Catering business, 201
CD business, 206, 289–90
CDNow, 289–90
Charles, Ray, 250
Chiropractors, 222–23, 267, 333
Chrysler Corporation, 321
Circuit City, 142
Client list(s), 256
 compiling, 259, 260–62
Client(s)
 attrition, 209–15
 benefit to, 19, 22, 105, 173, 212
 best interests of, 24, 57–68, 278,
  329
 comfort of, 65
 complaints, 213
 communication with, 328–35

368

Gardner, Tom and David, 290
Gates, Bill, 37, 40
General Electric, 155
Geometric growth formula, 5–6
Giant steps, 35–37
Goals, business, 336–40
   need for specific, 336–37, 339
   reverse-engineering, 337–39
   time line for attaining, 339
Goals, personal, 346, 356–57
Gould, Jay, 179
Growth formula, 5–6
Guarantee(s), 105, 109, 113
   better-than-risk-free (BTRF),
     105–108
   defined, 105
   insincere, 110–11
   length of, 111–12
   linked to sales, 108–10
   performance-based, 107–10, 112,
     114–16
   and sincerity, 110–11
   testing, 147
   types of, 114

Hair transplant business, 205
Hard-asset companies, 182
Headline ad, 86, 91, 153, 155, 238,
   247, 343
   testing, 146, 148–49
   Web site, 296–97
Health clubs, 107–8, 202
Health services, 114, 203, 247–48,
   290
Heating and air-conditioning business,
   203–4, 220, 311–12
Hertz, 19
High-quality prospects, 253–71
   finding, 255
   on Web sites, 295, 298
High-volume mass market, 93
Hines, Duncan, 27
Home Shopping Network, 308
Home teaching programs, 115–16
Host-beneficiary relationships, 26–28,
   143, 163–88
   approaching host in, 166–70, 188
   "automatic renewal and
   exclusivity agreement," 176, 177
   benefits to beneficiary, 164–71,
     172
   benefits to host, 171, 172–75
   defined, 165
   and E-mail and Web site links, 262
   examples of, 179–87

and financial arrangements, 166,
   168, 169, 175–79
honesty in, 176
inducements for clients, 167–68
middleman, becoming, 174, 183
negotiating, 175–79
renewal of, 176
setting up, 165–68
testing, 175, 178–79
HotBot, 302
Hotel industry, 320–21, 325, 332–33
Howser, Frank, 36–37
Human nature, 65–68

Iacocca, Lee, 22
Ice cream, 3
Inactive clients, 30–31, 209–26
   and competitors' lists, 259
   contacting, 219, 222
   identifying, 209–10, 219–20, 262
   reasons for, 210–15
   reinstating, 215–23, 231
Income
   increasing, 4, 10, 67, 114, 147
   multipliers, 15–16
Indemnification, 170
Industrial business, 12, 136, 258, 310
Infoseek, 302
Inserts, 177
Insurance business, 142, 201, 203,
   249
Intel, 294
Internal clients, 8–9
Internet, 33, 258–59, 287–306
   culture, 293, 295
   discussion groups, 300
   e-zines, 300
   "FAQ," 300
   getting rich quick on, 292
   global nature of, 304–05
   and high-quality, 288–89, 295
   as "information superhighway," 292
   local use of, 289
   lurking on, 300
   malls, 292–93
   marketing plan, 294–95
   myths and reality about, 291–94
   "netiquette" on, 300
   problems of business on, 291–94
   profitability of Web sites on, 289
   resource center, 359
   savings from use of, 293
   search engines on, 301–4
   success on, 288, 289–91
   testing on, 297

INDEX

National Cash Register, 353
National Energy Associates, 42
National Enquirer, 344
Neiman Marcus, 18
NETrageous, 304
New clients
  breaking even to acquire, 69–77
  and direct mail, 227–52
  and host-beneficiary relationships,
    163–88
  and Internet, 287–306
  and price reductions, 69–77
  and referrals, 189–208
  and risk reversal, 103–17
  and targeting, 253–71
  and telemarketing, 272–86
  and unique selling proposition
    (USP), 78–102
Newsletter business, 222
New York Times, 269
Niche market, 92–93, 301
Nickel-and-dime thinking, 44
Nike, 43
Nixon, Richard, 39
Nordstrom, 97
Northern Light, 302
NUA, 300

"Observed validation," 45
Obstacles, removing, 103–17. *See also*
  risk reversal
Olim, Jason, 289
100 percent solution, 6–7, 14
On-line servers, 71
Opportunity-based focus, 39–40
Optimum strategy, 355–57
Optometry business, 129, 206
Overhead, minimizing, 319

Package deals, 119, 132, 137, 183
Palm Springs, 325–26, 332
Parish, Will, 42
Park, Roy, 27
Past experiences, value of, 349–54
Performance-based guarantee,
  107–110
Performance-maximizing philosophy,
  38
Pest-control business, 100, 130
Photography business, 204
Physical therapists, 268
Pickford, Mary, 268
Pizza business, 96–97
Plant-growing systems, 269
Plastic surgery business, 137, 309

Point-of-purchase promotions,
  135–36
Polo magazine, 258
Possibility-based mindset, 39
Post-its, 41
Power equipment business, 115
Preemptive marketing, 82–84
Price Club, 141
Price(s)
  discount positioning, 87–89
  higher, 139–40
  lower, 80, 120, 125
  reductions, 69–77
  and telemarketing, 274
  testing, 147, 157–58
Printing business, 96
Problem solving, 10, 280, 339
  with client, 217
Professional
  accomplishments, 348, 352
  assets, 348, 352
  performance skills, 348, 352
Professional speakers, 122–23
Promotions, special, 94–95
  point-of-purchase, 135–36
Proposals, 31, 228
Prospect(s), 227, 229, 259, 262,
  303
  and competitors, 259
  defined, 253–54
  high-quality, 253–71, 298
  Internet, 300
  meeting with, 278, 280–81
  and other industries, 258–59
  prequalifying, 273
  vs. suspects, 253, 265
  targeting, 236, 253–71, 300–304
  and telemarketing, 272–86
  writing or calling you, 279–81
Public speaking, 206–7
Purchase
  larger unit of, 125–26, 261
  of company, 143
  options, 126–27

Qualifying prospects. *See* Targeting
  prospects
Quantum leaps, 35–37
Quick-freezing, 43–44

Radio Shack, 261
Raiders of the Lost Ark, 40
Real estate attorneys, 266–67
Real estate business, 205–6, 250
Recognition, 10

TFN ('Til Further Notice) basis,
129–30, 131
Thomas, George, 13
Thomas Register, 255, 258
Time options, 119, 129–31
Toilet paper, 3
Toulouse-Lautrec, 307
Tourism industry, 326
Toy business, 291
Trade shows, 75
Travel magazine business, 322
Tree trimmer, 138–39
Trial period, 154
Trump, Donald, 37
Turner, Ted, 37
Two-way valve effect, 174

Unfulfilled needs, 81–82
Unique selling proposition(s) (USP),
19–20, 25, 26, 78–102, 331–32
adopting multiple, 93
"broad choice," 80
clarity of, 84–87, 92
creating your own, 79–102
examples of, 96–101
fulfilling promise of, 80, 82, 93,
95–96
how to pick, 81–82
hybrid, 82
informing employees of, 93–94, 95
lack of, 80–81
"low price," 80
marketing, 82–101
multiple, 93
price-discount, 87
and risk reversal, 113
and salespeople, 85, 91–92, 93–94
selection-based, 80, 85–86
service-based, 80, 89–90, 93, 95,
100
snob-appeal, 80, 90–91
special promotions, 94–95
successes, 80
United Airlines, 174
Universal Studios, 28
Upscale markets, 140–41
Up-selling, 133–135

Vacation packages, 142
Value
better, 137, 173

market, 309
perceived, 309
retail, 311
Victoria's Secret, 261
Video stores, 183–85
Virtual community, 298–99
Visa, 28, 165
Volume options, 119, 125–29,
130
benefit of, 128–29
examples, 126–27, 141–42
suggestions for, 131

Wall Street Journal, 148
Warehouse business, 100–101, 141
WebCrawler, 302
WebMD, 290
Web site(s), 288
bulletin board, 299
changing, 297–98
cheap price of, 297–98
contests, 299
creating, 295–99
editorial page, 299
free samples, 298
headline, 296–97
interactive, 298–99
keywords, 303
page titles, 303
plurals, 303
polls and surveys on, 299
profitability of, 289
and search engines, 303–04
simplicity of, 303
testing, 297
translating, 304–05
visitors' contributions to, 299
See also Internet
Weight loss business, 116
Weintz, Walter, 32
White House Office of Consumer
Affairs, 212
Winery, 138
Wozniak, Steve, 37
Wright, Orville and Wilbur, 21

Xerox, 353

Yachting magazine, 258
Yahoo!, 302
Yellow Pages, 79